Bloodstain Pattern Analysis

With an Introduction to Crime Scene Reconstruction

CRC SERIES IN
**PRACTICAL ASPECTS OF CRIMINAL
AND FORENSIC INVESTIGATIONS**

VERNON J. GEBERTH, BBA, MPS, FBINA *Series Editor*

Bloodstain Pattern Analysis

With an Introduction to
Crime Scene Reconstruction

Tom Bevel
Ross M. Gardner

CRC Press

Boca Raton   New York

Publisher:	Robert B. Stern
Project Editor:	Helen Linna
Marketing Manager:	Bill Boone
Direct Marketing Manager:	Becky McEldowney
Cover design:	Denise Craig
PrePress:	Kevin Luong
Manufacturing:	Sheri Schwartz

Library of Congress Cataloging-in-Publication Data

Bloodstain pattern analysis with an introduction to crime scene reconstruction/Tom Bevel
and Ross M. Gardner
      p. cm.
(CRC series in practical aspects of criminal and forensic investigations)
    Includes bibliographical references and index.
    ISBN 0-8493-8159-2
    1. Forensic science.   2. Law enforcement—criminal investigations.   I. Bevel, Tom. II. Title.
III. Series
QV817.H89G39 1997
616′.0149—dc20
                                            97-57102
                                            CIP

No claim to original U.S. Government works
International Standard Book Number 0-8493-8159-2
Library of Congress Card Number 97-57102
Printed in the United States of America 1 2 3 4 5 6 7 8 9 0
Printed on acid-free paper

Editor's Note

This textbook is part of a series entitled "Practical Aspects of Criminal and Forensic Investigation". This series was created by Vernon J. Geberth, New York City Police Department Lieutenant Commander (Retired), who is an author, educator, and consultant on homicide and forensic investigations.

This series has been designed to provide contemporary, comprehensive, and pragmatic information to the practitioner involved in criminal and forensic investigations by authors who are nationally recognized experts in their respective fields.

Contents

11 Automation Applications in Bloodstain Pattern Analysis and Crime Scene Reconstruction 251

12 Presenting Evidence at Trial 267

13 Dealing with the Risk of Bloodborne Pathogens 275

Foreword

Bloodstain Pattern Analysis with an Introduction to Crime Scene Reconstruction is a clearly and concisely written text. It is the most complete and comprehensive handbook to date from the perspective of the investigator on the subject of bloodstain spatter analysis.

The authors have provided the reader with an articulate and practical guide to the interpretation of bloodstain patterns and crime scene analysis reconstruction. In fact, this text may very well form the bases for future standardization of blood spatter analysis.

The textbook begins with a chapter on the function of bloodstain analysis with an excellent historical perspective to acquaint the reader with the significant chronology of the application of this technique. The authors then provide an excellent section on distinguishing crime scene analysis from behavioral analysis and discuss the considerations involved in the reconstruction of the crime. There is an entire chapter dedicated to the important subject of proper terminology to be utilized in these analyses. The text then delves into the complex mechanics of blood spatter analysis with chapters which address the dynamics of reconstruction, such as determining motion and directionality, convergence and the point of origin, evaluating impact spatter bloodstains, the characteristic patterns of blood which aid in analysis and the proper documentation of blood stains and the reconstruction of a crime. The authors have included a chapter on automation application in bloodstain pattern analysis, presenting bloodstain analysis evidence at trial and dealing with bloodborne pathogens. The book is well illustrated with photos, practical applications, case histories and excellent appendices.

The authors bring 50 years of practical experience to this text. Tom Bevel, my friend and colleague for many years, is a retired Captain from the Oklahoma City Police Department. Tom holds a Master's Degree in Criminal Justice and has extensive training in the area of criminal investigation both in the United States and Europe. Tom has acted as a police consultant in over 29 different states and six foreign countries. He has personally participated in over 2500 criminal investigations in which bloodstain spatter evidence was the issue and has testified in numerous trials as an expert witness.

Ross Gardner, United States Army Criminal Investigation Command, has over 20 years of criminal investigative experience. He holds a Master's Degree in Computer and Information Resource Management and has extensive training in the area of criminal investigation through the United States Military. He is also certified as a Senior Crime Scene Analyst with the International Association of Identification and has published as a recognized expert in the field of bloodstain pattern analysis.

In my textbook, *Practical Homicide Investigation: Tactics, Procedures, and Forensic Techniques,* Third Edition, I point out that; "Solving homicides, especially those without witnesses are extremely more difficult to solve because your main witness, the deceased, is dead. One must develop the ability to "absorb" the crime scene, and be able to read the uncollectible nuances of the event." The interpretation and analysis of bloodstain patterns within the crime scene oftentime provides the investigator with the critical information to reconstruct the crime.

I personally believe that without scene experience there is a deficiency in crime scene reconstruction. Seasoned practice necessitates that the practitioner have that ability to "absorb" the crime scene, and be able to read the uncollectible nuances of the event. This is what we refer to as "scene experience" as opposed to a strict "laboratory" mentality. Tom Bevel and Ross Gardner both have this "scene experience" as well as the necessary knowledge to evaluate and apply the scientific methodology to the reconstruction process.

Bloodstain Pattern Analysis with an Introduction to Crime Scene Reconstruction is a masterful blend of practical crime scene knowledge and the application of scientific methodology to the process of crime scene reconstruction. It is organized in such a manner to allow the reader quick and easy reference into specific areas of blood spatter.

Vernon J. Geberth, M.S., M.P.S., B.B.A., FBINA
SERIES EDITOR

Preface

The goal of forensics and crime scene reconstruction is simply to seek the truth. In pursuing this end, we revisit what we hope is a not too distant past, and attempt to recreate the events that unfolded. The task is not simple, and the tools employed are all of the forensic disciplines.

Each area of forensics provides insight and a glimpse back into this past. Each has its place in evaluating the aftermath of crime — the physical evidence. In the most classical sense, the majority of the forensic disciplines provide us knowledge as to the "who" of crime. Fingerprints, serology, and trace and fiber evidence all give us the ability to associate people or objects with a crime scene. Forensic pathology, on the other hand, has always been our primary link to the "what" of crime, providing insight to some of the events that occurred during the incident.

Due to the efforts of people such as Dr. Paul Kirk and Herbert MacDonnel, bloodstain pattern analysis has reawakened to its role in modern forensics as another method of illuminating the "what" of crime. Used properly, bloodstain pattern analysis helps establish events associated with violent crimes. In this capacity, bloodstain pattern analysis acts as a critical bridge between classical forensics and crime scene reconstruction.

Although not a young discipline, bloodstain pattern analysis is just beginning to recognize some of the universal rules that define it. We still see aggressive discussions among analysts over what can or cannot be inferred from a specific stain. More often than not these arguments consume our objectivity. They lead us to a darker side of forensics, where subjective analysis reigns. To fight this tendency, our continuing goal must be to understand the discipline, its underlying scientific basis, and how best to objectively apply this knowledge to cases in the field. The investigator's mission is to always illuminate the truth, not shroud it in shadows.

Athough the authors come to you from two distinctly different backgrounds, both have considerable experience in "on scene" crime scene evaluation. One, a career civilian law enforcement officer, is internationally respected as an expert in bloodstain pattern analysis. The other is a career Criminal Investigator for the United States Army. Two very different roads that led to the same destination. Interestingly enough, those roads cross outside the City of London, at the Metropolitan Police Detective Training School. Although several years apart, both attended the Scenes Of Crimes Officer Course (SOCO).

The SOCO approach to scenes of crime, at the very least, is one of the most methodical in the world. This five-week course teaches the students to understand and incorporate all forensic evidence in the evaluation of crime. It places responsibility for understanding the interrelationship of that evidence on none other than a generalist — the crime scene investigator.

Perhaps, then it is the SOCO course which serves as the wellspring of the authors' shared passion and belief: conduct crime scene evaluations using a holistic approach.

Inherent in this thought is that case resolution is critically dependent upon proper crime scene analysis. However, case resolution is not just a matter of proving someone guilty. The investigator seeks the truth, no matter what it may be. This demands a consideration of all evidence available and the correlation of such evidence in an attempt to identify reasons for contradictory results when they happen to occur.

In the criminal justice system, it is not uncommon to encounter a lawyer who adamantly believes, no matter what the nature of the testimony, that the investigators have established in their own minds the innocence or guilt of a subject even before completing the crime scene evaluation. It appears incomprehensible to counsel that an investigator can take the often subjective information reported and conduct an objective investigation. Such a reaction should not surprise us, as the idea of objectivity is relatively foreign to law. No matter what the underlying truth, lawyers highlight that information which best serves their position and attempt to diminish that which works against them.

The crime scene analyst, however, can ill afford to pursue his or her end with the same mindset. Choosing what evidence one will or will not consider in the analysis is heresy. Unfortunately, that trap is far too easy to fall into.

Within the crime scene lies the evidence, which if properly analyzed provides everyone with an ability to define specific facts and certainly infer others. Based on the totality of this information, it may well be possible to determine the most probable events surrounding the situation. Even if one is unable to define the overall event, proper analysis still allows for the elimination of certain events, which alone adds clarity.

No forensic discipline has the potential to provide as much clarity regarding the occurrences at a crime scene as does bloodstain pattern analysis. That cannot, however, lead to an expectation that the bloodstain evidence should stand alone. Yet, in the right hands, bloodstain pattern analysis is an effective tool for defining the truth.

Bloodstain pattern analysis is not for the casual investigator who intends only to graze the surface, find a quick answer, and move on. The bloodstain pattern analyst is truly one who reconstructs crime scenes. As such, he or she must understand all the forensic disciplines. The analyst must be able to objectively apply each category of evidence to the situation, inferring as little as possible, but recognizing the whole. In this fashion, the *evidence* establishes a knowledge base from which the analyst reaches the "truth".

In part, the oath of office for a U.S. Army Criminal Investigation Special Agent states: "*I shall at all times seek diligently to discover the truth, deterred neither by fear nor prejudice....*" We dedicate this book to the men and women, analysts and investigators alike, who recognize and understand the importanance of their role as objective truth seekers.

The Authors

Tom Bevel is a Captain on the Oklahoma City Police Department. He is currently the Commander of the Homicide, Robbery, Missing Persons and the Unsolved Homicide Units. He has over twenty-six years of experience in law enforcement with twenty-two years in violent crime scene investigations.

Captain Bevel holds a Master of Arts degree from the University of Central Oklahoma in Criminal Justice. He is a graduate of the Scenes of Crime Course, Hendon, England; the Technical Investigations Course, Central U.S. Police Institute, Oklahoma State University at Oklahoma City, OK; the FBI National Academy, and the Post-Graduate Medical-Legal Course, London Medical College, London, England.

Captain Bevel was the Charter President for both the International Association of Bloodstain Analysts and the Association of Crime Scene Reconstruction.

Captain Bevel has been a crime scene consultant to over thirty U.S. States and six foreign countries. He has been qualified in many courts of law as an expert in crime scene reconstruction and bloodstain pattern analysis.

Ross M. Gardner is a Command Sergeant Major and Special Agent with the United States Army Criminal Investigation Command. He holds a Masters degree in Computer and Information Systems Management from Webster University, and a Bachelors degree in Criminal Justice from Wayland Baptist University. During his 22 years as a Military Policeman and Criminal Investigator, Special Agent Gardner has attended over 30 technical courses relating to criminal investigation. This includes the Scenes of Crime Course, Metropolitan Police Training Academy, Hendon, England from which he graduated top in his class. Special Agent Gardner is a member of the International Association of Bloodstain Pattern Analysts (IABPA), the Rocky Mountain Association of Bloodstain Pattern Analysts (RMABPA), the Association of Crime Scene Reconstruction (ACSR), and Compuserve's Technical Crime Association (TCA). He is certified as a Senior Crime Scene Analyst by the International Association of Identification (IAI), a rating he has held since

1990. Since 1988, Special Agent Gardner has been an active instructor in crime scene investigation, bloodstain pattern analysis, and computer crime investigation, teaching classes for police organizations, police consulting firms, and community colleges. He has authored five articles and in 1990, with co-author Tom Bevel, published *Bloodstain Pattern Analysis: Theory and Practice — A Laboratory Manual.*

Acknowledgments

In considering a project of this nature, it is rarely the effort of the authors alone which ensures success. We would like to offer thanks and acknowledgment to the following individuals for their support and effort:

- Rudi Jaehser of Frankfurt, Germany for his untiring efforts in leading Ross through the bowels of the Frankfurt University library those many late evenings.
- Regina Dearborn, for her expert translations of many of the articles discussed in Chapter 2. Without her skill in German and her ability as a legal translator, many of these articles would have remained unknown.
- Toby Wolson of Miami, Florida for his support in providing excellent examples of the *Roadmapping* concept.
- Sgt. Ron Wortham with the Oklahoma City Police Department, who designed and constructed equipment used in bloodstain pattern research, the results of which appear in this text.
- Jouni Kiviranta of the Helsinki Police, whose outstanding photography skills produced many of the enclosed figures.
- Dr. Martin Fackler of Florida, for his support and critical eye. Dr. Fackler readily shared his knowledge and research with us, providing important information to Chapter 7.
- Leonard Conn, formerly with the University of Oklahoma Police Department, who assisted in building equipment for both the stop-motion photography of blood impacting at various angles and for the high-speed photographs of a bullet impacting into a bloody target. Examples of both are included in this book.
- Vernon Geberth, who believed in our ability and helped bring the project to fruition. Without his support the book would still be a dream.
- Victoria Miller of Miller Forensic Computing, for her unselfish loan of a full-function copy of *No More Strings III*© for a separate project. That help and support ultimately led to the inclusion of many critical parts of Chapter 6.

- Dr. Alfred Carter of Carleton University, Ottawa for remaining patient and calm in the face of Ross' repetitive need for physics instruction.
- Dr. Kenneth Beard of Urbana-Champaign, IL whose original research led to our five-year search to better understand droplet impacts. Much of our understanding from Chapter 4 would not exist without Dr. Beard's initial assistance.
- Don Coffey, of the U.S. Army Criminal Investigation Command, for sharing his approach and knowledge on dealing with pattern transfers.
- John Anderson, Sheriff of El Paso County, CO for his untiring support and friendship. Whenever the project took a detour or seemed off track, John would offer a word of encouragement or support. Finally, he reminded us that nothing good is ever gained without some level of risk.
- Dr. Ronald O. Gilcher, M.D. and Arlene Wilson with the Oklahoma Blood Institute, who over many years have provided much information about blood components and the processing involved in blood products provided for research.
- To all the students from the 46 basic bloodstain pattern schools conducted by Tom. They have constantly demanded more and more knowledge which has caused the teacher to continue to grow within this discipline. From each and every class Tom gained knowledge and learned new techniques.
- Lt. Travis Witcher, (Retired) Oklahoma City Police Department for securing funding from outside sources that allowed Tom to attend training Hendon Police College in England. Lt. Witcher required at the end of this training that Tom start his own research and training courses to pass on the knowledge gained to OCPD officers. We can all benefit from the insight in his comment, "Teaching will force you to really learn the discipline." His wisdom is more than evident and serves as a challenge for each of us.
- William Turner, formerly of the USACIDC, who sparked a flame in Ross by sharing the knowledge he gained from a Corning Institute bloodstain pattern course. Bill probably has no idea of the events he set in motion, but we thank him anyway.
- The many instructors of the Scenes of Crime Officer Course, Metropolitan Police Detective Training School, Hendon, England. Their insight and knowledge is responsible in a large part for forging Tom and Ross' shared passion.
- Three units of the Oklahoma City Police Department and their respective members through the years: Technical Investigations, the Forensic Lab, and Homicide. All of them helped focus this discipline and develop Tom's "scene sense". Thank you for your never-ending support.

- Scott Hector, whose computer and late nights helped create many of the illustrations/figures used in the book.
- The following agencies and individuals for supplying various photographs in support of the project: Henry Muse, E-Systems; Lt. William D. Gifford, Anchorage Police Department; Donald R. Schuessler, Eugene Oregon Department of Public Safety; Tom J. Griffin and Barie Goetz, Colorado Bureau of Investigation; John Graham, Arvada Police Department; Helena Komulainen, curator of the Finnish National Gallery; Lt. Johnny Kuhlman, Oklahoma City Police Department; the Edmond Police Department, Edmond Oklahoma; Doug Perkins, Oklahoma State Bureau of Investigation; Ray Clark, the Oklahoma City Police Department; Heikki Majammaa, National Bureau of Investigation, Helsinki, Finland; Peter Barnett; Dr. Daniel Davis; *The Journal of Forensic Identification*; Mark Nelson, Springdale Police Department, Springdale, AR; T. Daniel Gilliam, Larimer County Sheriff's Department, Ft Collins, CO.
- The International Association of Bloodstain Pattern Analysts, the Rocky Mountain Association of Bloodstain Pattern Analysts, and the Association of Crime Scene Reconstruction for establishing an environment in which we can all grow.
- There are many more who may not be named here. All have contributed to this discipline in some fashion, which in turn assisted in the writing of this book. We salute them for their individual effort, insightfulness, and resulting research in support of bloodstain pattern analysis and crime scene reconstruction.

Dedication

Our love and thanks go out to our families for their support of this project. In particular, we wish to thank our wives, Elizabeth and Karen, for putting up with us during the long periods we spent behind the keyboard.

Bloodstain Pattern Analysis: Its Function and a Historical Perspective

1

"And Cain quarreled with Abel his brother: and it came to pass, when they were in the field, that Cain rose up against Abel his brother, and slew him.

And the Lord said unto Cain, Where is Abel, thy brother? And he said, I know not: Am I my brother's keeper?

And the Lord said, What hast thou done? The voice of thy brother's blood crieth unto me from the ground. And now art thou cursed from the earth, which hath opened her mouth to receive thy brother's blood from thy hand. When thou tillest the ground, it shall not henceforth yield unto thee her strength; and a vagabond shalt thou be on the earth.[1] "

Genesis 4:10

Reading these passages one might wonder, was God really unaware of what transpired between Cain and Abel? Was He then convinced of the crime only by the presence of Abel's blood? This seems unlikely given the nature of the Judeo-Christian God. Rather, it would appear that God was reminding Cain that no matter what Cain's denial, the physical evidence of the deed spoke in as strong, if not a more convincing voice. In these few short paragraphs, we find the historical basis and very likely the first usage of bloodstain pattern analysis in a judicial setting.

The Function of Bloodstain Pattern Analysis

What is the function of bloodstain pattern analysis? Like any forensic science or discipline, bloodstain pattern analysis seeks to define the facts surrounding some incident which is in question. The examination of the physical nature of bloodstains provides information specific to the events that occurred during the incident.

We often refer to what the analyst evaluates as the "static aftermath" of an event.[2] Dispersion, shape characteristics, volume, pattern, the number of bloodstains and their relationship to the surrounding scene are part of this aftermath. This information provides the investigator with a window to the past. Clarity is not a guarantee, for it is possible the information present in the bloodstains will fail to illuminate any of the issues in question. Often, however, the analyst finds direct and convincing information that makes the role of the fact finder much easier.

The information we are likely to discover through an examination of the bloodstains includes:

- The direction a given droplet was traveling at the time of impact.
- The angle of impact.
- The probable distance from the target from which the droplet originated.
- The nature of the force involved in the bloodshed and the direction from which that force was applied.
- The nature of any object used in applying the force.
- The approximate number of blows struck during an incident.
- The relative position in the scene of the suspect, victim, or other related objects during the incident.
- Sequencing of multiple events associated with an incident.
- In some instances, which hand delivered the blows from a beating.

The Relationship of Bloodstain Pattern Analysis to Crime Scene Reconstruction

Crime scene reconstruction demands that we evaluate all physical and testimonial evidence to derive some conclusion as to what occurred. As Geberth reminds us, for homicide investigations, case resolution hinges on "*careful and intelligent* [italics added] examination of the scene."[3] Much as does the reporter, the investigator attempts to define the who, what, when, where, how, and why of a crime to assist in reconstructing the events. There is an unfortunate problem associated with this process: there is no standard by which we can test our ultimate conclusions. An archaeologist once made an analogy about this difficulty: discussing a dig and the conclusions drawn from it, he said, "It's something like putting together a jigsaw puzzle without having access to the box. You really don't know what the picture is supposed to look like."[4] The investigator's box top is not available either. Despite this limitation, crime scene analysis and crime scene reconstruction attempt to define the nature of actions that are so dynamic that even if we had a videotape of the incident, they might not be fully understood.

In their most classic use, the majority of forensic disciplines provide the investigator with information regarding the "who" of the crime. Blood typing, DNA evaluations, fingerprint evidence, and hair examinations help us decide who was or was not present at the scene. In this concept of "who", we also include areas such as forensic chemistry, biology, geology, and trace evidence examinations, as they help associate items to our player and to the scene. This, too, ultimately serves the function of defining the "who" of the reconstruction.

Our answers to the "what", the actions that occurred during the crime, are sought most often through the application of forensic pathology. As Dr. James Luke stated: "From the standpoint of forensic pathology, the two major parameters that form the basis of any case investigation are (1) identification and documentation of the postmortem findings present, and (2) interpretation of those findings in the context of the *circumstances* of death." [Italics added.][5]

In the past two decades, bloodstain pattern analysis has reawakened to its role in documenting these circumstances. Bloodstain analysis brings to the investigation the ability to define those events which could or could not have occurred during the course of bloodshed. Once identified, these facts are considered in light of all other evidence as a means of corroborating or refuting statements, confessions, or investigative theories.

Thus bloodstain pattern analysis mirrors in many ways the role of forensic pathology. Once again quoting Dr. Luke, "It is the responsibility of the forensic pathologist finally to construct a scaffolding of factual information against which 'witnesses' and 'suspects' statements can be evaluated."[6] Bloodstain evidence in this role (acting as a scaffolding or part of the lattice) to stand apart from other evidence.[7] Reconstruction demands that we consider all evidence. Viewed from a holistic approach, all the evidence available should lead those who view it to a preferably similar conclusion.

This concept of a generally agreed-upon conclusion should not be a foreign thought, particularly when considering bloodstain patterns. They are, after all, graphically oriented. For example, in describing a pattern transfer as "consistent with" something, any analyst should be able to point to some physical characteristic of the stain and then to the correlating item which created it. The analyst should then be able to create some generalized reproduction of the pattern using the item. Having done so, another analyst cannot simply ignore this information. Granted, we may discover a secondary method of creation but this simply adds a responsibility to discover which is the more likely event. If a stain is observable and reproducible, it is difficult for two analysts to rationally argue their beliefs from mutually exclusive positions. When this occurs it is very likely the result of subjective analysis on the part of one or both. Unfortunately, subjective analysis is a fact of life. To help preclude subjectivity, the analyst should attempt to achieve several things.

First, the analyst must understand all areas of forensic science and have been directly exposed to crime scenes. Tom Griffin of the Colorado Bureau of Investigation often remarks that analysts need a "scene sense". This sense gives the analyst a more rounded perception, taking into consideration the many subtleties and interrelationships found at scenes. Evidence viewed from the confines of a white-walled laboratory is far too sterile. It leaves the viewer lacking a realistic perspective of crimes and crime scenes. It is this perspective which makes up "scene sense". As the SOCO course at the Hendon Detective Training School teaches, we gain much from viewing evidence *in situ*. This is true not only from a case perspective, but also for the long-term development of the investigator.

Do not construe the necessity for understanding these disciplines as meaning the analyst is an expert in all of them. Far from it — crime scene analysts are generalists. They have, much as does a manager, the knowledge to take the experience and expertise of the other team members and put them all together. This process is at the heart of crime scene reconstruction. As we will constantly remind the reader, it is not enough that the analyst can reconstruct the bloodstain evidence. A reconstruction that fails to consider all known evidence is no reconstruction at all.

Second, analysts must understand their discipline. Bloodstain pattern analysis is far from being a static field. Our understanding changes every day due to research and experimentation. As we base bloodstain pattern analysis on the application of physical laws on blood, there are certain universal rules we can apply. These rules are as true today as they were when first observed. Understanding these universal applications, and then seeking those areas that require further study, should be the lifetime goal of every analyst.

A Historical Perspective of Bloodstain Pattern Evidence

In seeking an understanding of bloodstain pattern analysis, it is important to look back at its evolution. In his book, *Blood Evidence*, Craig Lewis wrote: "The science of bloodstain pattern analysis, a field in which the only textbook in existence was written by MacDonell, was little known"[8] This viewpoint, although inaccurate, is not uncommon. Out of ignorance, authors, judges, and investigators continue to proclaim the discipline as something "new".

To those who spend time at scenes of violent crime, it seems unimaginable to ignore the presence of blood or not ask some simple questions as to its relationship to the crime. Bloodstain pattern analysis, as we will see, is anything but new. It is only in the last several years that we've discovered some of the more important historical documents relating to bloodstain pattern analysis. The existence of these documents alters the somewhat biased view held of our investigative predecessors.

The mere presence of blood, excluding any formal analysis, has long been held as evidence of foul play. For example, in the development of early Germanic law, tribal code (private, as compared to state) was often created. One of the surviving documents of this nature is the *Sachsenspeigel*. Compiled as a record of Saxon custom, a knight named Ritter Repkow wrote the document during the period of 1220–1235. Common Law II, 63, Article 1-3 dealt in part with the raising of the "hue and cry" and the necessity of proving one's innocence for acting against a criminal caught in the act. He who had acted was required to prove an incontestability of the criminal's deed.[9] Examples of this proof, although not quite *beyond a reasonable doubt* included "a criminal caught red handed".[10] The *Sachsenspeigel*, with its detailed illustrations, makes reference to the criminal having been caught with blood on his hand.

The work of William Shakespeare, although not the typical reference material of the criminalist, is filled with references to blood and the prejudicial nature by which its discovery is viewed. Shakespeare's various works, written between 1582 and 1616, like all authors, reflect the perceptions of his time. For example, in Act II, Scene II of *Macbeth*, after stabbing King Duncan, Macbeth says:

"What hands are here! Ha! they pluck out mine eyes. Will all great Neptune's ocean wash this blood Clean from my hand?"[11]

Though of little concern to modern bloodstain analysis, the *Sachsenspeigel* and Shakespeare's plays do reflect the consideration of bloodstains as a basic issue, preceding the formal development of forensic science. They also reflect the prejudicial manner in which bloodstains are often viewed. An interesting artistic example of the prejudicial nature of bloodstains hangs in the Central Art Archives of Finland. The work is entitled *Fratricide*, by Akseli Gallen-Kallela (*circa* 1897). It shows a young man with a bloodied sword and clothing as his mother points to numerous stains on his clothing (see Figure 1).

Another author whose writings reflect man's inquisitive nature with blood evidence is Sir Arthur Conan Doyle. In 1887, Doyle wrote *A Study in*

Figure 1 "Fratricide," by Akseli Gellen-Kallela, photographed by Hannu Aaltonen. An 1897 painting owned by the Anteneum, the Antell Collection, and the Central Art Archives of Finland. Beyond the issue of his bloody sword, the pattern transfer and blood spots on the young man's garments speak his guilt to his mother. (Photo courtesy of National Art Archives Museum, Helsinki, Finland.)

Scarlet, introducing the world to his brilliant character Sherlock Holmes. In this story, the master of deduction concerns himself not only with discovering a reliable reagent test for blood, but also in the examination of "gouts and splashes of blood, which lay all around."[12] Again, we see artistic indications that those concerned with the early investigation of crime considered the relationship of bloodstains to such crime.

Early Scientific References

Having considered several literary references, it seems appropriate to turn our attention to the scientific evaluation of bloodstain patterns. Your authors intend to discuss some of the more critical and insightful research conducted over the last century, however, there are many references that may not be mentioned or discussed in detail. The analyst should recognize this and consider seeking these historical references for greater enlightenment.

In Germany and Austria, the universities at Kiel and Vienna appear to have been academic hotbeds of activity in bloodstain pattern analysis. Two significant authors of the time were Eduard Piotrowski and Ernst Ziemke, followed soon after by Dr. Baltzhazard of France.

The primary periodical through which many of the continental authors expressed themselves was the *Viertaljahresschrift fur gerichtliche Medizin* (Quarter-Year Writings for Forensic Medicine), published in Germany. Although much of the concern between 1850–1940 dealt with the identification of blood, scattered throughout these discussions are references to patterns observed at scenes.

Before proceeding, it is important to note that in German the term "blutspritzen" was widely used by various authors. This term is translated most often as "blood sprinkles".[13] There is, however, no absolute translation and the terms sprinkle, spatter, splash, or spurt are all in acceptable usage.[14] It becomes difficult, then, to always understand the specific context intended by any author. A caution is in order when considering the translations offered here.

In 1856, J. B. Lassaigne wrote *Neue Untersuchungen zur Erkennung von Blutflecken auf Eisen und Stahl* (New Examination to Differentiate Bloodspots From Iron and Steel). In the latter section of his paper, Lassaigne discusses marks which appeared similar to bloodstains, but were caused by insects.[15]

Although, Lassaigne made it clear he believed "crushing" of dead flies created such stains, he implied having found such stains at scenes and associated their presence to the presence of flies. Based on the description, these stains seem similar to what we might refer to as "fly specks". Unfortunately, the translation and overall description of Lassaigne's cannot satisfy the issue. Had Lassaigne found "fly specks"? Was he then establishing a causal connection without considering the regurgitation of blood by flies at bloodstained scenes? Whatever the case, Lassaigne's observations establish his attention to detail and concern for differentiating such stains from normal bloodstains.

In 1863, John Beck and Theodric Beck wrote *Elements of Medical Jurisprudence*. The article, as reviewed by Herbert MacDonell, discussed various cases in which bloodstain pattern analysis was utilized. Specific references were made to the "situation" of wounds, and as MacDonell noted, the authors also used the term "blood sprinkles". The latter term tends to indicate a German influence, although the article originated in Philadelphia.[16]

In 1880, Dr. Henry Faulds published *On Skin-Furrows of the Hand*, describing bloody fingerprints and their likely usage to identify the criminal.[17]

In 1882, Professor Charles M. Tidy of London published *Legal Medicine*, in which he stated:

"… few things hold so important a place as, or involve investigations of a greater nicety, than determining the precise nature of various [blood] spots or stains found on fabrics, instruments…"[18]

Perhaps one of the most impressive treatises written on the subject of bloodstain pattern analysis is *Ueber Entstehung, Form, Richtung und Ausbreitung der Blutspuren nach Hiebwunden des Kopfes*, (Concerning Origin, Shape, Direction and Distribution of Bloodstains Following Blow Injuries to the Head) written by Eduard Piotrowski in 1895 at the University of Vienna.

Dr. Piotrowski's application of science to his observations and evaluations of bloodstains is unequaled in the known writings of the time. He reconstructed his scenes to model those in question, controlled and adjusted various variables to determine their specific effect on his experiments, and used live rabbits! Although the latter issue would not sit well with many modern groups, Dr. Piotrowski recognized the dynamic nature of what he was studying.

Dr. Piotrowski considered this dynamic nature and used it as one of his variables. Calling the concept a "*complicirtem morde*" he used multiple methods of attack against his study subjects (rabbits); thereby ensuring to himself he was considering all possibilities and their effects.[19]

In considering this *complicirtem morde*, Dr. Piotrowski properly recognized bodily reactions of his subjects when struck. In the following example he observed small stains "similar to dots" which radiated out from the rabbit's head, and concluded:

"As far as their position is concerned, they spread out in a radiating pattern. The center of this outward radiating droplet [pattern] was the nostrils and mouth from which the accumulated blood was forced out … [expiratory blood]."[20]

Evident to Piotrowski was the correlation between the location of the stain's tail and the direction the droplet was traveling at impact. Also, he recognized the causative factors of cast-off stains. He included in his evaluation of the first the effect of a parabolic arc on the resulting stain. In the latter, he isolated not only the fact that blood flung from a weapon would create a specific stain, but also correlated this with stain directionality, giving him an ability to define the direction in which the weapon was being moved.[21] In this work's concluding statement, Dr. Piotrowski commented: "the formation, shape, and distribution of bloodstains follow specific rules and that these, allowing for many modifications considering the nature of the case, are not to be underestimated and are of great value in the judgment…"[22]

Jurgen Thorwald, in describing the efforts of Professor A. Florence stated:

"[Florence] had worked out a whole system for classifying bloodstains caused by dripping, splashing, spurting, or grazing contact. Round stains, or roundish jagged stains, for example, indicate that blood fell vertically; oblong stains result from impact at various angles."[23]

Thorwald based his discussion on Florence's article "Les Taches de Sang au Laboratoire De Medicine Legale De Lyon". This article originally appeared in the *Archives De Anthropolgie Criminelle* in 1901.

In 1904 Hans Gross wrote *Handbook fur Untersuchnungsrichter Als System Der Kriminalistik* in which he provided a detailed discussion of not only the evaluation of bloodstains, but also their collection and documentation.[24] Gross felt bloodstains were of critical importance in the investigation and he devoted some 30 pages of the book to his considerations of blood and bloodstain patterns in the investigative process.

In 1914, Haberda wrote, *Eine besondere Form von Blutspritzen* (A Special Form of Bloodstain), discussing a specific pattern observed in airway injuries. He described such stains as droplets of various shapes which contained small air bubbles mixed with the blood. Beyond his consideration for this particular stain, Haberda offers many insightful lessons which are still applicable. Consider the following:

"The discovery of quantity, spread, form, and arrangement of bloodstains at a blood spattered crime scene can be of high importance. Evaluation requires many years of experience, usually learned little by little through practice, but never from books. Never the less, experts are often not careful enough when it comes to the necessary evaluation.

Forced by precise questions of police, jurisdictional or governmental authorities, the experts sometimes answer too exclusively and draw the wrong conclusions about the bloodstains on a corpse or in the surrounding crime scene."[25]

We would agree wholeheartedly that oftentimes analysts make conclusions which are far too exclusive.

Haberda also made reference to bloody fingerprints, clothing pattern impressions, and his particular stain: the foamy bloodstain. In describing the shape of stains which might be encountered, Haberda said:

"Even though the distance of the fall, or the angle with which the blood hits the ground influences the shape of bloodstains, which are for example more or less round, bear paw like, club or bottle like…"[26]

How similar to modern descriptions are Haberda's? *Round* and *bear paw* are still adjectives used to describe stains, while *elliptical* replaced terms like *club* or *bottle-like*. There can be little doubt Haberda was observing and classifying the very things we still look for today.

Ernest Ziemke is another author of interest. His work is found in *Gerichtsarztliche und polizieartzliche Technik,* a book written by Theodor Lochte in 1914. Chapter 7 entitled "Die Untersuchung von Blutspuren" (The Examination of Blood Tracks) was written by Dr. Ziemke. The work includes 14 pages of text with numerous pictures; it details various stains and the information represented by those stains. Ziemke dealt with a wide range of issues affecting bloodstain pattern analysis.

In the chapter preamble, Dr. Ziemke states:

> "Blood tracks [effects or evidence] are the most important tracks that stay behind after a crime is committed. Very often they alone have been of significant enough importance for the conviction of the suspect, and have been the focal point in a trial with only circumstantial evidence... Their evaluation should be efficient, because during an investigation it may be hard to foresee what might be of importance later during a court trial.[27]"

In discussing the search for blood, both for serological and bloodstain pattern evidence, Dr. Ziemke offers that:

> "The suspect, his clothes, all items he carries, or which are in his pockets should be carefully examined for bloodstains."[28]

This is sound advice which some of the best bloodstain pattern analysts in the country continually stress and teach today. Far too often such minute traces are simply overlooked by investigators.

In discussing pattern analysis and the conclusion drawn, Dr. Ziemke comments:

> "Very important conclusions can be drawn from the arrangement, location, size, and form of bloodstains ... Based on our own experience and experiments we want to point out that it is necessary to be cautious and not draw conclusions from a single or very few blood tracks. This happens quite often... Only when a large number of bloodstains are examined and compared, is it possible to exclude errors [in logic]."[29]

Dr. Ziemke provided detailed descriptions of various types of bloodstains. His terminology followed that of Piotrowski, but he added terms such as "thorn apple shaped" to refer to the bear claw stain. He acknowledged that secondary droplets (wave cast-off stains) in these instances would indicate the direction of motion of the blood droplet. He included figure examples of cast-off blood and drip patterns in which he described how to define

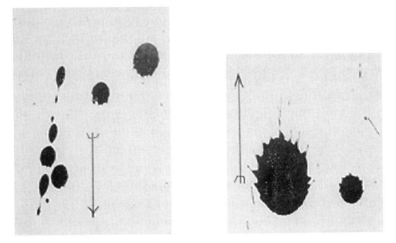

Figure 2 Illustrations from Dr. Ziemke's chapter on bloodstain patterns which relate to defining directionality. The two figures (Ziemke's Figures 42 and 43) demonstrate a drip effect from walking and running. Ziemke added the arrows to show the directionality evident in the stains.

directionality. Figure 2 is an example of one of these illustrations. In closing his discussion of bloodstain patterns, he said:

> "When the examination of bloodstains is done efficiently and carefully, and if all possibilities are exhausted, shape, location, and the site of the bloodstain can give important details about the circumstances of the deed, eventually even be of importance for the conviction of the suspect."[30]

Dr. W. F. Hesselink, writing in 1931, considered various issues related to bloodstain analysis in his article "Blutspuren in der Kriminalistchen Praxis." For example, Hesselink considered the subsequent condition of the dried stains on clothing as a manner of differentiating whether such clothing had been worn or in use since the deposit of the stains. He also considered a method of dissolving the bloodstain to determine its relative age when compared to some other stain. Hesselink eventually concluded this technique was inaccurate, indicating that the manner in which each droplet dried and coagulated would impact on the results.

He also considered whether a suspect would or would not be stained in a violent murder, making the following observations:

> "The answer depends upon two main circumstances: one, if many bloodstains are found at the scene, and two, what instrument was used. Regarding this I did several experiments. When using the hammer, the liquid squirts in all four directions, and will also cover the suspect. If a stick is used, the blood squirts left and right, and the suspect might not show any blood

marks. When a forward bent file is used, the blood squirts only to the front. The foreground [of an illustration] shows many spatter while only a few went towards the subject. While the suspect of a bloody murder, performed with a hammer, usually will be bloodstained, the suspect, in case of death caused by hitting with a bent file might have few or no bloodstains on the clothes."[31]

Hesselink then described the use of a pattern transfer he discovered, stating:

"In one murder, I found a blood spot on the bedroom floor. First, it did not look too informative, but when I examined it later with a very strong light, I found remarkable prints of about 14 shoe nails."[32]

Hesselink sought not only to define the nature of the stains found, but to define the manner of the event creating the stains. He then correlated the information with other forensic evidence, resulting in a partial reconstruction of his scene and the crime. His recognition of the importance of bloodstain pattern analysis for this purpose is reflected in his closing statement:

"Therefore, when examining blood, the blood investigation [to identify a substance as blood] itself is not as important as the clarification of surrounding circumstances."[33]

In 1939, at the XXII Congress of Forensic Medicine, one of the most insightful papers relating to bloodstain pattern analysis was presented by Dr. Victor Baltzhazard, R. Piedelievre, Henri Desolille, and L. Derobert. Entitled Etude Des Goutes De Sang Projecte the proposed purpose of the research was to pinpoint characteristic elements of a bloodstain which might "give decisive hints" as to its origin.[34]

Baltzhazard et al. felt it necessary not only to examine the resulting spatter and stains, but also to understand the manner in which blood exits wounds, the trajectories of such blood, and the manner in which the blood droplet changed to become the resulting stain. As with Piotrowski, Baltzhazard recognized the importance of the dynamics involved in bloodshed, and realized bloodshed could not always be mimicked under laboratory conditions. To provide more realistic data, Baltzhazard utilized rabbits to produce actual bleeding injuries.[35]

Baltzhazard's consideration of the length-to-width ratio of a stain as a function of impact angle is one of the most important contributions of this work. Analysts repeat his experiment in nearly every 40-hour bloodstain pattern analysis course taught today. Professor Baltzhazard offered a caution in considering impact angle estimations, however, stating:

"In practical application, it [impact angle evaluations]should not be looked after for an illusionary accuracy... Nevertheless, this curve permits an esti-mate of the impact angle with an acceptable accuracy, sufficient for practical purposes."[36]

Another important consideration was determining the point of origin. Baltzhazard furthered the cause and process for making such estimations. His group's efforts established the basis for current "stringing" techniques. Yet in considering the issue of the unknown parabola of the droplet, Baltz-hazard stated:

"Practically these methods can only be applied in a limited manner. [For instance] sometimes it is necessary to find out whether a victim, at the moment he was injured, stood on his feet or was lying."[37]

Finally, Baltzhazard's group considered the nature of the target on which a droplet fell. They found that many deformations would be possible, given various target characteristics. In summary Baltzhazard stated:

"These modifications [deformations caused by the target] are sometimes obvi-ous, but we must constantly remember that on an apparently homogeneous target, uneven areas can occur which may cause slight disfigurations."[38]

Dr. Paul Leland Kirk, of Berkeley, California also added immeasurably to the knowledge of bloodstain pattern analysis. Dr. Kirk, a Professor of Criminalistics and Biochemistry, was active in assisting law enforcement organizations in the U.S. between 1935 and 1967. Kirk's book, *Crime Inves-tigation*, published in 1953, included a chapter entitled "Blood: Physical Investigation". In that chapter Kirk discussed the application of bloodstain pattern analysis to criminal investigations.

Another source for Kirk's beliefs on the subject is evident in his affidavit filed in the Court of Common Pleas, Criminal Branch, in the case of State of Ohio v Samuel H. Sheppard. This document provides immense insight on his approach to bloodstain analysis.*

In the Sheppard case, Dr. Kirk considered the drying times of blood and the evaluation of blood trails as evidence. He specifically sought to evaluate plausible causes for such trails. Further, he identified a void in the bedroom of Mrs. Sheppard that others missed, which established the most likely posi-tion of the attacker. He then correlated the cast-off patterns found in the

---

* We must make one point when considering this document — whereas Dr. Kirk's knowl-edge and consideration of bloodstain analysis are unquestionable, we feel his reconstruction in the Samuel Sheppard case is difficult to defend. He managed to interweave extremely subjective information into his opinion of what was or was not a "fact".

room to the position of this void. Dr. Kirk clearly utilized a whole-scene approach.[39]

Modern Works in Bloodstain Pattern Analysis

Having dealt with a "historical" view of bloodstain pattern analysis, we arrive at a more recent history. Following Dr. Kirk's efforts through the 1960s was what might be considered the modern renaissance of the discipline. The number of authors writing on this subject increased dramatically, professional associations related to the field were established, and the discipline as a whole took on a far more accepted status in court.

Many proclaim Herbert MacDonell as the father of modern bloodstain pattern analysis. Whether this is accurate depends upon your individual perspective. What cannot be denied is that Herbert MacDonell brought about a distinct reawakening of this discipline.

In 1970, after conducting extensive research, MacDonell and Lorraine Bialousz coauthored *Flight Characteristics and Stain Patterns of Human Blood*. As the two were working under a Law Enforcement Assistance Administration (LEAA) grant, the LEAA published the report. The LEAA document remained available for nearly 12 years before going out of print. In 1982, the revised paper was released as *Bloodstain Pattern Interpretation*. MacDonell subsequently completed a third work on the subject in 1993, entitled *Bloodstain Patterns*.

In 1983 Dr. Henry Lee, Peter Deforest, and Dr. R. E. Gaensslen wrote *Forensic Science: An Introduction to Criminalistics*.[40] Included in this work is a 12-page section dedicated to explaining bloodstain patterns.

In 1983, the International Association of Bloodstain Pattern Analysts (IABPA) was formed. The association's stated purpose is to promote the general knowledge, techniques, and understanding of bloodstain pattern evidence.*

In 1986, the *Journal of Forensic Medicine* published two papers by Peter Pizzola, Steven Roth, and Peter Deforest, entitled "Blood Droplet Dynamics I and II". The group sought to examine the dynamics of liquid droplets in flight and photographed droplet impacts, providing a more accurate understanding of the action which is often called "wave cast-off". In "Blood Droplet Dynamics II", Pizzola et al. clearly demonstrated that motion in the target could mimic characteristics of an impact at a greater angle than that which occurred. Their findings are extremely important in our efforts to understand dynamic scenes of crime.[41]

---

* In support of this role, each year the IABPA hosts training seminars dealing with bloodstain pattern analysis and other related forensic disciplines.

In 1989, William Eckert and Stuart James published *Interpretation of Bloodstain Evidence at Crime Scenes*. Although the book received a very critical review in the *Journal of Forensic Science*, it was the first attempt in almost seven years to tackle bloodstain pattern analysis as a single reference text. The following year, the International Association of Identification accepted bloodstain pattern analysis as a tentative discipline, removing it as a subcategory of crime scene analysis. That same year, we wrote *Bloodstain Pattern Analysis: Theory and Practice — A Laboratory Manual*.

Summary

Whatever we might say of bloodstain pattern analysis, it has a rich history; one that indicates the consideration of bloodstains in solving crime predates even modern forensics. As to the issue of being a "new" discipline, the examination and consideration of bloodstain patterns and their historical acceptance in forensics is well documented. Long recognized for its ability to support the evaluation of scenes of crime, bloodstain pattern analysis serves the investigator by illuminating "what happened". It cannot tell us in all cases "who", but as Piotrowski and Hesselink discussed, the ability to define the "situation" or "circumstances" of the crime is often just as important.

Working with an understanding of all areas of forensics and with experience in evaluating crime scenes, the investigator can often use bloodstain pattern analysis to reconstruct the events surrounding a given incident. More and more, this process of crime scene reconstruction is being tested in our judicial system, but it is only through the application of quality objective analyses that the discipline can hope to serve its intended function. As analysts, our purpose must always be to guard against subjective analysis.

As we wrote in 1990…"each day, blood from scenes of a crime cries out to investigators. The use of proper bloodstain pattern analysis simply enhances the criminalist's ability to be an active listener to this very vocal witness."

References

1. Anon., *The Bible*, Genesis, 4:10.
2. MacDonnel, Herbert L., *Bloodstain Pattern Interpretation*, Laboratory of Forensic Science, Corning, NY, 1982, pg. 4.
3. Geberth, Vernon J., *Practical Homicide Investigation*, 2nd ed., Elsevier, New York, 1990, pg.12.

4. Anon., From a public television program. Our apologies to the author and show as they were not identified.

5. Ressler, Robert K. (et al.), *Sexual Homicide Patterns and Motives*, Lexington Books, Lexington, MA, 1988, pg. 155.

6. Ibid., pg. 162.

7. Bevel, Tom and Gardner, Ross M., *Bloodstain Pattern Analysis: Theory and Practice — A Laboratory Manual*, TBI Inc., Oklahoma City, OK, 1990, pg. 1.

8. Lewis, Craig A., *Blood Evidence*, Berkeley Books, New York, 1992, pg. 168.

9. Hinckeldey, Christopher, *Criminal Justice Through the Ages*, Druckerei Shulis, Heilbron, Germany, pg. 55.

10. Ibid., pg. 74.

11. Ibid., pg. 922.

12. Doyle, Arthur C., *The Original Illustrated Strand Sherlock Holmes*, Wordsworth Editions, Hertforshire, England, 1990, pg. 21.

13. MacDonell, Herbert L., Segments of History: The Literature of Bloodstain Pattern Interpretation, *International Association of Bloodstain Pattern Analyst News*, Volume 8, Number 1, March 1992.

14. Dearborn, Regina, Personal communications, January 1993.

15. Lassainge, J. B., Neue Untersuchung zur Erkennung von Blutflecken auf Eisen und Stahl, *Viereljahresschrift fur gerichtliche und offentliche Medicin*, 1856, pp. 285-289.

16. MacDonell, Herbert L., Segments of History: The Literature of Bloodstain Pattern Interpretation, *International Association of Bloodstain Pattern Analyst News*, Volume 8, Number 1, March 1992.

17. Ibid.

18. Ibid.

19. Piotrowski, Eduard, *Ueber Entstehung, Form, Richtung u. Ausbreitung der Blutspuren nach Hiebwunden des Kopfes*, Golos Printing, Elmira, NY, 1992, pg. 8 (German version).

20. Ibid., pg. 18 (German version).

21. Ibid., pg. 16 (German version).

22. Ibid., pg. 32 (English version).

23. As quoted by MacDonell, Herbert L., Segments of History: The Literature of Bloodstain Pattern Interpretation, *International Association of Bloodstain Pattern Analyst News*, Volume 8, Number 4, December 1992.

24. Gross, Hans Dr., *Handbuch fur Untersuchungsrichter Als System Der Kriminalistik*, J. Swietzer Verlag, Munchen, 1904.

25. Haberda, H., Eine besondere Form von Blutspritzern, *Vierteljahresschrift fur gerichtliche Medizin*, Volume 47, Supplement IX, 1914, pp. 380-381.

26. Ibid., pg. 381.

27. Lochte, Theodor and Ziemke, Ernest, *Gerichtsarztliche und polizieartzliche Technik,* J.F. Bergmann, Wiesbaden, 1914, pg. 152.

28. Ibid., pg. 153.

29. Ibid., pp. 157-158.

30. Ibid., pg. 164.

31. Hesselink, W. F., Blutspuren in der kriminalistischen Praxis, *Zeitschrift fur die angewandte Chemie*, Volume 44, Number 31, 1931, pp. 653- 654.

32. Ibid., pg. 655.

33. Ibid., pg. 655.

34. Balthazard, Victor, Piedelievre, R., Desoille, Henri, and Derobert, L., *Étude des Gouttes De Sang Projecte,* XXII Congres De Medicine Legale, Paris, France, June 1939, pg. 1.

35. Ibid., pg. 6.

36. Ibid., pg. 8.

37. Ibid., pg. 25.

38. Ibid., pg. 27.

39. Kirk, Paul L., Affadavit Regarding the State of Ohio vs. Samuel H. Sheppard, Court of Common Pleas, Criminal Branch, No. 64571, 26 April 1955.

40. Lee, Henry L, Deforest, Peter and Gaensslen, R. E., *Forensic Science: An Introduction to Criminalistics*, McGraw-Hill, New York, 1983.

41. Pizzola, P. A., Roth, S. and Deforest, P. R., Blood Droplet Dynamics — II, *Journal of Forensic Science*, JFSCA, Vol. 31, No. 1, Jan. 1986, pg. 58.

Crime Scene Analysis and Reconstruction

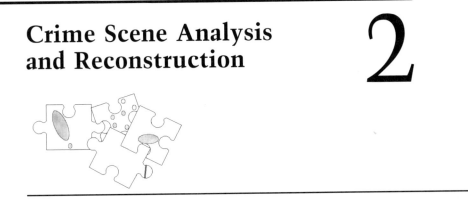

Discussions on crime scene analysis abound, but few defined methodologies exist to provide the analyst with a reference or beginning from which to understand what crime scene analysis really entails. Before proceeding to the specifics of bloodstain pattern analysis, it seems appropriate to consider crime scene analysis and reconstruction in their own right.

Distinguishing Crime Scene Analysis From Behavioral Analysis

To consider crime scene analysis we must first define the authors' consideration of analysis; specifically contrasting it from the work of the Federal Bureau of Investigation's Behavioral Sciences Unit (BSU).* This distinction is important as many people closely associate the BSU's methods of criminal profiling with the modern usage of the term "crime scene analysis".

The BSU provides an outstanding service in serial and violent crimes, which often assists the investigator in narrowing the search for a suspect. The process consists of three stages:

- Profiling inputs: crime scene, victimology, forensic information, police reports and background information, and photos.
- Decision process models: homicide style, primary intent, victim risk, offender risk, location and escalation.
- Crime assessment: reconstruction of the crime, crime classification, staging issues, motivation, and crime scene dynamics.[1]

---

* The Behavioral Science Unit was recently incorporated into the FBI's National Center for the Analysis of Violent Crime (NCAVC).

This evaluation, which considers the crime scene, the victim's actions and background, and the apparent actions of the suspect, provides information that may define the suspect as an individual. The information derived from the process is invaluable and has often proven its worth. It is also a subjective process; the BSU fully explains to prospective clientele (police agencies) that the method is not without fault and is anything but completely accurate.

Our discussion of crime scene analysis includes the evaluation of the scene, considering specific facts and any information we may safely infer from those facts. We base such an analysis on evidence that has been tainted as little as possible with subjective information. It is our position that having defined the crime in this fashion, we may always expand out to consider the more subjective information available and any hypothesis based on such information.

Crime scene analysis, then, is the process of defining those events supported directly by physical evidence. The first step in accomplishing this is the proper recognition and collection of such evidence, which is followed by a formal analysis.

Reconstruction is the end purpose of analysis; it requires not only the consideration of the events identified, but whenever possible the sequence of those events. Reconstruction in this sense does not demand the analyst identify a motive or intent behind some action. As we have stated, understanding human behavior during a crime is an issue fraught with subjectivity. Attempts to assign motive or intent to the specific events within the crime adds immeasurably to the problem.[2] We do not offer exclusion of this concern as an alternative, rather we simply think it best to conduct an objective evaluation, delaying our consideration of motive to the latter stages of the investigative process. Much as in the BSU's criminal profiling method, objective clear information must be the basis and foundation of any initial reconstruction or analysis.

In this chapter, we will first consider a conceptual model of analysis; looking at the function of collection, evaluation, assessment, and integration of evidence from the scene examination. Later, we will offer a methodology by which the analyst breaks down each crime into events, event segments, and their supporting evidence; considering each part in and of itself, then together as a whole. Lastly, we will consider the function of logic and its effect on decisions the analyst makes.

Limitations in the Reconstruction of Crime

Before progressing further we must accept the limitations of the reconstruction task. Much as in the archeologist's dilemma, we seek to revisit a past event and define it accurately for the court. The problem is that no true standard will ever exist to compare our conclusions to.

Just as limiting to the reconstruction is the fact that no matter how smoothly the investigation proceeds, in the end what we know is often far less than what we don't know. In part this is due to limitations in the available evidence. To accomplish the reconstruction we have only the evidence discovered and evaluated, and that evidence provides us with but mere glimpses back to the actions and events that encompass the crime.

The Rodney King incident in Los Angeles in 1989 is perhaps the best example of how truly limiting the reconstruction process can be. In the subsequent trial, jurors had to decide if the police officers acted appropriately during the apprehension. In this particular instance, the jury had an additional advantage, a video tape of many of the critical portions of the incident. The problem seemed simple enough: watch the tape and decide who was right and who was wrong. For example, was Mr. King struck full force in the face by a baton? The opposing counsels presented valid and convincing evidence claiming opposite positions.[3] Even with the tape, decisions of whether this action transpired were anything but simple for the jury.

Investigators rarely have the luxury of a videotaped beating, shooting, or murder from which to develop a concise picture of the actual events involved. Lacking such evidence, the court still expects us to shed light on what did or did not transpire during any given incident. We attempt to do this by using whatever evidence is available.

In viewing our scene to define these events, the evidence encountered will likely fall into one of three broad categories. Without alluding to legal definitions, we might name these categories: Direct, Circumstantial, and Peripheral.

Direct evidence is that which gives us clear direction and focus relevant to some event or action. For example, a contact gunshot wound indicates the weapon was in contact with the victim, thus whoever operated the weapon must also have been in an appropriate proximity. A latent fingerprint tells us clearly that the depositor of the latent had contact with the item it was found on. This type of evidence speaks clearly and concisely to everyone.

Following direct evidence is the *circumstantial evidence*, which provides direction but lacks distinct focus. Consider a swipe pattern made with the victim's blood. Obviously, it occurred after the victim received some bleeding injury, yet the specifics of who made the swipe and how it was made may still be lacking. This evidence is still important, but it demands that we carefully consider any conclusions we draw from it.

On the heels of this second category comes the *peripheral evidence*. For instance, consider a single hair or fiber found at the scene. Can we relate it to the incident or is it perhaps some accidental deposit totally unrelated to the situation being investigated? This type of evidence may or may not assist in the reconstruction. The problem is in determining where and how it fits into the overall picture. Nevertheless, it may be critical to our understanding of the event. Oftentimes this type of evidence creates major distractions, not only during the investigation but also in the subsequent judicial proceeding. As we are not clear as to how it relates to the scene, wild and insupportable claims are often made regarding that relationship.

In pursuing a reconstruction we seek to define physical events that we were not present to observe. Therefore, we must always remember that:

- These events are dynamic. This is to say that any number of similar events may produce the result which we observe. These similar events, however, may deviate in slight but important ways.
- The nature of the evidence to support our decisions on these events, even in the best of circumstances, will probably provide a glimpse back to this past.
- Rarely, if ever, will we have a standard to which we can objectively compare our conclusion.

Therefore, neither we nor the court can ever be absolutely certain as to all of the specifics encompassing an incident. We may be able to define individual moments with near-absolute clarity, but in the end our overall picture is simply the most probable definition available based on experience and the evidence available to us. For this reason we should never attempt to define too narrowly the events surrounding an incident. Our responsibility is to make this an objective picture, inferring as little as possible.

A Conceptual Model for Analysis

The process of analysis involves four stages when considering any piece of information. (In the following section information and evidence may be considered synonymous.) These stages are

- Collection
- Evaluation
- Assessment
- Integration

The first is perhaps the investigative benchmark, for without collection there is nothing to analyze. The latter three serve specific functions in deciding whether some piece of information has value to the investigation.

In discussing analysis, we need to introduce three terms which relate to a reconstruction process called Event Analysis. We'll discuss the terms in greater detail later in the chapter, but a definition of each is helpful at this point. The terms are

- **Incident:** the incident encompasses all actions related to the crime.
- **Events:** each event is some part of the crime. Each event can be defined by either specific actions (event segments) or specific items of evidence.
- **Event Segments:** distinct moments of the crime defined by some specific action and supported by physical evidence.

Collection and the Generalist Attitude

Obviously, evidence which is neither recognized nor collected has no value to the investigative process. If responsible for the initial scene processing, the analyst must know what to look for and what it can tell them. Knowledge and experience in all areas of forensics and criminalistics is a must for any analyst. A "generalist" attitude must prevail in the analyst's mind: that is, to become familiar with and remain current on forensic advancements. As any area of forensics may affect the consideration of evidence found at a given crime scene, the analyst must be able to interrelate the various disciplines. This ability combined with a "scene sense" is an absolute prerequisite to becoming a crime scene analyst.

Evaluation

The first stage in a formal reconstruction is evaluation. In the process of evaluation the analyst considers two sub-issues, reliability and credibility of the evidence or information. Reliability impacts on crime scene analysis in a very minimal sense as it considers the source of the item or information. In most instances the source for any given piece of evidence is the scene itself. If we find the evidence within the scene, we accept its trustworthiness unless issues of staging or contamination are evident or possible. Learning to be cognizant of such issues is an integral part of the investigator's scene sense.

In view of this concern we need to ask two questions of those who respond to the scene (e.g., officers, firemen, EMT): (1) What did you do there and (2) what did you move in the scene? Failing to ask these questions is a failure to properly consider the reliability issue.

Staging of the scene, situations in which the criminal creates false evidence to mislead us, presents an odd contrast. Staging certainly impacts on issues of reliability for reading the scene as it was left for us to view. Yet, staging is an integral part of the scene and represents reliable, distinct evidence in and of itself. Our concern, then, is to recognize the investigative "red flags" which point to staging.[4] Once the issue of staging is on the table we must then attempt to differentiate the evidence which is accurate as a reflection of the true event from that which the subject designed to misguide us.*

Another reliability issue may be the evaluation of the condition of evidence observed but not recorded for subsequent viewing. In such instances we must consider the ability of any source (e.g., witnesses, officers) to effectively observe, register, and then report the information. It would be preferable to see such evidence firsthand, but if it was moved, destroyed, or otherwise damaged our source's observation of such evidence may be all that is available. If we reasonably assume our sources are reliable we cannot dismiss their observations, nor should we.

After considering source reliability, the next sub-issue in evaluation is to consider the credibility of the information or evidence in question. Credibility considers issues such as:

- Is the action or evidence in its current condition possible?
- Is there corroboration to the evidence?
- In considering the other evidence available, does this item present any specific contradictions?
- If such contradictions exist, can we reconcile them, or is one inherently less accurate than another?

Credibility, as evident from the preceding questions, has a direct relationship to establishing issues of staging or inadvertent contamination. This step assists in considering if a particular piece of evidence found at a given scene is related to the event in question. In effect, we apply a "tree vs. forest" approach — evaluating the specific item first in view of itself, then contrasting it against other evidence known to us.

Having considered reliability and credibility, at the end of the evaluation phase we should feel reasonably sure which information is trustworthy and which is less reliable. It is important to note that although we may place some piece of evidence in a less than admirable light following evaluation, we should not discard it entirely.

Assessment

Following the evaluation phase, the analyst must assess the information. Assessment considers the information in light of what it does or does not

---

* To a great extent we would agree with Professor Haberda regarding the ability to read a scene:[5] the analyst learns this ability not from books nor classroom lecture, it is learned singularly through experience.

prove. We start asking simple questions regarding the evidence, and by answering them we establish the specific events or event segments that will eventually make up our overall reconstruction of the crime.

Rynearson and Chisum, in discussing crime scene analysis, considered all evidence against two things: time and surroundings.[6] Although this approach to assessment is functional, we prefer several modifications.

The analysis will eventually bring us to a point of defined actions, or what we call event segments. Each item of evidence speaks to some event segment where it was created or used. In reconstructing the incident, we must consider each event segment and the information which supports it with three objectives in mind:

- The basic nature of the segment and evidence.
- The relational aspects to other segments and evidence.
- Time and sequencing aspects.

In considering the basic nature, we seek to describe the event segment or evidence in its simplest form. In describing evidence we start simply with: What is it? In answering this question for an event segment, our answer is likely to consider: What was the nature of the occurrence? We also look at the function or purpose the evidence or action served. This often leads to the question: Was it used as intended, or did it serve an alternate function? (See Figure 3.)

Our next consideration is to see what relation the event segment or evidence has to other events, event segments, and evidence found in the scene. What interrelationships exist between the various articles of evidence or the scene as a whole. (See Figure 4.)

Such considerations help us link the evidence in some fashion to the scene, victim, subject, or other involved parties. Here the classic linkage triangle is important.[7] (See Figure 5.) Our function is to relate the three primary players (scene, victim, and subject) to one another by considering how each of the actions may tie any one of the three together. With regard to the event segments, a specific concern is to determine which segments appear related or result from a common event.

Other obvious relational questions emerge: Is this item foreign to the scene? If so, Why and how did it come to be here? This further demands a reevaluation of the basic nature issues. As in the Figure 4 example, the presence of the wire in the scene seems to indicate it is foreign. This may eventually point to some link (e.g., an occupational link) between the wire and the subject.

Throughout the evaluation and assessment the analyst must consider not only what is found but also ask what is missing from the scene; constantly

Basic Nature Issues

At a rape/homicide scene we discover two items of specific concern:
  - a wire which is fashioned in a loop and left in place in the victim's mouth.
  - a small bloody mark on the victim's thigh.

What is it?
We determine the wire is heavy gauge electrical wiring, similar to that used for AC wiring.

The blood spot is a swipe mark. It holds limited characteristics of a fingermark.

What function did it serve?
The looping device is not the mechanism of death. It appears to have served as some mechanism of control. What we are not sure of, is if this was a true mechanism of control or a prop related to the subject's fantasy.

There is no blood source evident for the swipe. It doesn't appear to be a ritualistic marking and gives the appearance of being an accidental contact.

Figure 3 In answering basic nature issues, we ask simple questions regarding the items of evidence we find. What is it? What function did it serve? We keep our focus clearly on the item itself, without drawing broad conclusions based on other evidence.

watching for negative evidence issues and documenting the presence of such a condition. Negative evidence may play a distinct role in evaluating a situation where there are several possible events. It serves as an auditing method, which we'll discuss later in the chapter.

Having dealt with the basic nature and the relational aspects of the evidence, this information will lead the analysts to a point where they can define specific event segments. (See Figure 6.) The next concern is that of time and sequencing effects. In what manner will this evidence establish or define:

- Specific information related to the actual or relative time of the crime.
- The sequence of events or event segments associated with the crime.

Sequencing information is extremely important as it assists the analyst in ordering the events segments during the integration stage of the analysis. Time and sequencing aspects, however, are distinct. For instance, rigor follows a basic time line in its onset and departure from the corpse. Identifying the stage of rigor present at some point, often gives indications of when the individual was killed. In other words, it places the time of the crime. Granted we cannot take the rigor time line as absolute, but it does point to the passage

> ### *Relational Aspects*
>
> #### Relationship to the Scene
> We find no similar wire anywhere in the scene. It appears to be foreign. We do find small traces of similar insulation on the floor in the scene.
>
> There is no other blood present in the scene.
>
> #### Relationship to Other Evidence
> Examination determines the wire and insulation exhibit similar toolmarks.
>
> The blood is inconsistent with the victim. But small blood traces under the victim's fingernails are found to be of a similar type.
>
> There are no usable latent characteristics in the swipe, other than to verify the likely source as a finger.
>
> The tool, wire source, a minor injury, and the subject's blood type represent future means of linking our subject. Certainly the wire itself may indicate an occupational link to our subject.

Figure 4   Considering our evidence against all other evidence, we attempt to establish links between the various items we find. It also provides future focus for evidence we may need to seek out.

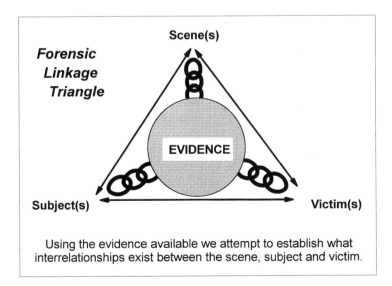

Using the evidence available we attempt to establish what interrelationships exist between the scene, subject and victim.

Figure 5   The crime scene analyst uses the concept of the linkage triangle in considering every item of evidence found. In what fashion will it establish specific links between the victim, scene, and subject?

Event Segment Definition

Relating to the loop:
The loop was likely cut and fashioned on scene, which tends to indicate the subject already had control of the victim.

This makes it more likely the loop is a prop and served no true control function.

Relating to the swipe:
The victim apparently scratched or scraped the subject during the assault, resulting in a minor bleeding wound.

This occurred some time after she was undressed, as no blood is found on her clothing, which was forcibly removed.

This defines some attempt by the victim to fight off her attacker.

Figure 6 All of our prior considerations eventually lead us to a point where we can define specific actions or aspects of the crime, the event segments. They also help us answer our basic nature question: What function did it serve?

of time since the crime. A broken watch may point to the time of an altercation; this of course assumes we have sufficient reason to believe it broke during the incident in question. We often seek to identify interruptions of daily schedules to give us information relevant to when the crime may have occurred. Each of these types of evidence or events points to the actual time of the incident. They serve only a limited purpose in sequencing the events which encompass the incident itself.

Sequencing, on the other hand, helps define where the various events and event segments belong in the overall picture. For example, distinguishing a stain as a wipe indicates the deposit of the blood first, followed by its disturbance. The analyst must constantly seek out information which will assist in the sequencing process for it is the very heart of the reconstruction.

In considering time, Rynearson and Chisum identified three effects related to time which are of specific concern:

- Predictable effects.
- Unpredictable effects.
- Transitory effects.[8]

We look at things such as the progression of rigor and livor as predictable effects. Perhaps a good example of a predictable effect in bloodstain pattern analysis is the time required for skeletonization to begin. As Pex and Hurley noted, this time is very short in individual spatter or stains, beginning within 30 to 60 sec. after the stain deposit.[9] If we find disturbances within such stains without evidence of skeletonization, this places the action of disturbance very close to the time of deposit of the stain.

Rynearson and Chisum considered unpredictable effects to be those things that we cannot control. Such effects tend to destroy the value of evidence at the scene. Inadvertent contamination, destruction, and altering of evidence are examples. Unpredictable effects most often impact on how the analyst views the evidence and incorporates it into the analysis.

Transitory effects include those things which are fleeting. If unrecognized, they may well be lost forever. Often referred to as fragile evidence, a failure to recognize and record their condition could also be disastrous. Reliability issues become important in dealing with such concerns. We cannot ignore reports of evidence of this nature, but we must be confident of the source's ability to have effectively observed and remembered this evidence.

During the assessment phase the investigators will generally establish a set of questions that are of immediate issue. They then seek to answer these questions using the assessment process described. This is not to say the investigators are looking for "his or her answers" and nothing else, but without some basic questions to consider, assessment serves no logical function nor for that matter would the investigation. Examples of initial assessment questions might be:

- How did the subject enter the dwelling?
- What instrument was used in the assault?

Often after viewing the scene and considering the analysis, the investigators may find they are asking the wrong questions and have an inappropriate focus. To correct this the investigators must be willing to reformulate their questions, considering any new knowledge. The only limiting factor in assessment is the analyst's willingness to clear the slate and start the process again. Much as Geberth commented that "flexibility and common sense" are key ingredients to successful homicide investigation, these elements are also critical to any attempt in crime scene assessment.[10]

What is unfortunate is that often we find ourselves aligned to ideas that too narrowly define the questions being asked. The analyst must be willing to consider any possibility. As Dr. Jon Nordby wrote "Detectives are not ordinarily in the habit of reasoning to generate novel hypotheses … instead they habitually reason to select the best model from among a given set of fixed alternatives."[11] In effect, we attempt to fit our observations of the evidence into narrowly defined conclusions. For example, we may attempt to define a death as murder, without considering suicide, autoerotic, or accidental causes.

Failing to find corroboration to the analyst's initial set of questions invariably leads the investigation in some new direction. If we lack evidence that a "subject" entered our death scene, then our focus should shift to questions of whether evidence is present to support suicide or accidental death. Remember, the questions asked in assessment are simply a guide: the analyst must be ready to readjust the focus at any time.

Another consideration in assessing evidence is giving credence to both the positive and negative aspects of the evidence. The analyst must ask, In what fashion does this evidence support some position, and how does it refute the same position? Inexperienced investigators often make the mistake of assuming evidence singularly proves or disproves some issue. This might occasionally be true, but it is more often the case that an item of evidence may support several points of view.

We must also consider the relevance of the information or evidence, considering all questions at issue. Simply accepting the evidence for what it apparently proves or disproves on its face, may lead to overlooking valuable links. This is particularly true if one considers scenes of crime from the point of view that nothing "just happens". Every event has some series of actions which lead up to it.

These background actions may have no specific relevance to the crime, nor will they in every instance be of concern to the investigation. In some instances, however, the relevance of these actions may be to determine which of two possible event segments is the more likely occurrence. This process can be refered to as auditing, as it represents a means by which to cross check the evidence. Auditing can often assist the investigator in establishing the staging of a scene by identifying situations in which evidence simply "appears" within the scene.

To understand this process, imagine a situation in which we are faced with two possible events sequences which might explain evidence discovered at the scene. The evidence related to what happened supports both possible events equally. We are left, then, to objectively choose from between these events the one we feel is the more probable.

If we look beyond the immediate issues and find background evidence supporting the occurrence of Event A but no such evidence to support Event B, from the reconstruction perspective Event A is the more probable event. Later in the chapter we'll give the reader a more detailed example of this auditing process.

By the end of the assessment phase the analysis should have distinct form. The questions asked by the investigator have been revised and a primary focus found. Much as a jigsaw puzzle half finished, certain portions of the reconstruction are clear in form, content, and context. We have defined events and event segment sequences which are based on the evidence discovered. Based on the evaluation and assessment, we know how reliable the information is and we have a clear view of what each proves in and of itself. Remaining are the sections where we think we see patterns in the event segments or have some hazy focus of which we are not yet confident. Of course, we also have those pieces that fit in no fashion to the content and context as we understand it.

Integration

Our final task in analysis is to integrate the information and evidence with all other known information and seek "to form a logical picture or hypothesis."[12] We have reached the ultimate goal of the analysis: How do these pieces fit together and in what fashion did the events unfold? It is here that our analysis begins the transition to a reconstruction. The sequencing information developed during the assessment process is the primary foundation of integration. We combine it, of course, with a simple common-sense approach.

In accomplishing integration, we must consider that crimes do not occur instantaneously. From our facts and evidence we will establish "time snapshots or windows".[13] Each window has a set of facts that ultimately support our belief for that snapshot's occurrence. (See Figure 7.) The increments for such windows may begin as large chunks of time, in that we attempt to define gross aspects of our reconstruction. As individual pieces of information begin to fit into the overall picture, we enhance our ability to break up the time increments. This process is a simple extension of the long-honored use of "time lines", which investigators apply in most serious crime investigations.

As the reconstruction develops, our time increments for one section may be small and precise in defining the events which occurred, yet for another period the increment may remain large. The distinction between the two is our ability to accurately define the detail present in the evidence. Obviously, the smaller the increments the more detailed the analysis, and the more likely our reconstruction will be an accurate representation of the incident.

In terms of serving the reconstruction process itself, these snapshots, when considered sequentially, may help us identify some part of a missing picture. If we have a factual beginning and end to some event of the reconstruction, the "logical" missing piece in-between may identify what direction we need to focus investigative efforts to prove or disprove our beliefs about this missing piece.

One final caution is appropriate when considering the integration phase. What has been a logical development of the crime scene analysis is at severe risk of becoming garbage in this latter stage. When asked to pull the pieces together, we tend to go overboard. Subjective considerations creep into what

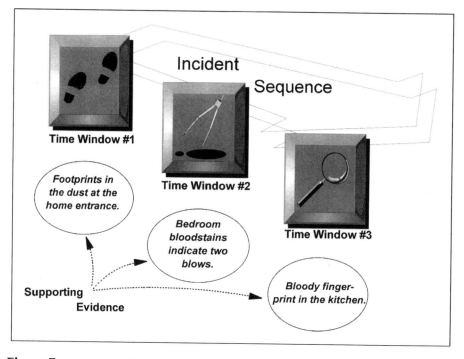

Figure 7 Our crime does not occur instantaneously. Thus we attempt to establish "Time Windows" or "Snapshots" of the actions which encompass the Incident. We then sequence these snapshots using the available evidence.

should be a relatively objective process. In trying to build a neat and tidy package, we begin to make assumptions about what the participants thought, felt, or even said. By doing so we also inappropriately fill in gaps in our knowledge.

Our goal should be to remain unattached to issues of intent or motive unless they are clearly proven by concise knowledge. We should concentrate our efforts on piecing together the event segments which we can factually prove as having been accomplished during the crime. Thus when viewing the crime as a series of actions it may be easier to subsequently define motives, or perhaps recognize anomalies.

As an example of this issue consider what the BSU defines as the "signature". We differentiate signatures from the *modus operandi* (MO) in that most often the MO is a set of actions necessary for the accomplishment of the crime. As criminals learn and gain experience, MOs often change to exhibit this criminal maturity. A signature is some action taken by the criminal which, considering the crime, is quite unnecessary. Signatures tend not to change with time and often have significance in a very personal manner to the criminal.[14] We may recognize the action as a signature, but its significance to the subject may totally evade us.

If we fail to consider the crime, as a series of subset actions (events or event segments), as a whole, the needlessness and thus the identification of the signature action as a "signature" might go unnoticed. On the other hand, should we become too focused on the signature by seeking the action's significance to the criminal, we may lose sight of other important evidence while chasing what may be a minor point in terms of reconstructing the event. Even worse, we may incorrectly assume its significance and end up tainting the overall reconstruction.

Integration takes each piece of the puzzle and attempts to place them together to form a whole picture. Just as in the jigsaw puzzle, the analyst cannot try to force information into what looks like the "right" place. If some portion of the evidence contradicts its usage, we may need to set aside that information until we can establish its rightful place. We must also recognize that as our puzzle's box top is not available; we may never fit each piece into the picture. Long after the case closes and the trial ends, specific questions relevant to evidence discovered may remain in the investigator's mind.

By applying the steps of the reconstruction process, the analyst may define more accurately those events associated with the incident. These events become the definition of the crime as a series of actions in which motivation, intent, or other subjective factors have no effect. The why of the event, (e.g., *why* the subject chose to cut the victim three times) in no way effects the fact that the event occurred (e.g., the victim *was* cut three times).

As simple as this seems, by sequentially ordering as many of the events and event segments as possible the reconstruction takes shape objectively rather than subjectively. After we have defined all available events, what should not occur, as it often does, are completely contradicting recreations. In using this model, whether some particular event is favorable to the prosecution or defense is of no concern. If it occurred, and physical evidence exists to prove its occurrence, we cannot argue its existence. We can only reformulate our beliefs regarding how and why the crime proceeded as it did. Having defined the crime in this fashion, we may then turn to the more subjective issues and attempt to resolve them.

The model is just a concept for analysis — a process to apply to all information and evidence considered in the investigation. In the following section we'll present a specific methodology to apply that concept to.

Event Analysis: A Process for Crime Scene Reconstruction

In Event Analysis, recall that the overall crime is the *Incident*. The incident encompasses all actions related to the crime. Within this incident there are specific *Events*. Each event is some part of the crime. Each event can be defined by small, specific actions taken which are in turn supported by the presence of specific items of evidence. Each of these smaller actions we refer to as *Event Segments*. Consider these events and event segments to be slices of the time window; moments of the crime defined by some physical action or form. Since the reconstruction attempts to define the crime or incident by establishing these events, we call the overall process Event Analysis. The steps taken to create a crime scene reconstruction model using event analysis are as follows:

- Collect data and using all evidence establish likely events.
- Establish from the data specific snapshots or event segments of the crime.
- Consider these event segments in relationship to one another in order to establish related event segments.
- Order or sequence the event segments for each identified event.
- Consider all possible sequences and, where contradictory sequences exist, audit the evidence to determine which is the more probable.
- Final order or sequence of the events themselves.
- Flow-chart the overall incident based on the event and event segment sequencing.

As an example, consider an assault and rape in a home. The incident likely consists of approaching the house, gaining entry, making contact with the victim, assaulting and raping the victim, and subsequent departure. These *events* are simply large chunks of our time window. The crime or *incident* encompasses all of these processes or events. (See Figure 8.)

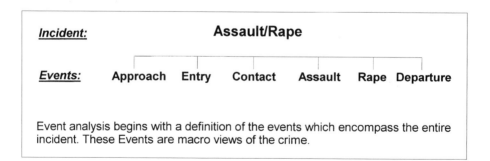

Figure 8   Establishing events requires that we consider what must occur for the incident to transpire. For instance, besides approaching and departing the scene our subject must gain access to the victim and overpower her in order to commit the rape. Oftentimes the analyst can surmise these events before they know specifics of the crime.

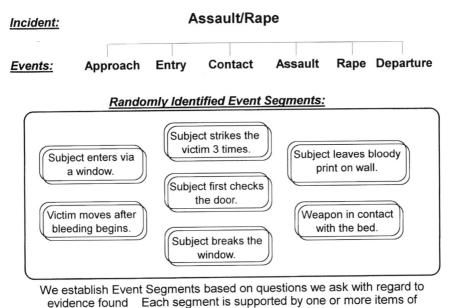

Incident: **Assault/Rape**

Events: **Approach   Entry   Contact   Assault   Rape   Departure**

Randomly Identified Event Segments:

Subject strikes the victim 3 times.

Subject enters via a window.

Subject leaves bloody print on wall.

Subject first checks the door.

Victim moves after bleeding begins.

Weapon in contact with the bed.

Subject breaks the window.

We establish Event Segments based on questions we ask with regard to evidence found   Each segment is supported by one or more items of evidence.

Figure 9   Event Segments are the "snapshots" of the crime. They detail specific actions and are based on our evaluation of specific items of evidence. Initially we may only know they occurred, without understanding their sequence or relationship to the events themselves. Eventually the event segments will help define what actually occurred during any given event.

Any event, such as "entry", is composed of individual segments (more precisely defined time slots). For example, the rapist may check the door or window in question to see if it is unsecured; then, using a crowbar to break the glass, reach through and unlock the entry and climb through the entry point. Each of these actions result in the creation of individual items of evidence. Our subsequent discovery and analysis of the evidence helps us establish that the event segment occurred. Examples of this evidence might be fingerprints on the outer surfaces of the entry point, glass fractures in the pane of glass, glass fragments on the subject's clothes and shoes, and dust footprints or disturbances in the broken glass where the rapist stepped.

As more and more of these event segments from the evidence are defined, they are considered in relationship to each other and the identified events. (See Figure 9.) Based on these relationships, the various segments which we believe are associated with a given event will be identified.

Our function now is to order, if possible, these related event segments. This ordering gives a structure and an understanding of how the specific event transpired. Again, all known information must be considered to place these segments in a logical and supportable order. Typically, very obvious

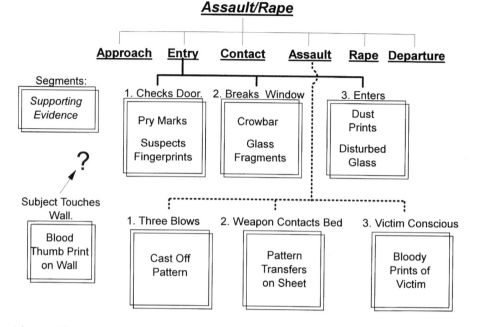

Figure 10 In time we will seek to relate the Event Segments to a specific Event and then sequence them. This gives us a clearer picture as to how the incident transpired. Each Segment is based on some grouping of evidence. Not every event segment will have a clear and obvious position in the reconstruction. For instance, the segment related to the subject touching the wall might well belong to the Assault, Rape, or Departure event; unfortunately there is insufficient evidence available to establish where it belongs in the overall reconstruction.

beginning and ending event segments are found. There may also be several segments that fit together in a very logical and functional order as well as segments that appear to fit the sequence loosely, but we may be uncomfortable as to their exact sequence. Of course we will also find segments which are believed to relate the event, but for which we do not understand the sequence or order in any fashion. (See Figure 10.)

Considering all the information remember, too, that each event or event segment either has some action which leads to or follows it. Nothing just happens. There is no "*Beam me up Scotty*" as in Star Trek; our players must arrive, act, then depart. As an example, consider the rape/assault event of "break glass with crowbar". In order to break the glass with a crowbar, our rapist must first procure one. In order to procure one, he must either find it on scene or bring it with him. If found on scene, it must have existed there previously for some reason, or have been brought by someone else. If brought by the rapist, he must have brought it from somewhere. Obviously, these issues become convoluted and lose relevance to the investigation as a whole;

but if for some reason the issues were important, background evidence may well exist to prove their occurrence.

Oftentimes the investigation will present the analyst with contradictory evidence which support two or more possible events, event sequences, or event segment sequences. By looking at this background evidence, we can audit the crime in order to help establish which of the events or sequences is the more probable.

Consider a case example of auditing. Imagine a situation in which we have two possible locations in a scene for a shooting. Based on evidence present, either location could conceivably be the location for the shooting. Testimony by the defendant indicates the shooting occurred at the first location (a bathtub). He claims he placed the weapon on the floor there and never again moved it. This information supports his overall claim of self defense. The barrel of the weapon was bloodied by contact with the victim when it was fired. We also find a bloody pattern transfer consistent with the weapon on a pillow at the second location of interest. In considering the pillow in relation to the defendant's claim, it is possible that:

- Previously the pillow was at the location claimed by the defendant, it made contact with the weapon, and was later moved by someone.
- The shooting occurred where the subject claimed, the weapon was moved, came in contact with the pillow, and was then returned to the original site.
- The shooting occurred at the second site, where the weapon made contact with the pillow, the weapon was then returned to the first location which was staged after the fact by the subject.

The analyst's issue becomes one of finding some means of deciding which of these possible events is more probable. In examining the pattern transfer we are confident the weapon caused it. The pillow exhibits no other stains. We also find that at the first location, where the subject claims the shooting occurred, watered-down stains are present from another event. These watered-down stains appear to be related to the splashing of bloody water in the tub. The subject is adamant that these occurred just before the shooting and relate to a minor injury. The other evidence and facts support this claim. These stains are evident on all surfaces and objects present near the first location.

Given the presence of these splash stains all around the bathtub and the lack of similar stains on the pillow, it is obvious the pillow was not subjected to this earlier event. If the subject is being truthful and location 1 is the site of the shooting, then the splash event occurred, causing the stains on the walls and surfaces, the pillow was then moved to this location, the shooting occurred, the weapon came in contact with it, and the pillow was removed and replaced in the second location.

Unfortunately, our subject neither claims this, nor in his overall description had sufficient time to take such action. This precludes the pillow's presence at the first location before the shooting; as such, the more probable events are:

- The weapon was moved from the first location, came in contact with the pillow at the second location, and was then returned.
- The second location is the actual site of the shooting.

Although auditing does not answer absolutely which event segment sequence is the actual sequence, it establishes that the subject's story, as told, is false and certainly points us back to the second location. In this instance the watered-down stains, which did not relate directly to the shooting event, provide a means of discriminating between the various possibilities for the shooting. Auditing can be an extremely effective tool for reconstruction, but it demands that we look beyond the immediate issues.

The final step in the crime scene reconstruction process is to order the events and segments themselves, first mentally, then later using a more formal event flow chart. We use the same process to order events as we did to order the individual event segments. We look for sequencing evidence within the events, applying an objective and logical view to them.

In the end, the result may look something like Rynearson and Chisum's storyboard or an ANACAPA process chart. (See Figure 11.) With all the time-windows or snapshots sequenced, we define the crime in as much detail as possible. Of course the ordering may not be as simple as our illustration and the end result may have many segments for which we are unsure of their sequence.

In considering the entire process of event analysis, it's important to keep two issues in mind. First is the "generalist" view for analysis and the second is flexibility.

To revisit the "generalist" viewpoint, remember that the crime scene analyst cannot be an expert in every forensic field. Yet, any forensic field may establish some part of the event segments. To conduct an analysis, then, the analyst must have a strong working knowledge of the major forensic disciplines, including crime scene processing.

The entire investigative package consists of information and efforts emanating from the crime scene processors, investigators, and forensic scientists of every nature. Their products contain varying experts opinions, reports, witness and subject testimony, and the scene evaluations. Someone must

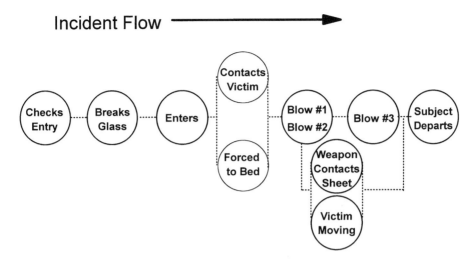

Figure 11   Event Flow charting. Using a supportable order or sequence we can lay out the Events and Event Segments in a flow chart model. In effect the flow chart is a graphic representation of the reconstruction.

apply all of this knowledge to the incident and mold from it the best view or most probable definition of the crime. This role should and must fall to the analyst who has both a criminalistics background and investigative experience.

The second consideration is that of flexibility. As we acquire new evidence we must reevaluate the entire event sequence, or a specific segment based on that new information. Remember that no matter how detailed we may be, we will never have a "standard" of our crime to which we can compare our analysis. We need to be ready to wipe the slate on a particular sequence order if we discover contradictory physical evidence.

In the end, it is the evidence at the crime scene and our application of event analysis to that evidence which allows us to set a foundation for the crime. On top of this foundation we can ultimately build our understanding of the case using the more subjective information discovered during the investigation.

The Role of Logic in Analysis

John Locke in *An Essay Concerning Human Understanding* remarked, "God has not been so sparing to men as to make them barely two-legged creatures, and left it to Aristotle to make them rational." Locke believed the study of logic and reasoning served no function, that man was a rational creature by nature.

We recognize reasoning as a skill used to resolve problems encountered daily. It provides a practical approach by which analysts weigh options and ultimately make conclusions about events they were not present to observe.

Much as Locke believed, the application of a raw talent may be sufficient in some instances. Yet, by refining our reasoning skills and recognizing the dynamic nature of the events we seek to explain, we strengthen our ability to define the most probable conclusion. Therefore, it is important for analysts to consider logic and reasoning as they relate to the reconstruction task. As Dr. John Nordby says: "The purpose of the expert is to refine the context of the situation using the expert's understanding."[15] Lets explore the application of logic and its purpose in refining this "context" during the process of crime scene reconstruction.

Expectations and Predictions

Every day of our lives we encounter situations in which we have expectations. We expect our positions to await us at work or to receive a handshake when we offer one. Although subjective, we base these expectations on experience. In any situation, the expectations or context we have (which we base on our personal experience) influence our perceptions and observations in that situation.[16]

As investigators we also have expectations and a context of observation. The moment we walk into a crime scene our mind begins to process data. The context and expectations we apply play an important role and help define our early investigative focus. For example:

- The room is locked from inside, was this a suicide?
- That looks like a high-velocity spatter pattern, where is the gun?

Such expectations are usually the result of study and personal experience. They typically serve the function of providing initial momentum to an inquiry and may guide us in the investigation.

Unfortunately, these expectations are nothing more than simple predictions. As *predictions,* they may prove to be without factual basis. Dr. Nordby, in this regard, writes, "Inappropriate expectation laden observations can lead to observation errors. Recall that nothing is self evident unless the detective happens to be looking for it."[17] As we discussed in the assessment role, the investigator may need to ignore early beliefs or concerns if evidence to support such beliefs is not forthcoming. Flexibility must be a cornerstone of the investigator's approach.

Consider this concept of expectation-laden observation in relation to a teaching incident. While instructing a bloodstain course in Helsinki, the students asked the author to explain a pattern which they created while completing an impact spatter experiment. Present on the target was a somewhat U-shaped void in the middle of the pattern. In examining the pattern, the author considered the experiment as he had explained it to the group, yet could not immediately explain the void: the instructor's expectation being that the group used the targets, blood, and mousetrap as told, and somehow managed to cause the pattern. In reality, the students introduced another element into the experiment by taping a balloon onto the target area.

The instructor's expectation was simple: they were students, they were told to do something specific, they had always done so before, so the situation could be explained given these circumstances. Such expectations created a type of tunnel vision, which precluded just asking "What did you use to cause the void?" Expectations guide the analyst, but they must always be viewed in their proper light. They are not absolute, and they may limit our thinking.

Impact of Dynamic Events on the Reconstruction

The dynamic nature of our world also affects our reconstruction attempts. By dynamic we mean simply that in any event there are countless ways in which two components may interact. In essence, a reconstruction tries to establish a previous state of a set of components. Our ability to define this previous state is directly related to our ability to determine the relative positions and interactions of the components. Our typical components are the victim, subject, weapon, and blood. We may be able to infer the velocity of the weapon and we know that gravity and air resistance have a constant effect on the blood in flight. Unfortunately, the nature of how the components interact (e.g., exact positions of victim and subject, the angle of the weapon striking a body) leave a lot of room for error in defining their specific motions. As we will never define in absolute detail the positions and actions of these components, we are likely to limit our conclusion and reconstruction to general parameters of possible and impossible events.

This issue directly affects experiments in which we try to replicate bloodstain patterns. Imagine a recreation attempt of a simple hair swipe. To absolutely reconstruct the swipe we would need information pertinent to exactly how many hairs were bloodied, by what volume of blood, and in what order and at what angle did they then contact the surface involved. Given the detail required, it is unlikely our attempt at a pattern recreation will produce a Xerox copy of the original stain. It is far more likely we will only create an approximate simulation, the specific characteristics of which may or may not "match" the stain in question. Again we must emphasize that no one has an ability to define in absolute detail the specifics of such dynamic events! Anyone who would claim to do so should seriously reconsider their position.

Deductive Vs. Inductive Reasoning

Sir Arthur Conan Doyle's fictional character, Sherlock Holmes, often utilized complex reasoning to reach his investigative conclusions. In truth, the manner of reasoning used by the fictional master of deduction was often more inductive than deductive. This distinction is of little importance in fiction, but to the investigator the difference is real.

Deductive and inductive arguments may appear on the whole as similar. There is, however, a distinct and important difference in the conclusions which follow each. Deductive arguments are those in which the conclusion must logically follow from the premise. If the premise is true, the conclusion **must** also be true.

> **Premise:** "A" fingerprint, in A's blood, is on a knife. The print belongs to "B".
> **Conclusion:** "B" was in contact with the knife after "A" began to bleed.

The premise establishes all information in the conclusion. The conclusion must therefore be true. It does not exceed the knowledge presented in the premise.

Inductive arguments, on the other hand, allow for exploration by the analyst. If the premises are true, the conclusions are also likely to be true. As Morris Engel explained in his book, *With Good Reason*: "...the conclusion is presented as following the premises with a high degree of probability."[18] Accepting the previous deductive argument and its conclusion, lets expand the situation.

> **Premise:** "A" was stabbed at point "Z". The knife containing the incriminating print was also found at point "Z".
> **Conclusion:** "B" was involved in the assault of "A".

On its surface, the basis for the argument looks sound. If the premise is true, it is probable the conclusion is true. The conclusion, however, contains information not completely established by the premise. An obvious possibility is "B" having found "A" after the assault, and then touching the knife. Although the argument and the conclusion may well be true, the inductive nature causes the conclusion to exceed the knowledge presented in the premise.

In analysis, we must distinguish deductive arguments from inductive arguments. Inductive arguments are a valuable tool for investigators, leading to that which is not always apparent. We cannot, however, treat an inductive argument as a deductive argument as this excludes possibilities and leads to unsound reasoning. Far too often in crime scene and bloodstain pattern analysis, investigators accept inductive arguments as deductive and define too narrowly the likely events in their reconstruction of the crime.

Informal Fallacies Encountered in Analysis

Any analysis, at its heart, is an argument. Before we accept any argument, we should be clear on three things:

- What does the argument choose to establish?
- Is the evidence presented correctly, without weighting in either direction?
- Is the reasoning of the argument valid?[19]

There are three categories of fallacies which deal with these questions: fallacies of ambiguity, fallacies of relevance, and fallacies of presumption. Although we may encounter any of the fallacies, the presumptive fallacies tend to be more prevalent in our discipline. This group deals with incorrect arguments disguised to look like correct arguments. The following represent a sampling of such fallacies and illustrate their deceptive nature.

The first presumptive fallacy we will discuss is bifurcation. It presumes that something is either true or it is not. There is no in-between. Lawyers who ask us to "Just answer yes or no" use this fallacy in their favor. They know the witness cannot adequately answer all questions so easily. This allows the lawyer to receive the answer they want, without delving into background detail that might better reveal the truth of the matter. Analysts have a bad habit of accepting or including bifurcated positions about events and event segments in their reconstruction; rarely is such a position warranted.

Sweeping generalizations are another fallacy of concern. In this case a rule which is applicable in some instances is applied to all instances. For example, a well-intentioned bloodstain axiom states: "Correct interpretation of the spattering of a bloodstain is *impossible* [italics added] without first considering surface texture of the target upon which it impacted."[20]

Although in many instances the analyst must consider surface texture to properly understand a pattern or stain, this axiom is certainly not true for every instance. Specifically, in determining directionality of the stain, surface texture will not in and of itself affect the conclusion drawn. Thus it is possible to correctly interpret a bloodstain in this regard without considering surface texture.

As an example of a combined argument (both a bifurcated argument and a sweeping generalization) imagine a question about the origin of a spatter following a gunshot. We know that shotguns often produce considerable back and forward spatter. Having found a small stain that is consistent with a gunshot spatter, must we exclude it from having been produced by the shotgun simply because it is not "large"? Analysts have argued exactly that, claiming that shotgun wounds only produce large spatter patterns. A less presumptuous position demands we look at the empirical data. Gunshots, to include shotguns, do occur where there is little or no spatter. Between the parameters of "a lot" and "very little" reside many possibilities. The sweeping generalization attempts to apply a rule (e.g., shotguns often produce large stains) to a situation in which the rule may not be applicable. The bifurcated position bolsters the argument (e.g., shotguns only produce large stains) to make it look incontestable.

The ultimate issue, that is, can a small spatter stain be produced by a shotgun, remains unanswered based on this information alone. Is it possible to produce such a stain by firing a shotgun? Yes. Obviously, it is not the most frequently occurring event, but the argument uses the bifurcation and sweeping generalization position to force a decision on the issue without exploring the possibility.

Another fallacy encountered in crime scene analysis is that of false cause. In these instances the analyst draws a causal connection between two actions or an action and some item of evidence. Consider arriving at the site of a homicide and discovering bloodstains of various types. We observe the victim and note wounds that might account for these stains. If we simply assume all the stains to be the result of the victim's injuries, the fallacy of false cause has presented itself. We have not considered the possibility that other people (particularly the perpetrator) were injured and then created the stains. Using other evidence, we may reach the same conclusion later, but at this point the argument is unsound.

An irrelevant thesis is another fallacy encountered. Simply stated, an irrelevant thesis attempts to prove something that is not at issue. It is then offered as proof that another issue is false. Imagine the question: Could a particular event "A" create bloodstain "Z"? The answer is likely to be put forth as a "yes" or "no". The irrelevant thesis answers this question by offering an alternate set of circumstances, "B", which could also create stain "Z".

The most deceptive thing about an irrelevant thesis is that it may offer valid information which could be of importance to the investigation. Yet the approach veils the answer in such a manner as to exclude or rebut the original issue without having dealt with it at all. Whether circumstance "B" could produce stain "Z" says nothing about the question of whether circumstance "A" could produce stain "Z". Although event "B" may well be the circumstance which produced the stain, it does not disprove "A" in and of itself. Event "A" must still be considered, and either excluded or included based upon the physical evidence available.

We've discussed only a few of the logical fallacies, there are others. To properly conduct analysis, the analyst must consider the nature of the arguments they attempt to support or rebut. Although the analyst may not know or remember the proper names of these fallacies, our point is simple — to be accurate the analyst must recognize and eliminate erroneous arguments.

Putting the Pieces Together

The limitation in the reconstruction task is evident — the analyst seeks to look back in time. In many instances there is no one, beyond the subject, who can provide details regarding what occurred. Even in situations where eye witnesses exist, the seasoned investigator realizes they often give conflicting testimony for various reasons. In the end, proper analysis of physical evidence shoulders the greatest burden of proof in establishing these past events.

Often, when presented with less than clear circumstances, investigators depart from objective concerns and turn to subjective issues. Statements like "That's not logical, why would he do that?" begin to appear. It is not that we aren't concerned with motive, but once we stray to subjective issues in order to define our crime we lose touch with our most authoritative asset. Perhaps Herbert MacDonell put it best in the title of his book: *The Evidence Never Lies*. We can best define our incident by considering the physical evidence in a clear and objective manner. From this solid platform we may always reach out to explore the more subjective concerns.

In most instances, the deceptive nature of the fallacies and subjective traps discussed occur without intent on the part of the investigator or analyst. We are all capable of these failures and fall prey to unsound reasoning as a matter of our basic human nature. To avoid these subjective traps, the analyst must try to understand a basic application of logic, then seek to define their arguments using acceptable reasoning. The basis of our ultimate reconstruction conclusion rests on earlier conclusions made about items of evidence. Point "A" leads to Point "B", which leads to Point "C", … ad infinitum. If we infer Point "A" based on poor reasoning, we may taint the entire conclusion. As such it could also be wrong. Only with clear, logical thinking are we likely to stay the course and reach acceptable solutions.

Given the dynamic nature of our world and its interactions, no one can establish every action related to crime with certainty. Paraphrasing Voltaire, only a charlatan is absolutely certain of everything. We must recognize that although they are valuable tools, our expectations or predications are subjective in nature. As such they cannot form the cornerstone of our conclusions. We must follow a proven path of evaluating the evidence present in our scenes, applying event analysis whenever possible. To accomplish this, the reconstructionists must refine their context of observation which they do by "assess[ing] the entire scene, noting all competing explanations [and] refusing to be guided by inappropriate preconceived expectations."[21]

In this manner our crime begins to emerge as a series of objective moments, which we then link and sequence to produce the most probable view of events which encompass the incident. Once defined in this fashion, we may always turn to the more subjective issues and, using sound reasoning skills, attempt to define the "why" of the crime.

References

1. Ressler, Robert K. (et al.), *Sexual Homicide Patterns and Motives*, Lexington Books, New York, 1988, pg. 137.

2. Gardner, Ross M., The Role of Logic in Bloodstain Pattern Analysis and Crime Scene Reconstruction, *International Association of Bloodstain Pattern Analysts News*, Vol. 8, No. 3, September 1992, pg. 19.

3. Courtroom Television Network, *The Rodney King Case: What the Jury Saw In California V. Powell*, 1992.

4. Douglas, John E. and Munn, Corinne, Violent Crime Scene Analysis: Modus Operandi, Signature, and Staging, *FBI Law Enforcement Bulletin*, February 1992, pg. 6.

5. Haberda, H., Eine besondere Form von Blutspritzern, *Viretaljahresschrift fur gerichtliche Medizin*, Volume 47, Supplement IX, 1914, pp. 380-381.

6. Rynearson, Joseph M. and Chisum, William J., *Evidence and Crime Scene Reconstruction*, 1989, pp. 92-93.

7. Bevel, Tom, Crime Scene Reconstruction, *Journal of Forensic Identification*, Vol. 41, Number 4, 1991, pp. 248-254.

8. Rynearson, *op. cit.*, pg. 93.

9. Pex, James O. and Hurley, Michael N., Sequencing of Bloody Shoe Impressions By Blood Spatter and Droplet Drying Times, *International Association of Bloodstain Pattern Analysts News*, December, 1990.

10. Geberth, Vernon J., *Practical Homicide Investigation*, 2nd ed., CRC Press, Boca Raton, FL, 1996.

11. Norby, Jon J., *Bootstrapping While Barefoot (Crime Models Vs. Theoretical Models in the Hunt For Serial Killers)*, Kluwer Academic, Netherlands, 1989, pg. 377.

12. U.S. Army, Intelligence Analysis FM 34-3, Headquarters, Department of the Army, Washington, D.C., March 1990, pg. 2-17.

13. U.S. Army, Intelligence Analysis FM 34-3, Headquarters, Department of the Army, Washington, D.C., March 1990, pg. 5-5.

14. Douglas, John E. et al., *Crime Classification Manual*, Lexington Books, New York, 1992, pg. 261.

15. Nordby, Jon J., The Lady in the Lake. Presentation to a joint training conference of the Association of Crime Scene Reconstruction and the International Association of Bloodstain Pattern Analysts, Oklahoma City, OK, Oct. 6, 1995.

16. Ibid.

17. Nordby, Jon J., Can We Believe What We See, If We See What We Believe, *Journal of Forensic Sciences*, Vol. 37, No. 4, July 1992, pg. 1121.

18. Engel, Morris S., *With Good Reason: An Introduction to Informal Fallacies*, St Martin's Press, New York, 1982, pg. 7.

19. Ibid., pg. 11.

20. MacDonell, Herbert L., *Bloodstain Patterns*, Golos Printing Inc. Elmira Heights, NY, 1993, pg. 15.

21. Nordby, Jon J., Can We Believe What We See, If We See What We Believe, *Journal of Forensic Sciences*, Vol. 37, No. 4, July 1992, pg. 1122.

Terminology

3

There are several schools of thought on the use of "technical" terms for bloodstain pattern analysis. One voices the concern that in using these terms the analyst may well alienate the intended audience, the jury. Such analysts speak in laymen's language so that the jury is neither offended by their expertise nor lost by the subject matter itself.

A second position argues that analysts, being analysts and being accepted as knowledgeable in their trade, must speak in a manner which conveys that knowledge. Technical terminology is simply another way of exhibiting ability.

The two positions present a classic bifurcated argument, as neither is totally wrong nor completely right. The possibility of alienating your audience is real and must be considered when testifying. Yet the discipline has a generally accepted vocabulary which is relatively clear and concise. Failing to use the accepted vocabulary could easily damage the credibility of the analyst. Counsel may try to imply that speaking as a layman indicates a lack of knowledge in the subject matter.

Between these two positions lies the ability of the analyst to use a combination of laymen's explanations along with an underlying infrastructure of the technical terminology, skillfully taught and explained beforehand to the jury.

The analyst gains several things through this process. First, the analyst's credibility is better established by the use of "technical" knowledge. This applies not only to courtroom situations, but also in dealing with other investigators and analysts. Understanding and accurately using the accepted terminology of the discipline eliminates the ability of anyone to disparage the speaker.

Another positive aspect in using such terminology is that the process of testifying becomes easier. Once introduced, a term does not change in definition. Explained in detail to the court, a term such as swipe is easily brought back to mind by gentle reminders of the previous discussion. As the jurors begin to grasp the vocabulary they too may feel more confident in their own ability to understand the testimony. The courtroom becomes, as is often the case with expert testimony, a classroom.

The reader must accept, however, that no strict set of terms is available. Unfortunately every analyst has a way of adding and customizing those terms in use. In this chapter we (Bevel and Gardner) offer our own perspective of terminology. This terminology should not be construed as all-inclusive nor absolute.

Referring to the Discipline

Perhaps the first term to deal with is the name of the discipline itself. In discussing bloodstain pattern analysis one is likely to find both trained and not so well-trained analysts using terms such as:

- Bloodstain pattern interpretation
- Bloodspatter analysis
- Bloodstain spatter analysis
- Bloodsplatter analysis/interpretation
- Bloodstain pattern analysis

The term preferred by the authors is the latter: bloodstain pattern analysis. This wording is preferable for numerous reasons, some subjective, others not so subjective.

Analysis implies a structured approach in evaluating that which is to be examined. Analysis is an examination in detail in order to determine the nature of that examined or to determine interrelationships present.[1] *Interpretation,* on the other hand, alludes to a more subjective viewing. An example of this difference might be in the area of questioned documents. At any side-street carnival you may have your handwriting interpreted to reveal your "true personality". At a crime laboratory, however, the examiner of the document analyzes the physical nature of the writing in an attempt to identify the originator.

So, too, must the bloodstain pattern analyst examine the physical nature of stains. It is not that acceptable "interpretation" of a crime scene is bad, it is simply that we need to exclude, whenever possible, references to actions that can be construed as subjective and therefore unscientific.

There is a reason to use *pattern* vs. *spatter* or *splatter,* for analysts evaluate all bloodstain patterns. Spatter is a specific type of bloodstain pattern; properly, a bloodstain spatter analyst would be one who analyzes only spatter. Bloodstains found at scenes of crimes run the gamut for their source of origin.

Stains such as swipes, pattern transfers, or blood pooling are not technically spatter.

Thus a bloodstain pattern analyst examines patterns of bloodstains in detail to determine their nature and interrelationships, no matter what their source.

As we have introduced the terms spatter and splatter, it seems appropriate to tackle what are likely the most misused terms in bloodstain pattern analysis today. When discussing bloodstain pattern analysis with someone newly introduced to the subject, the term "splatter" is likely to be heard.

There are two reasons for not using this term. First, the term lacks an aesthetic value: "splatter" in a sentence goes over about as well as castor oil. If one can be prejudiced to a word, then we are. To say the least, splatter is obtrusive and rough. It is not one of the more fluid words found in the English language.

A second, less subjective concern is that splatter has usage singularly as a verb, whereas spatter has usage as both a noun and verb. When discussing bloodstain pattern analysis, it can be said that most references to a splatter or spatter are to some "thing" being evaluated. Thus the noun spatter is the only proper usage in those instances. In a few isolated situations the speaker or writer may well be discussing the act of causing spatter, during which splatter (or more likely, splattered) could be properly used.

General Terms Relating to Bloodstain Pattern Analysis

The terms, definitions, and discussion which follow are intended to assist the analyst in understanding and conversing in the discipline of bloodstain pattern analysis. Although perhaps not absolutely complete, they certainly serve as a basic vocabulary for anyone interested in the discipline.

Grouping Stains

We can generally group bloodstains into three basic categories: passive stains, transfer stains, and projected or impact stains. This categorization was originally suggested by Jozef Radzicki.[2]

Passive stains include clots, drops, flows, and pools, while impact stains include patterns such as spatter, splashes, cast-off stains, and arterial spurts and gushes. Transfer stains include patterns such as wipes, swipes, pattern transfers, and other contact bloodstains.

These groupings allow a basic categorization of a stain or pattern for purposes of discussion early on in the investigation. For the long-term purpose of analysis, of course, a more specific categorization is necessary.

Droplet Vector

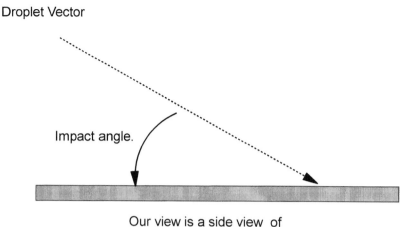

Impact angle.

Our view is a side view of
the target surface.

Figure 12   Impact angle. The acute angle (less than 90°) at which a droplet strikes a given target.

Angle of Impact:

> The acute angle as viewed from the side, created by the intercept of the target by the droplet's vector. (See Figure 12.)

When blood drops strike a target they do so at some angle. The angle of impact is relative to the surface of the target itself. For instance, drops or spatter traveling straight downward and impacting the floor, have an impact angle of 90°. Drops traveling across the room and impacting a wall may also have a 90° impact angle. The possible measurements of the impact angle can be expressed in a range from the most acute angle, 1°, to a maximum of 90°.

Much of the application of mathematics to bloodstain pattern analysis deals with defining these impact angles and determining the point of origin for the stains evaluated. It is imperative in considering these issues that one remembers the angle of impact is relative to the target at the moment the blood impacts.

Arterial Gushing and Spurts:

> The escape of blood under pressure from any breach in an artery, showing pressure, pressure fluctuations, or both. (See Figure 13.)

Blood in the arteries flows under greater pressure than blood present in the veins. If an artery is breached through some wounding mechanism while the

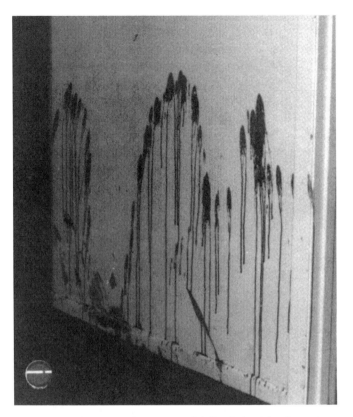

Figure 13 An arterial spurt. The rise and fall of the blood pressure is evident by the arc of the pattern.

heart is functional, the resulting pattern will very likely exhibit both the increase and decrease of the arterial pressure as it flows from the wound and the force of projection behind the flow.

Arterial gushes are large-volume patterns in which the pressure variations are less distinct due simply to the volume of blood gushing out of the wound. Arterial spurts usually represent a smaller volume (volume refers to the amount of blood escaping the wound at that particular moment, not the total volume lost).

The most typical arterial pattern reflects this rise and fall of pressure in up-and-down trails of blood on surrounding surfaces. The pattern may have a zigzag appearance with distinct termination points, or a more wave-like appearance.

In instances where the artery spurts directly into the target, the patterns found may exhibit the appearance of a meandering trail with many spines. (See Figure 14.) The pattern is similar to that encountered when one directs a stream of water into dirt.

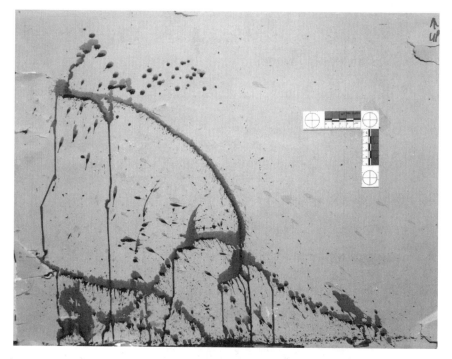

Figure 14　This stain resulted from a cut carotid artery. In this instance the blood was projected more directly into the target, resulting in the "trail" appearance. Still evident in the stain are spines (indicating the force of the projection) and several small indications of pressure fluctuations. (Photograph courtesy of T. Daniel Gilliam, Larimer County Sheriff's Department.)

Atomized Blood/Misting:

> Bloodstain patterns characterized by a mist-like appearance, which are generally associated with explosive force such as gunshot. (See Figure 15.)

When sufficient force or energy is applied to a blood source the blood may be reduced to a fine spray, resulting in atomized bloodstains. Such an effect is also referred to as a misting effect or misting stain. These stains are most typical of situations in which there is an explosive force such as gunshot.

The resulting pattern consists of many small, generally circular stains. The individual stains may be macroscopically indistinguishable within the overall pattern, producing an area that appears as a reddish hue, as if lightly spray-painted. The number of these individual stains may be in the teens or it can exceed hundreds. The actual number found at a given scene is dependent upon several factors including but not limited to the nature and site of the injury, intermediate targets such as clothing, and the nature of the wounding projectile(s). Atomized stains follow the general principle that as the

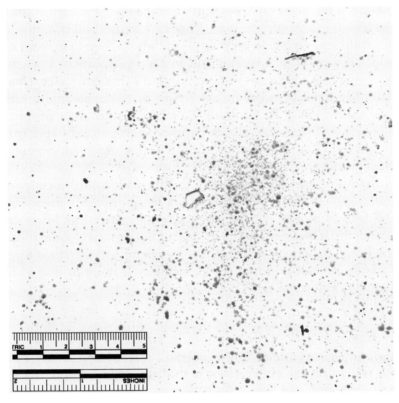

Figure 15 Atomized blood. The central area of the pattern surrounding the hole exhibits a "misting" effect.

energy or force applied to the blood source increases, a decrease will be observed in individual stain size. Typically the overall diameter of such stains will measure a fraction of a millimeter.

Spatter:

Spatter are those stains created as a result of some impact.

There are two types of spatter: forward and back spatter. The impact, whatever its nature, causes a breakup of the blood at the source into smaller droplets (impact spatter). In contrast, blood droplets which simply fall as a result of gravity as in venous bleeding (often referred to as low-velocity stains) are stains, not spatter.

In instances where impact spatter is produced, the spatter projected outward, away from the item creating the force or energy, are considered to be forward spatter. Back spatter are obviously those spatter which are projected to the rear or back towards the item creating the force.

The size of the spatter is dependent upon the nature and force associated with the impact. Although not an absolute, back spatter will generally consist of fewer stains and slightly larger stains than those present in forward spatter. This is particularly true in instances of impact spatter created by gunshot. On impact, a projectile creates a conical path of particles which expands out from the impact site. Blood and tissue are projected out along this path, not only in the direction of the projectile but also rearward towards the source of the projectile.[3] The width of both paths expands as the distance from the impact site increases. The effect is similar to that observed in gunpowder residue deposits.

In these situations the majority of the projectile's force is concentrated along the vector of the projectile, resulting in the tendency toward a more symmetrical and intense pattern in the forward spatter. The forces causing back spatter are still considered questionable, but one may be the collapse of the temporary wound cavity created in the wound track.[4] These forces are not as intense as those present in the projectile itself, resulting in less breakup and less blood being projected rearward.

Clot:

> A gelatinous mass formed by the collection of blood cells in fibrin; this mass will usually exhibit separation of the liquid and solid materials.

A clot is considered to be any mass of congealed blood and other contaminants created through the natural clotting mechanisms of the body. Blood under normal conditions within the vessels maintains its liquid state; however, when drawn from the body it thickens to form a gel. The clot consists of the cellular components of the blood. Serum separation is often observed late in the clotting process. At this stage a straw-colored liquid is evident around the congealed mass. This serum is simply plasma without the blood solids.[5]

Capillary Action:

> The force exhibited in the attraction of a liquid to surfaces it is in contact with and its own surface tension. This attraction often results in stain characteristics for which no corresponding defect may exist.

When discussing capillary action in bloodstain analysis it is evident that the definition does not strictly follow the scientific definition of capillary attraction. The latter is the force resulting from surface tension and adhesion of liquids when in contact with solids. In bloodstain pattern analysis this term is used to describe two observed actions which are related to capillary attraction.

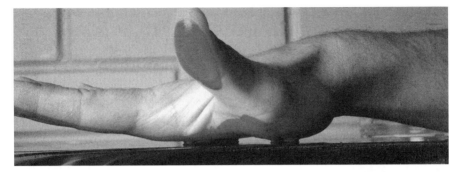

Figure 16   An example of capillary action. As the hand is withdrawn the surface tension of the liquid in conjunction with its adhesive quality causes a bridging effect. (Photograph courtesy of Jouni Kiviranta, National Bureau of Investigation, Helsinki, Finland.)

The first is the action evident when two objects in contact are separated, while blood is in-between. An example may be a bloodied hand in contact with a floor or wall, which is then lifted. The adhesive force of the blood with the surfaces of the solids acts to anchor the blood on both objects. At the same time, the surface tension of the liquid attempts to hold the blood together as a single entity. This anchoring, combined with the action of the surface tension, causes the liquid to be stretched across the expanding gap as the objects separate. Obviously, the surface tension of the liquid will eventually be overcome, but in the process the liquid is drawn together between the objects causing a line or demarcation which has no correlating trait on either of the objects creating the stain. As in the case of the hand, the stain may reflect linear characteristics for which no correlating defect exists. Figures 16 and 17 demonstrate this action, while Figure 18 shows the result.

A second usage encountered is to describe blood flow around objects. An example might be a flow of blood from a wound which then comes in contact with the victim's arm. Obviously, the arm acts as a barrier, but the adhesive nature of the liquid to the arm may also give rise to what could appear as unnatural blood flow.

Cast-Off Stains:

Stains created when blood is flung or projected from an object either in motion or which suddenly stops some motion. (See Figure 19.)

The pattern, referred to as a cast-off stain, is the result of blood being flung from some secondary object. The nature of this object may be a weapon (e.g., a club or hammer) or perhaps the victims or subjects themselves (e.g., a hand

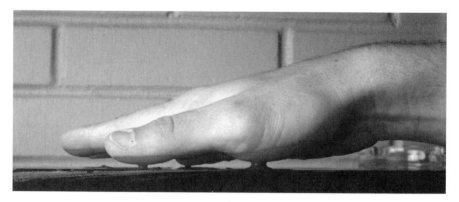

Figure 17 Here the bridging of the liquid between the two surfaces is even more evident. (Photograph courtesy of Jouni Kiviranta, National Bureau of Investigation, Helsinki, Finland.)

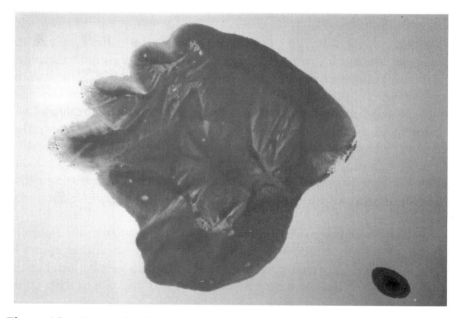

Figure 18 The result of Figures 16 and 17. Distinct linear features are present in the pattern as a result of the capillary action. (Photograph courtesy of Jouni Kiviranta, National Bureau of Investigation, Helsinki, Finland.)

or hair). Cast-off stains create linear patterns that reflect the general position of the item they were flung from; they may identify at least the minimum number of blows struck, and will likely provide some information as to the direction or motion involved in their creation.

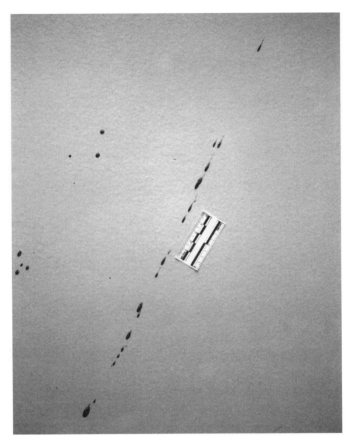

Figure 19 A cast-off pattern. The distinctly linear pattern on the right exhibits a motion moving up the wall, while the more elliptical droplets show motion going down the wall.

The size of the cast-off stain will most often be smaller than those found in a drip stain. In the drip, the weight and volume of the blood collecting at the drip site will eventually overcome the surface tension, affected simply by gravity. In the cast-off stain, motion in the form of centrifugal force carries the blood out and away from the object. Once set in motion, the level of force present is more likely to overcome the surface tension earlier, resulting in smaller-volume drops. Cast off patterns are discussed in greater detail in Chapter 8.

Directionality:

Relating to, or indicating the vector a droplet follows in relation to a target.

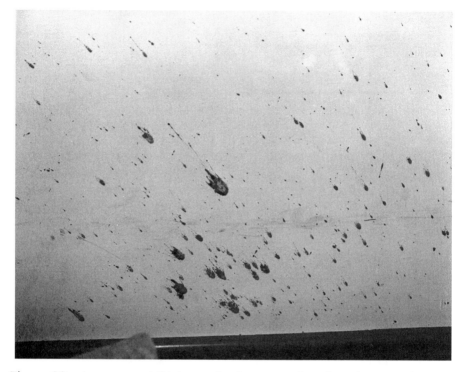

Figure 20 A pattern exhibiting multiple impacts based on directionality. The majority of the spatter evident on the wall indicates downward directionality. Intermixed within this spatter are smaller elliptical stains which indicate another trajectory different from the first.

One of the most important pieces of information available to the analyst is the directionality of the stain in question. Directionality denotes the path or vector the droplet was following at the time it impacted the target.

Directionality is evident by a tail which is often created by the impact of the droplet. In all instances except satellite spatter, this tail points in the direction of travel of the droplet. Figure 20 depicts spatter showing indications of opposite directionality.

Directional Angle:

> The angle, as viewed from the front of the target between the long axis of the stain and a standard reference point. (See Figure 21.)

The directional angle defines directionality of a droplet in relation to the target. This is measured as a degree for the purpose of defining the flight path using forensic software.

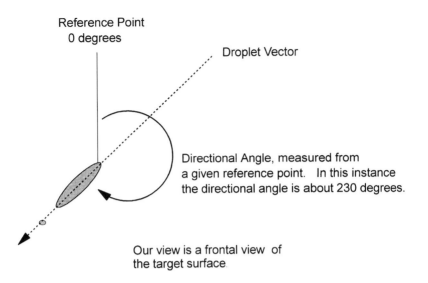

Reference Point
0 degrees

Droplet Vector

Directional Angle, measured from
a given reference point.   In this instance
the directional angle is about 230 degrees.

Our view is a frontal view of
the target surface

Figure 21   Directional angle. The angle between the long axis of a stain and a standard reference point. This angle describes the droplet directionality, but does so from a standard point, allowing it to be used by forensic software to establish point of origin.

Drawback/Blowback Effect:

The process in which blood is deposited inside the barrel of a weapon after discharge. (See Figure 22.)

In instances of gunshot injuries involving close or near contact wounds, blood will often be found within the barrel of the weapon. This is a result of the drawback effect. Whether drawback is directly related to back spatter is still questionable. Most explanations have been based on claims that an overpressure in the wound coupled with a near vacuum in the barrel cause contaminants (blood and tissue) to be sucked up the barrel as air rushes back in to fill this void. Probable correlations to the temporary wound cavity and the creation of back spatter are likely. Whatever the specific cause, blood and tissue have been found as much as 10 in. up a barrel. This distance of penetration in the barrel may provide information relevant to the distance between the wound and weapon when it was fired.[6]

Drip Patterns:

A pattern of blood caused when liquid blood drips into another liquid. (See Figure 23.)

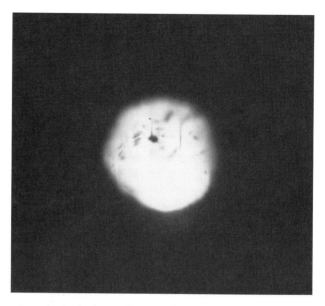

Figure 22 An example of the result of drawback. Stains are evident in the barrel of this 357 revolver. The weapon was used in a suicide, with hard contact to the head. The depth of the drawback in this instance was 18 mm. The photograph was taken using a fiber optic light, which was inserted into the breech of the barrel. (Photograph courtesy of Don Blake and Bill May, Norman Police Department.)

In instances where blood drips into standing blood (particularly in instances of pooled blood), a specific pattern is created. These patterns have characteristic traits whether found on vertical or horizontal surfaces.

When created in proximity to a vertical surface such as a wall, a voided area may be found in the pattern on the wall. This pattern resembles a funnel or is V-shaped.

On a horizontal surface the drip pattern causes random, somewhat irregular stains all about the pooled or standing blood. If these satellite stains from the drip pattern intermix with impact spatter it may be difficult to differentiate between the two. Chapter 8 discusses drip patterns in greater detail.

Expiratory Blood:

> Blood forced from the mouth, nose, or respiratory system under pressure, resulting in spatter. (See Figure 24.)

In situations which result in mouth, throat, or lung injuries a spatter pattern is often created which may mimic impact spatter from other circumstances.

Figure 23 A drip pattern. Note the small irregular droplets among the larger drops. The majority of these resulted from satellite spatter projected out by the liquid-to-liquid impacts.

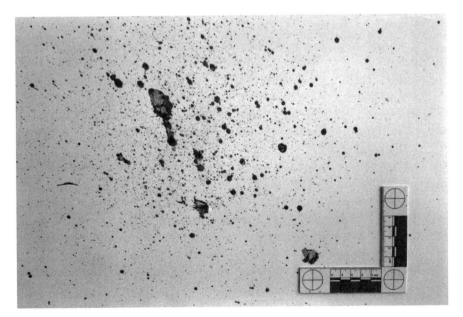

Figure 24 Blood forcefully expelled from a nose. The subject was on his hands and knees, with the face about 2 ft above the target. (Photograph courtesy of Tom J. Griffin.)

The mechanical process of breathing acts on the blood as it is introduced into the airways of a living victim. The blood is broken up into relatively small stains. The process is analogous to an atomizer which creates a mist by forcing liquid out using air pressure. Coughing, gasping, and the basic nature of the victim's breathing pattern obviously affect the nature of the air pressure involved, which in turn affects the appearance of the resulting stain. The ranges of size in expiratory stains can mimic both medium- or high-velocity spatter patterns.

A failure to recognize expiratory blood and its misidentification as spatter from another event can easily cloud the resulting analysis. Although not an absolute rule, expiratory blood may be less vivid in color (from being diluted by saliva) or contain evidence of where small air bubbles were prior to bursting.

Flight Path:

The overall orientation of how a droplet strikes a given target. Flight path is defined by both the impact angle and the directional angle in consideration with the point of origin.

Impact Site:

The point where a given force encounters a blood source.

In discussing bloodstains and their relationship to scenes of crime, references are made to point of origin, impact site, target, or origin. All seem related, but used in specific contexts they have distinct definitions and meaning.

Although numerous references are made to drops impacting a surface, an impact site is not the point where a drop impacts. Impact site generally denotes the point on the body which received the force or blow which then creates the resulting bloodstain.

Perhaps a more accurate description would be the *point or location* which receives the force of a blow, resulting in a bloodstain. For example, an injury was received which then bled to a secondary surface — should that surface then be struck by some object (making it the impact site), spatter is likely to occur. No body is involved.

This term is occasionally used to describe the drop's impact point, referring simply to the point where the drop struck the target, resulting in the observed stain or pattern. Although it is not inaccurate to use the term impact site to denote this point, it often leads to confusion. In discussing such terms, simply ensure that your audience is aware of which "impact site" you are referring to.

Origin/Point of Origin:

The point in three-dimensional space where a blood drop originated.

It might seem that origin and impact site go hand in hand, but origin and impact point are distinct concepts.

In most instances, the impact site is the origin of any given stain or spatter. One particular example of when this is not true is a cast-off stain. A weapon coming in contact with a body creates an impact site and thus a source for blood. This blood is transferred to the weapon and, as previously discussed, is carried with the weapon as it is swung. At various points along the arc of this swing, blood may be cast-off and impact some target surface. In tracing the origin of these stains, using principles to be discussed later on, the point of origin will identify that point in space where the drop detached from the weapon. Point of origin then, refers to where the drop originates in regard to its flight path.

Parent Stain:

The main stain from which satellite spatter originates.

When encountering stains at a scene, the analyst is very often concerned with directionality of the stain. To distinguish directionality, the stain being examined must be identified as being either a parent spatter/stain or a satellite spatter/stain.

When a drop impacts a target, surface tension, molecular attraction, inertia, and velocity all act in their own way to either hold the drop together or break it apart. When the surface tension is overcome in the main drop, as it collapses smaller droplets detach. Both result in stains. The larger stain is the "parent" while the smaller are the "satellite" stains. A parent may spawn multiple satellite stains, but a satellite has only one parent stain. (See Figure 25.)

The primary reason for making a distinction between the two is found in the tail of the stain. Satellite tails point towards the origin, whereas the tail of the parent stain points away from the origin.

Projected Blood:

Blood which impacts a target or surface under pressure and in volume. The most obvious incidence of a projected bloodstain is the arterial spurt or gush.

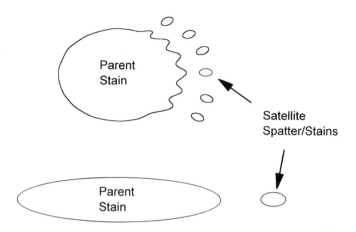

Figure 25 Identifying parent from satellite. The major portion of the stain resulting from a drop's impact is referred to as the "parent stain". Small droplets often detach during the impact creating smaller stains, referred to as "satellite stains".

Ricochet Stain:

> Blood which impacts a secondary object and then bounces or falls to another target.

Bloodshed in a violent confrontation is a very dynamic situation. We always see the result, but rarely the event. The ricochet stain represents another stain which, if not recognized, can lead to distinctly false conclusions.

On impact, the drop shows the directionality evident as it struck the target. If we assume this to be the original direction of the blood without some consideration for the possibility of a ricochet, the resulting analysis is likely to be tainted. As directionality is the easiest information to glean from a given bloodstain, it is also often taken for granted.

Satellite Spatter:

> Small stains created when droplets detach from a bigger drop as it impacts a target.

When a blood drop strikes a surface, at any angle, the drop is subjected to extreme shifts in the liquid. During these shifts the surface tension acts to contain the liquid as an integral entity. Often, due to the nature of the force involved this is impossible. During these shifts, smaller droplets may form which are connected to the parent drop by a spine-like structure of blood.

If the velocity of these smaller droplets is sufficient they may break from the parent, forming a smaller individual stain. Whether these newly formed droplets are attached or detached, one (as in the case of the "wave cast-off stain"[7]) or many (as in the case of a drip pattern), they are the result of a single action and may be classified as satellite spatter.

As stated, the primary difference between satellite and parent drops is that directionality will be opposite in each. Recognizing the satellite and parent relationship, however, is a relatively easy process. In overcoming the surface tension of the spine(s), linear tails on either the parent or satellite may be evident. These tails will help in matching parent to satellite.

Shadowing/Ghosting/Void:

> An area within a generally continuous bloodstain pattern that lacks blood-stains.

If, while a target is being exposed to some form of bloodstain-producing event (e.g., a blow, a drip), a secondary object is either present or introduced between the blood source and the target, the secondary object is likely to receive some of the stains. Should this secondary object then be moved from its position, the remaining target may exhibit a voided area. Beyond its mere presence, this voided area may also exhibit characteristics of size and shape that will help identify the nature of the object which caused it. The terms ghosting or shadowing are used to describe a pattern of this nature, as the voided area casts a "shadow" of the object onto the target.

At a minimum, the presence of a void indicates some secondary object was involved. The mere location of the voided area helps place this item (if identified) back into the crime scene at the moment of the bloodshed. Depending upon the nature of the event creating the void, its size, shape, or location may provide more specific information. As an example consider a spatter pattern present on a shooting victim's pants. The victim is found sitting in a chair. We locate a voided area across the upper pant leg which correlates in size and relationship to the victim's arm, which is now hanging to the side of the chair. We then find matching spatter on the arm of the shirt. This information helps place the victim's arm in a specific position when the spatter was created.

Skeletonized Stain/Skeletonization:

> A bloodstain that although disturbed still reflects its original shape and size.

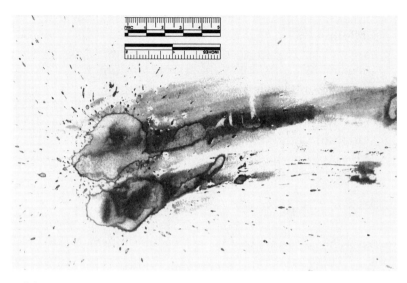

Figure 26   Evidence of skeletonization in a smear pattern. The ring surrounding the wiped out bloodstain is referred to as skeletonization and indicates a period of time passed between the blood's deposit and the wiping action.

Once deposited, blood will usually begin drying from the outer perimeter inward toward the center of the stain. Should the stain be disturbed prior to completion of the drying process, the resulting effect is referred to as skeletonization. In this effect, those portions of the stain which have dried remain undisturbed, while the wet blood is either wiped away or smeared. Figure 26 shows an example of a large deposit of blood which was wiped through. The border of the bloodstain, its skeleton, is still apparent.

Skeletonization not only helps us recognize the stain's original size and shape, but also helps in sequencing actions. Obviously, it illustrates that some subsequent action has followed the deposit of spatter or stains. It may also provide parameters of the time during which this disturbance occurred.

Spines:

Linear characteristics evident in both single drop stains and volume stains.
(See Figure 27.)

As discussed previously, the surface tension of a liquid is a viable force which attempts to hold the liquid together as a single entity. In the process of overcoming this surface tension, long narrow spine-like formations form between a parent drop and the secondary droplet attempting to break from it. This spine formation is found not only in the breakup of a single drop of blood, but also when larger quantities of blood are disturbed. When these

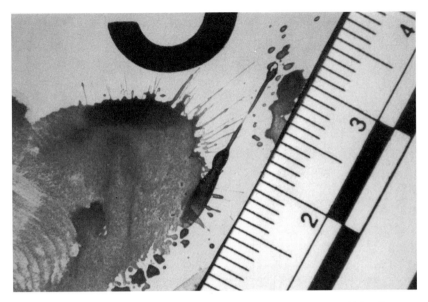

Figure 27 Spines occur even in instances of small volumes of blood. Note the linear features at the tip of the finger pattern transfer.

structures fall to the target they create linear stains which are referred to as spines.

In large stains which exhibit spines, this may indicate some measure of force was applied to the blood. A good example is a quantity of blood present on a floor, which is then stomped in by a shod foot. (See Figure 28.) Spines often result in this instance. The length of the spines themselves are dependent upon the quantity of blood present in the stain and the nature of the force applied.

Splash:

> The stain pattern created when a volume of blood impacts a target with minimal force. (See Figure 29.)

Splashes of blood are relatively uncommon to the crime scene. A splash is considered to be a pattern created when a volume of blood strikes any surface under conditions not amounting to projection. In other words, the force or energy behind the application of the splash is minimal. As a result, the splash stain tends to present a consolidated appearance.

The presence of splashes may lead to considerations of a staged scene, as the mechanism to create a splash is uncommon to the events associated with most violent crimes. An example of a naturally occurring splash may be found in a suicide, where the victim shoots himself in the head while sitting

Figure 28   A boot stomp into blood. Note the numerous spines present in the stain. As a general rule, the presence of spines in a stain tends to indicate that some level of force was used in the impact.

or standing. A quantity of blood can pool in the remnants of the lower skull and be thrown out when the body collapses, causing the splash.

Passive Flow:

> A blood flow created by gravity alone, with no circulatory action involved.

A common form of stain found at many scenes is the flow pattern. These patterns are found on the victim, on objects in the scene, or on surfaces in the scene.

Only the wound or body position can prevent gravity from creating passive blood flows. Depending upon the manner in which the body is moved and positioned, passive flows resulting from gravity may be extensive.

Pattern Transfer:

> Any stain created when a wet bloody object comes in contact with another surface.

Pattern transfers are very likely the most common form of stain present in any bloodstained scene. This should not be surprising based on the physical nature of liquid blood. Long recognized for its adhesive qualities, once an object is contaminated with blood in some fashion, the blood is difficult to

Figure 29 A splash pattern. This splash pattern was produced in a lab setting by tossing a small volume of blood against the target. Splash patterns tend to have a cohesive look, with little breakup of the blood into smaller stains.

clean up and will tend to contaminate (or stain) anything the first object subsequently comes in contact with. Figure 30 shows a pattern transfer caused by a hand, while Figure 31 shows the pattern caused by a pair of scissors.

As is evident from the figures, the pattern on the second surface often provides specific characteristics which help the analyst identify the first object. Examples of pattern transfers run a wide gamut, including bloody fingerprints, foot and shoe prints, wiping caused when a weapon (e.g., a knife or bludgeon) is cleaned, and stains caused by the weave or pattern present in bloodied clothing or bedding.

Wipes and swipes often exhibit characteristics of the item causing them, and as such also qualify as pattern transfers. Just as patterned injuries are an important aspect of forensic pathology, so too are pattern transfers to bloodstain analysis. Too often they are simply ignored by the analyst, who fails to see the relationship of the pattern to some other item of evidence.

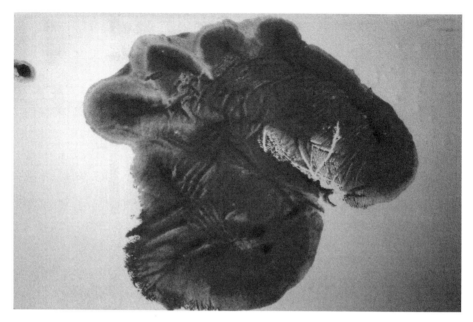

Figure 30 A pattern transfer which exhibits evidence of capillary action. Within the pattern, however, is sufficient detail to point to a friction-ridged surface as the pattern's source. (Photograph courtesy of Jouni Kiviranta, National Bureau of Investigation, Helsinki, Finland.)

Swipe:

> The transfer of blood onto a target by a moving object that is bloodstained. The motion involved is generally considered as some type of lateral movement. (See Figure 32).

Wipe:

> A wipe is a stain created when an object moves through a preexisting bloodstain on another surface. Again, the motion is assumed to be a lateral movement.

Figure 33 shows a wipe caused by the sliding motion of a shoe. The function of a wipe or swipe in analysis is usually one of sequencing. The first consideration is to distinguish what was bloodied by what (defining the stain as a wipe or swipe). Knowing this order may add overall clarity to the events surrounding the incident. Evaluating the nature of the lateral movement also adds to our understanding of the event, very often defining the direction of the movement.

Figure 31 A pattern transfer which exhibits distinct linear features. The pattern's source was a bloodied pair of scissors. (Photograph courtesy of Jouni Kiviranta, National Bureau of Investigation, Helsinki, Finland.)

Velocity Impact Patterns

Depending upon the analyst's background, the three velocity impact pattern definitions can be considered as anything from the Holy Grail to pure heresy. It is important to understand these three terms, as they are often used and abused. In discussing spatter and stains one will hear the terms: low velocity, medium velocity, and high velocity. Before considering these definitions, remember that the size range discussed is for the majority of spatter or stains present, in other words, the preponderant stain size. Rarely are there singularly sized stain patterns. In any pattern we will normally see varying sizes of spatter present.

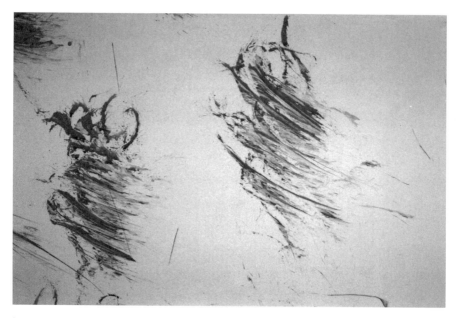

Figure 32   A classic swipe pattern created by bloody hair. Note that the motion of the hair (i.e., left to right) is evident by examining the feathering of the pattern. (Photograph courtesy of Jouni Kiviranta, National Bureau of Investigation, Helsinki, Finland.)

Figure 33   Wipe pattern. Evident in the lower right-hand section of the photograph is a wipe pattern coming from the small pool of blood.

Low-Velocity Stains

Low velocity is considered to be a force or energy equivalent to normal gravitational pull up to a force or energy of 5 ft/s. The resulting stain is relatively large, usually ranging 4 mm and up in diameter.

Medium-Velocity Impact Spatter

Medium-velocity impact spatter (MVIS) is usually considered to be a pattern of spatter in which the preponderant stain size ranges between 1 and 4 mm in diameter. The force or energy for creation of the stain is said to be between 5 and 25 ft/s.

High-Velocity Impact Spatter

High-velocity impact spatter (HVIS) is usually considered to be a pattern of spatter in which the preponderant stain size ranges 1 mm or smaller in diameter. The force or energy for creation of the stain is said to be 100 ft/s or higher.

There is an obvious consideration in using these terms. Are the demarcation points for the force scientifically valid? The issues surrounding velocity labels have plagued the discipline for years. However you view this issue, in discussing velocity labels, always be cautious. Velocity pattern definitions are discussed in greater detail in Chapter 7.

Summary

Language is a fluid and changing medium. This is particularly true for terms used in any technical field — as advances occur in the field, the language evolves to reflect those changes. We have presented a cornucopia of terms. It is not our contention that every analyst must use these terms and only these terms. Certainly, other authors may disagree with the inclusion of some terms in our listing or the exclusion of others.

We hope that by understanding the underlying concepts (which are unlikely to change with time) analysts can express themselves clearly and understand others when discussing any bloodstained scene.

When presenting evidence in court, the analyst may favor a more generic method of phrasing his or her responses, but technical terms are still useful. In the end, the analyst is responsible for ensuring that whatever message they send, it is received and understood. The specific manner of *how* that is accomplished is best left to the individual analyst to decide.

References

1. Guralnik, David B., Ed., *Webster's New World Dictionary*, William Collins, Cleveland, OH, pg. 49, 1979.

2. Radzicki, Jozef, *SLADY KRWI n Praktyce Sledczek* (Bloodstain Prints in Practice of Technology), Bibliotecka Kryminalistyczna, Warsaw, Poland, 1960.

3. Pex, O. J. and Vaughn, C. H., Observations of High Velocity Bloodspatter on Adjacent Objects, *Journal of Forensic Sciences*, Vol. 32, No. 6, Nov. 1987, pp. 1588.

4. Fackler, Martin, Penetrating Projectile Caused Disruption of Human Bodies Applied to Bloodstain Pattern Analysis, Presentation to the International Association of Bloodstain Pattern Analysts, Colorado Springs, CO, Sept. 24, 1992.

5. Tortora, Gerard J. and Anagnostakos, Nickolas P., *Principles of Anatomy and Physiology*, 5th ed., Harper & Row, New York, 1987, pg. 449.

6. MacDonell, Herbert L. and Brooks, Brian A., Detection and Significance of Blood in Firearms, *Legal Medicine Annual*, 1977.

7. MacDonell, Herbert L., *Bloodstain Pattern Interpretation*, Laboratory of Forensic Science, Corning, NY, 1982.

8. Kirk, Paul L., *Affadavit Regarding the State of Ohio v. Samuel Sheppard*, Court of Common Pleas, Criminal Branch, # 64571, 26 April 1955, pg. 8.

Understanding the Medium of Blood

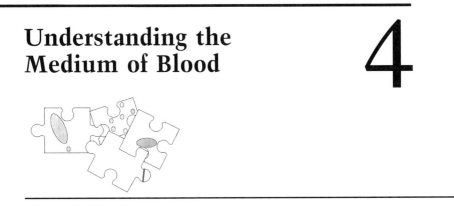

What is blood? What physical properties does it hold and how do they affect the resulting shapes of stains observed by the analyst? Must the analyst understand fluid dynamics and serology to properly conduct analysis?

The answer to the last question is a resounding NO. Yet understanding the properties of blood has a function for the bloodstain pattern analyst. In this chapter we will attempt to describe in laymen's terms the medium of the blood and how it reacts with its environment.

General Properties of Blood

Blood is a complex fluid that makes up approximately 8% of the total body weight of humans. As a rule, this equates to 5 to 6 l (liters) for males and 4 to 5 l for females.[1] Blood viscosity usually ranges between 4.4 and 4.7. Viscosity by definition is resistance to flow. Fluid viscosity is compared against water, which is considered to have a viscosity of 1. Blood, then, is more resistant to flow than water. Viscosity in blood is primarily the result of the hematocrit (the proportion of cellular material to fluid). Wider variances of blood viscosity are possible; however, whether distinctly higher or lower, such a variance would represent a major medical condition to the individual involved.[2] For this reason we can be relatively sure that the viscosity found in generally healthy humans, certainly for those up and walking about in a crime scene, remains somewhere within the 4 to 5 range. The issue of viscosity has a direct effect on the damping of oscillations in blood droplets, which we'll discuss in greater detail later in the chapter.

Blood has an adhesive quality. Although easily observed by the layman, this adhesiveness is also recognized medically.[3] This stickiness is of particular interest to the analyst, as this quality results in pattern transfers of every nature in the crime scene. A little blood can go a long way in contaminating everything it comes in contact with.

Blood serves many functions in the body. Obviously, a primary function is to provide the body with oxygen and nutrients while removing waste. Another function of particular concern to the analyst is protection against blood loss. The cardiovascular system is a closed system and breaching represents a major threat to survival. Blood will act through various mechanisms to reduce blood loss, thereby increasing overall survival chances.

Blood Make-Up

As a medium, blood is broken into two components: the formed elements and the plasma. The plasma makes up 55% of blood, while the formed elements make up 45%.[4]

Plasma, the fluid component of blood, is broken down into four general components. These are water, soluble proteins, organic acids, and salts. By volume plasma is 91% water, while the latter three components make up the remaining 9%. The proteins represent approximately 8%, with the organic acids and salts consisting of about 1% each. The proteins include fibrinogen which plays an important role in clotting.[5]

The formed elements are the true cellular material of blood. There are three basic blood cells: erythrocytes (red blood cells), leukocytes (white blood cells), and thrombocytes (platelets). All three cells develop from a single cell, the hemocytoblast; however, in its transformation each cell takes on properties which are of some interest to the analyst.[6]

Red blood cells represent the majority of the formed elements. There are about 4.8 to 5.4 million cells per cubic millimeter of blood.[7] Red blood cells have two properties of particular interest. First is the presence of hemoglobin within the cell. Hemoglobin is a red pigment which gives blood its color and, hence, red blood cells their name. As the oxygen content increases in the blood, so does the bright red pigment of the hemoglobin. The second property of interest is the absence of a nucleus in the red blood cell. In the process of maturing from a hemocytoblast, the red blood cell sheds the remaining cell material including the nucleus.

The analyst must consider that since all red blood cells present in the stain have no nuclei, they serve no function in current DNA analysis. In fact, when considering blood by total volume, about 99% contains no material of use to DNA analysis. The remaining 1%, which is of value, is randomly distributed throughout the total blood volume. Therefore, we should not be too surprised by inconclusive results. This knowledge doesn't preclude us from submitting all stains found at the scene. Remember, it is a random process which determines what proportions of cells are found in the stains. Also, as DNA procedures progress (e.g., PCR testing) we see better results from smaller samples.

White blood cells are the second type of cell present in blood. They are broken down into five additional subcategories. In general, they all act to fight infections, and destroy old cellular material and other invading microbes. White cells make up less than 1% of the total formed elements, which equates to about 5000 to 9000 cells per cubic millimeter.[8] White cells have nuclei and are the only material present in the blood by which DNA analysis is currently possible. Again, the random distribution or subsequent degradation of the sample may leave a serologist with little if anything from which to work.

The third and last type of blood cell is the platelet. It, too, lacks a nucleus. Although occuring in larger numbers than the white cells, there are substantially fewer platelets than red blood cells. Generally, there are about 250,000 to 400,000 platelets present per cubic millimeter of blood.

The platelet serves a single function, to help in the chain reaction of the clotting mechanism and thereby reduce blood loss. Platelets have irregular shapes and are quite small under normal conditions. They change drastically, however, when they encounter elements present in damaged blood vessels (e.g., collagen). Upon encountering a damaged vessel, the platelets increase in size and their shapes become even more irregular. At the same time, they become sticky and begin to adhere to surrounding fibers in the vessel wall. The resulting accumulation of platelets is known as a "platelet plug". In the instance of smaller vessels the plug, by itself, can effectively control blood loss.[9]

The Body's Response to Breaching of the Circulatory System

When breaching of the circulatory system occurs, the body reacts in three ways to control the blood loss. The first mechanism is the vascular spasm. Simply put, smooth muscles in the vessel wall contract to decrease the size of the vessel, thereby reducing the flow of blood through it. This mechanism is said to reduce blood loss for up to 30 min following injury, allowing time for the other blood loss mechanisms to occur.[10]

The second mechanism is the platelet plug. As discussed, platelets change their shapes when they encounter damaged blood vessels. Platelets and the platelet plug literally plug holes in the circulatory system, reducing if not stopping blood loss.

Coagulation or clotting is the third process. Present in blood are 13 different clotting factors. These factors can initiate clotting either intrinsically, that is, from within the blood itself, or in an extrinsic path which is based on trauma to surrounding tissue. Whichever the case, the process occurs in three steps.

The extrinsic pathway is shorter and occurs almost immediately after trauma is sustained. In the first step of the extrinsic pathway, the damaged tissues release substances which create what is known as a prothrombin activator. The first step of the intrinsic pathway takes longer, usually several minutes. The blood in contact with collagen begins a series of events involving the various clotting factors which ultimately releases this same prothrombin activator.

The second and third steps of both pathways are the same. The prothrombin activator, in the presence of calcium ions in the blood, converts prothrombin into thrombin. The thrombin in the presence of calcium ions converts soluble fibrinogen into insoluble fibrin. Thrombin accelerates the production of the prothrombin activator, which produces more thrombin, which in turn produces more prothrombin activator, and so on.[11] Once set in motion the process builds momentum on its own.

The clotting we observe at crime scenes gives us a glimpse at the result of this overall process. The fibrin takes on a very structured form, capturing within it the blood cells. As with blood left to clot at the scene, one sees only the serum (typically a clear, straw-colored liquid) which surrounds the clotted mass (the fibrin fibers and blood cells). (See Figure 34.)

Figure 34 Serum separation. The puddle located in the lower right-hand portion of the photograph exhibits separation of the formed elements from the serum.

Circulatory System Considerations

At any given moment the 4 to 6 l of blood present in the circulatory system is distributed as follows:

> 58% in veins, venules, and venous sinuses,
> 13% in arteries,
> 12% in the pulmonary vessels,
> 9% in the heart, and
> 8% in the arterioles and capillaries.[12]

Although not always of immediate interest to the analyst, understanding this blood reservoir concept may at times help explain the presence of a large volume of blood at a scene. For instance, lacking evidence of active bleeding, but finding a distinct injury to the heart, one should not be surprised to find 20% of the body's total volume of blood present in a passive flow. Nor should we be surprised that it all occurred as a result of a passive flow. The heart and major pulmonary veins easily hold this volume. On occasion the analyst may need to consider these reservoir amounts, correlating specific injuries sustained to the amount of blood present at the scene. This consideration may assist the analyst in differentiating blood lost from active bleeding and that resulting from passive flow following death.

Droplet Dynamics in Flight

Hopefully, the reader now better understands blood, at least from the aspect of its behavior in the circulatory system. More to the interest of the analyst is how blood reacts once shed. In flight, what characteristics does it have?

Much has been written about the so-called "normal drop" of blood. It should not be surprising that our first consideration is the droplet itself. What shape does a droplet of blood attain while in flight?

James E. McDonald, in discussing raindrop shapes and answering why a droplet is spherical, said: "surface tension always tends to reduce the surface of a free mass of liquid to the smallest area it can achieve... an isolated drop of liquid not distorted by external forces is pulled by its surface tension into a spherical shape."[13] In considering how internal pressures present in droplets impacted on the force of surface tension, McDonald found that small droplets (1 mm in diameter and less) were almost perfect spheres. Larger drops, however, were unable to maintain the perfect sphere shape in flight and often resembled nothing less than a "hamburger bun."[14]

Dr. Alfred Carter also commented on the issue of shape and surface tension stating: "With regard to the spherical shape of liquid droplets, it can be explained entirely by the surface tension of the liquid."[15]

Surface tension acts to shape a droplet into a sphere. Yet, surface tension is not the only factor in keeping it in this shape. As many author's have noted, water droplets oscillate to a great extent when falling in air. The surface tension of water is considered to be 70 dyn/cm, whereas blood has a surface tension of only 50 dyn/cm.[16] Thus, if surface tension alone were the force in effect, we might well expect blood droplets to oscillate considerably. In fact they do not, based on their viscosity. To understand viscosity's relationship in maintaining this sphere, we must first consider the force that disrupts this spherical tendency.

In seeking to explain the diverse shapes of raindrops evident in nature, researchers identified the primary force behind them as oscillations present in the mass of the droplet. As McDonald noted in his larger drops, oscillations were evident to the extent he could physically observe and photograph them. Such oscillations occur naturally in raindrops, particularly those with larger diameters. They result from various forces including but not limited to collisions with other droplets.[17]

Before going further its probably best to define these oscillations and their effect on the analysis. (Refer first to Figure 35.) To understand these oscillations, imagine for a moment that we could sit our droplet on a table (like a water balloon), and that it would retain its shape. If pressure were applied to either the sides or top, the shape of the droplet would change to accommodate the liquid volume moved by the pressure. The volume would not change, only the shape.

While in flight, oscillations in droplets have the same effect on shape, only the pressure or force for change comes from within the droplet. The closest analogy we can make is, that like a wave, the oscillation moves through the mass of the droplet, rebounding within it. The resulting change is cyclic, that is it causes a range of recurring deformations from the perfect sphere. This results in a somewhat evenly distributed shape deformation. (See Figure 36.) The overall level of this deformation will decrease with time.

With but one major exception, these oscillations have no effect on issues in bloodstain pattern analysis. The exception is in considering impact angle determinations. These angles, in part, are based on the belief that a droplet impacting a surface is in the shape of a sphere. If a blood droplet were to oscillate to any great degree at impact, the resulting deformation in the droplet's shape could alter the stain's ratio of width to length. Given this instance, the analyst could not rely on the resulting angle determination.

For all liquid droplets, size, viscosity, and time affect these oscillations. As analysts we must consider these factors and the resulting range of oscillations

Oscillations and Droplets

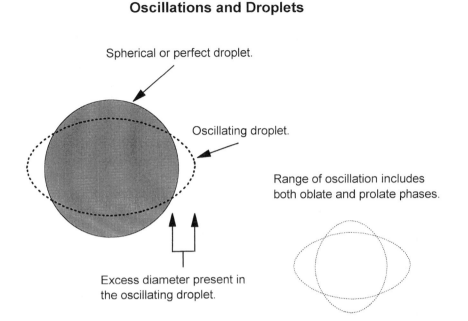

Spherical or perfect droplet.

Oscillating droplet.

Range of oscillation includes both oblate and prolate phases.

Excess diameter present in the oscillating droplet.

Figure 35   Oscillations in droplets. As a result of their formation, droplets oscillate. This causes a shift of the droplet's mass from a perfect sphere to an oblong spheroid. The oscillation is dynamic, that is, it shifts until the oscillation decays completely. As such, the droplet moves through a wide range of shapes as the oscillation shifts back and forth between the oblate and prolate phase.

Flight Path of the Droplet Over Time

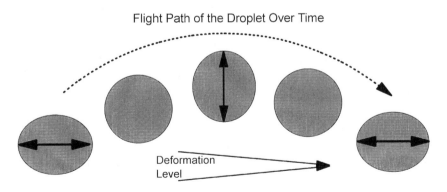

Deformation Level

The arrows indicate the plane of the deformation of the droplet from a perfect sphere.   The level or amount of the deformation present in the droplet decreases with time.

Figure 36   Oscillations in droplets move through an entire range of deformations. The most important aspect of these oscillations is that they decay with time. The longer the droplet is in flight, the smaller the remaining oscillation.

present in blood droplets to decide whether our impact angle results are generally accurate.

Ryan, in working with water droplets, observed these oscillations and remarked: " … drops smaller than 0.5 mm radius are essentially spherical regardless of surface tension."[18] Regarding drop instability as being a factor for breakup, Ryan stated: "Thus, the current experiments lend further credence to the now generally accepted belief that raindrop size is limited by breakup caused by drop interaction rather than breakup from individual drop instability."[19]

Ryan, working with artificially produced drops, created water drops 6 to 9 mm in diameter. He believed, however, a 5-mm-diameter drop would be the largest naturally occurring water droplet. Of particular concern to our issues, he noted that the larger the drop the greater the level of oscillation.

What size should we expect in the instance of a blood droplet? Pizzola et al. produced low-velocity drops with diameters of about 3.7 mm. They, too, noted that such drops oscillate.[20] MacDonell reported drop diameters up to 4.6 mm.[21] The authors observed drops on the order of 5.3 mm, but again these were the result of low-velocity events. Thus in situations where blood merely forms a drop as a result of gravitational forces (drips and similar actions), we may well expect stable drops with diameters as large as 5 or 5.5 mm. Such drops would have a volume of about 60 µl. This size of droplet exhibits distinct levels of oscillations.

We offer a caution in discussing a "standard" or "normal" range for drop size or volume. MacDonell was criticized for alluding to a "normal" drop volume, since the actual volume for any drop is in part determined by the surface area it drips from. Nevertheless, this 5.5-mm-diameter (0.06 ml) size is empirically evident to be the upper limit for a stable blood droplet, while MacDonell's 4.6-mm-diameter drop (0.05 ml) is probably more typical of free-falling drops resulting from venous bleeding.[22]

As one might expect, impacts result in significantly smaller drops. While studying impact events, we documented droplets (not the stain) with diameters ranging between 0.125 to 2 mm. Volumes for such impact droplets are significantly smaller, ranging between 0.008 to 4.18 µl. We are not saying this range is an absolute for all impact events. Just as in the argument against a "standard" blood drop, the range in droplet size for any given impact event would vary depending upon the nature of the impact involved. Nevertheless, considerations of stain size and droplet volume place the upper limit of this range at about 2 mm for droplets formed by an impact event. We found that droplets which create stains 4 to 5 mm in size (medium velocity spatter) have diameters generally not larger than this 2 mm range.[23] So when considering impact events we are looking at relatively small droplets which, as Ryan noted, oscillate at a much lower level.

As a result of Dr. Kenneth Beard's efforts in raindrop research, he reported that raindrop oscillations were related to collisions (analogous to Ryan's droplet interaction) between the larger, faster-falling drops with the smaller drizzle drops.[24] With the issue of collisions and oscillations in mind, we asked Dr. Beard to comment on oscillations in blood droplets and their effects. In considering this issue Dr. Beard stated:

> "Blood droplets should have initial oscillations of a rather large amplitude since the forces in the disruption process are not spherically symmetric. These oscillations will damp significantly in a fraction of a second for droplets of a few millimeters in diameter. Disruption of blood flow at the source of droplets should be the primary cause of oscillations since the forces from other influences are generally weaker (for example, that associated with air motions). It seems unlikely that droplets would collide far away from the source, to produce additional oscillations, because they become dispersed."[25]

Dr. Beard provided calculations for defining droplet oscillation which allow us a greater insight into droplet behavior while in flight.[26] He also indicated that a liquid's viscosity is a critical element in damping any oscillation in the droplet. The higher the viscosity, the faster the damping.

Based on this information we know that oscillations in blood droplets damp about four times as quickly as those found in water droplets. We can't absolutely discount these oscillations. At impact they may be quite distinct (up to 40% of the droplet's diameter), but the actual time it takes these oscillations to die out is relatively short.

Raymond, working with pipette-produced droplets, noted oscillations up to 10% of the droplet's diameter.[27] Gardner, working with droplets created by impact found similar data, in which the majority of oscillations damped below 10% of the droplet's diameter within 0.05 s after impact.[28] Thus, the high viscosity of a blood droplet helps eliminate oscillations, allowing surface tension to form the drop into a more perfect sphere. Droplets in flight will tend to maintain this spherical shape with few factors present to disrupt them.

In summarizing these concerns about droplet size, oscillations, and any resulting deformation of the blood sphere in flight, we can say that droplets created as a result of an impact:

- Generally have diameters not greater than 2 mm.[29]
- Have oscillations present in the mass of the liquid, but these oscillations damp very quickly.
- When impacting a target such droplets are close to being perfect spheres, which allows a level of confidence for the width and length ratios of the resulting stains.

Dr. Beard's belief that collisions among droplets are an uncommon event in blood impacts is also of some interest to the analyst. While studying oscillation damping, we captured photographic images of impact spatter in flight. In these photos the impact droplets randomly disperse, with less than 1% colliding in any fashion away from their source. The data sample used in this observation included 70 different impacts and in excess of 600 droplets.[30]

The lack of collisions between droplets in free flight speaks to an important issue. It indicates, as Dr. Beard suggested, that only the impact itself causes breakup in blood droplets. Collisions after creation are too few to cause instability of droplets in flight. Once set in motion, then, droplets do not spontaneously break apart.

Another interesting aspect of droplet behavior is that the droplet's size drastically changes its path in free flight. The effect of air resistance is inversely proportional to the size of the droplet. The larger the droplet the less the effect and the smaller the droplet the greater the effect. Thus, when given two droplets of differing diameters directed along a path at the same velocity, the larger drops will carry farther than the smaller one. Although projected in a common direction, their respective parabolas will differ. Figure 37 is a TRACKS© model of two droplets of different volumes.[31] The smaller droplet (Droplet #1) although projected at the same initial speed as the larger drop, quickly loses velocity and falls to the ground.

This is particularly noticeable in the instance of very fine droplets such as those associated with gunshot injuries. These droplets carry only a short distance before gravity and air resistance drag them downward. For such small droplets the total distance traveled from the origin will normally not exceed 4 ft.

Droplet Dynamics on Impact

We understand our blood droplet's behavior as it follows a given flight path to its destination, but what happens when the droplet impacts a given surface? What the human eye cannot see, the human mind often cannot fathom. So it is with blood droplet impacts. Almost every author has commented in some fashion on what occurs during impact. In many instances, false cause and effect relationships were established. Although these beliefs do not deter our understanding of the resulting stain, they are still in error. A particular point in contention is what occurs when a droplet impacts a rough surface. Nearly everyone, including your authors, have reported that droplets burst on contact when a rough surface ruptures the droplet's surface.[32-34] This certainly seems logical, but it is incorrect.

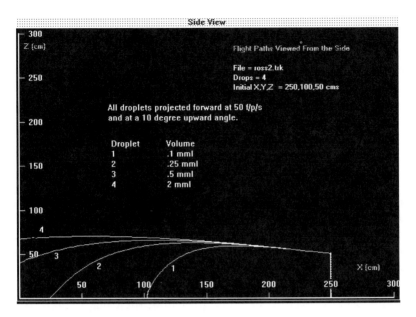

Figure 37   Air resistance is inversely proportional to drop size. This TRACKS(c) model shows four droplets projected out at the same angle. Droplet #1 has a small volume while droplet #2 is much larger. The smaller droplets, although initially traveling at a similar speed and angle, quickly drop as a result of the effect of air resistance.

One might question why the analyst should worry about what happens during these impacts. After all, the analysts concern themselves with the aftermath of the impact (the stains) not the impact itself. There are many antagonists of bloodstain pattern analysis. The discipline has been challenged both in and out of court based on a lack of research into blood droplet dynamics. Although only an initial step, the following observations provide a greater understanding of the droplet's dynamic shifts at impact.

Over a two-year period, Gardner studied impacts using both strobo-scopic photography methods and stop-motion video. The droplet impacts involved varying targets including coarse sandpaper, rough weave fabrics, poster board, and plexiglas. Impact angles were varied also. As a result of these observations, four distinct phases of the impact were identified.[35]

Some analysts may object to the specific labels used to describe this action, but what cannot be disputed is the physical action of the droplet during each phase. These phases appear independent of surface texture or impact angle, although all of these issues have some effect on the process. The phases, although slightly different, occur in all impacts. The only caveat we make with regard to these observations is that there may be a point of diminished volume in very small droplets at which the later phases are altered. This particular issue requires further study.

In considering our observations, accept them as just that — empirical observations which help us understand the shift and transitions the droplet goes through to create a stain.

Your authors choose to call these four phases of impact: Contact/Collapse, Displacement, Dispersion, and Retraction. For ease of discussion, the following assumes a solid substrate or target. Liquid targets do not dramatically change the considerations of the phases, but unnecessarily complicates them. As such, we'll deal with liquid to liquid impacts as an aside.

Contact/Collapse

This phase begins when the droplet (a sphere) contacts the substrate or target. The droplet begins to collapse in a very orderly fashion, from the bottom up. Those sections of the sphere not in direct contact with the target remain intact and generally unaffected until they too collide. As a result, halfway through the collapse one would see half a sphere or droplet centered about the point of impact.

As this collapse occurs, the blood present at the collapse point is forced outward creating a rim around the droplet. This rim or boundary grows as more of the droplet's mass is forced into it. The flow to the rim has been referred to as an "involution"; however, it does not appear to fit that definition well since the blood flows outward and not inward.[36]

The angle of impact affects the contact collapse phase by defining the nature of the rim and blood flow into it. For instance, in a stain impacting at 90°, the blood flow into the rim is equal on all sides. (See Figure 38.) As a result, we see a circular stain with a generally equal diameter.

In stains impacting at more acute angles, the droplet's momentum forces the blood from the collapse into a more directional outflow. Consider an impact at 20°. Although the rim is still evident across the entire periphery of the expanding stain boundary, the blood flows primarily into the area of the rim opposite the direction from which the droplet originated. (See Figures 39 through 41.) This directional outflow in combination with the droplet's skimming movement during collapse helps explain the elliptical shape of the stain.

Surface characteristics have an influence on the contact collapse phase. Surface irregularities may begin an irregular outflow of blood in the collapse; however, this irregular outflow is far more evident in the displacement phase.

Displacement

In this phase the sphere itself has collapsed against the target and the majority of the blood from the droplet has displaced to the boundary rim of the resulting stain. Dr. Balthazard, in his early efforts, also noted this particular

Figure 38 A droplet in late contact collapse phase. A small dimple is evident in the center of the developing stain, this is, what is left of the still-collapsing droplet.

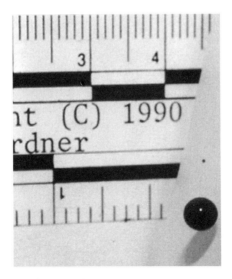

Figure 39 Free flight of a droplet just prior to its contact in an acute-angle impact.

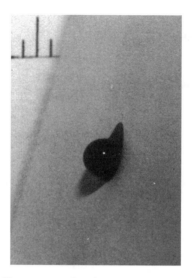

Figure 40 Contact collapse in a droplet impacting at an acute angle. This is early contact/collapse, nearly two thirds of the droplet is still intact and undisturbed.

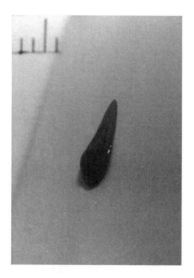

Figure 41 Late contact collapse in an acute-angle impact. In this photograph only about half of the droplet is still evident in the expanding stain. Note that the majority of the blood is being forced into the rim opposite the direction of origin.

phase or condition.[37] To this point there is no apparent disruption of the surface tension. The droplet, although exposed to considerable shifts in its shape, is still one mass and has not broken apart.

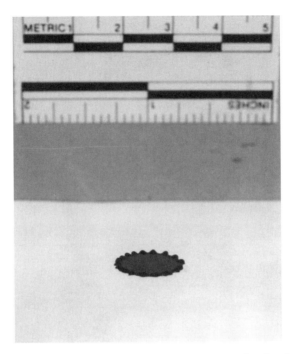

Figure 42 Displacement phase in a 90° impact. Note the displacement of the liquid to the rim of the developing stain. All motion up to this point in the collapse is lateral (outward).

Evident on the boundary rim of the collapsing droplet are dimples or short spines. (See Figure 42.) These appear to form as a result of the blood displacing from the central portion of the stain into the rim. The dimples may eventually lead to the creation of satellite spatter during the next phase of the impact. The central area of the stain retains some blood, resulting in a very evident sheet of blood which connects the entire structure. Nevertheless, nearly all of the liquid volume of the original droplet is now within the structure of the rim.

Although displacement is only the second phase of the impact, it's interesting to note that the area defined in the displacement phase will also define the overall dimensions (excluding any spines) of the resulting stain. If the liquid laterally displaces 4 mm in this phase, the resulting stain will measure 4 mm. Its important to note that displacement does not occur on a 1:1 ratio. That is, a 4-mm-diameter droplet does not create a 4-mm stain. We have yet to define the true nature of this displacement ratio, but it is often as high as 270% in larger drops (e.g., a 4-mm droplet creates a 11-mm stain). We believe the displacement ratio drops as the volume drops, but this area also requires further study. This ratio may have correlation to the effect of the oscillation

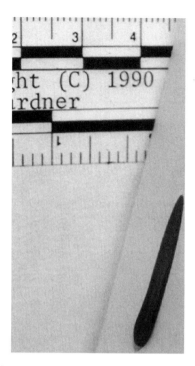

Figure 43 Early displacement of a droplet impacting at an acute angle. Note the distinct rim in the leading edge.

evident in the droplet at impact (e.g., a 0.06 mm excess oscillation at impact could result in as high as a 0.16 mm error in the length to width ratio).

Impact angle affects the displacement phase only in the nature of the dimples. As was evident in the contact collapse phase, 90° impacts result in development of a symmetrical rim. Thus in displacement, dimples will also appear symmetrically, surrounding the entire rim. Acute-angle impacts lead to dimples only in the forward edge of the developing rim. A single dimple, as found in a 10° to 20° impact, results in the classic wave cast-off stain. For example, Figure 43 exhibits the wave cast-off features during displacement, but prior to the development of dimples. Figure 44 shows a late displacement phase, in which the dimple is now evident and moving outward. Although often reported, there is no whip or backlash effect evident in the wave cast-off.[38]

Any dimple evident in displacement can result in an individual satellite spatter or spine. For instance, in 50° impacts one often observes a bear claw effect in the resulting stain. Each claw is the result of a single spine and each spine results from one of the several dimples that developed in the rim.

The surface texture of the target plays a prominent role in the displacement phase. It is not that a rough target "bursts" the droplet, resulting in the irregularly shaped stains we so often find. In fact, the typical balloon analogy

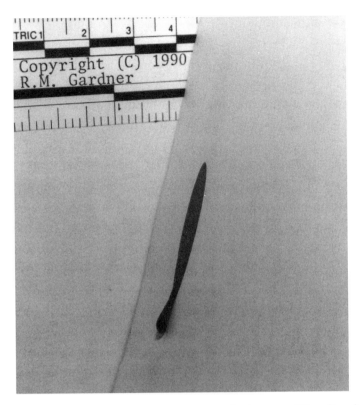

Figure 44   Late displacement in an acute-angle impact. The dimple in this photograph is well formed and beginning to show upward movement off the target plane.

is severely lacking, since in the balloon the skin is not an integral part of the fluid. In the blood droplet, however, the "skin" created by the surface tension is actually the fluid. It doesn't burst, it simply shifts its shape.

As a result of this shifting, on a rough surface the blood flows irregularly into the rim. The volume in one part of the rim may be large, while in another it may be small. The spines that eventually form will also be irregular, based on this difference in volume. This irregular flow will usually result in an abnormal or asymmetrical collapse of the entire structure later in the retraction phase.

This eventually results in what analysts would likely call a distorted or excessively spattered stain. Figure 45 shows stains created by similar droplets falling the same distance, but to different surfaces. The droplets falling to the rougher surface display distinct distortion. We cannot ignore the effect of the target surface on the collapsing droplet as it may limit any subsequent analysis.

Droplet velocity also plays a role in the displacement phase. As other authors have indicated, terminal velocity is reached for a given droplet when

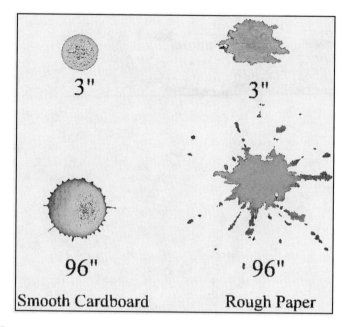

Figure 45 Target surface effect. These stains resulted from droplets falling 3 and 96 in. onto two different surfaces (e.g., a rough paper towel and smooth cardboard). Although the blood droplet does not "burst" on contact with a rough surface, the surface does cause an irregular outflow of the liquid in the displacement phase. This asymmetrical outflow can lead to distinct distortion, abnormal spines, and irregular development of satellite spatter. The end result is a distorted stain.

the effects of gravity are countered by air resistance.[39] This results in a constant velocity.

If we drop similar-sized drops from different heights the resulting stains will exhibit different overall sizes (different levels of displacement). A stain caused by a drop falling 3 in. will be smaller than one caused by a drop falling 3 ft. This is due to the increase in velocity of the droplet as it falls. The farther it falls the faster it falls, up to its terminal velocity.

However, dropping distance experiments also indicate that before the droplet reaches this terminal velocity, no further lateral spread (displacement) will be evident in the resulting stain. For large drops the maximum lateral spread occurs at about 20 ft/s.[40]

In the 1970s correlations were often drawn between the size of a stain and the distance which it fell. These correlations were based on the effect of velocity on the droplet (e.g., the lateral spread in displacement) and an assumed constant volume for a drop. Subsequent efforts show that the volume of a drop varies greatly depending upon the nature of the surface on which it forms. Unfortunately for the analyst, the many combinations of

Figure 46   Early dispersion in a droplet impacting at 90°. Note the surface tension is still intact although the droplet's mass has shifted dramatically.

droplet volume and droplet speed leave too many variables for this knowledge to be of any precise use in analysis. The only point we can conclude is that increasing the velocity beyond the terminal velocity (as in the case of blood projected by some force) does not cause a greater displacement of the droplet.

Dispersion

The dispersion phase offers a glimpse at perhaps the most elegant behavior of the droplet during impact. Results include the crown or blossom effect (Figures 46 and 47) and the wave cast-off (Figure 48).

This phase is easily categorized by the action of the rim. Blood is forced into the rim and dimples, which continue to rise upward and in a direction opposite to the original momentum. As the volume of liquid in these structures increases they become unstable. If sufficient force (inertia) is present, the structures break apart, resulting in the creation of satellite spatter.

The angle of impact plays an important role in defining the dispersion phase. In droplets impacting at or near 80° to 90° the result is a blossom effect. In this instance the rim and dimples rise upward around the entire periphery of the stain. (Refer back to Figure 46.) Whereas the liquid's motion in displacement was lateral, in dispersion it is upward and outward.

Figure 47 Late dispersion. Note the small dimples present on the rim of the blossom. In some cases these may detach and cause satellite spatter. Also note that the movement of the liquid in the dispersion phase is upward and outward.

In stains impacting at the more acute angles, the blossom builds more like a wave on one side of the rim. This wave in turn creates one or more spine-like structures. As the wave builds, surface tension once again pulls the liquid together. This causes a droplet to form at the end of the wave. As the wave and droplet rise off the target, surface tension pulls the liquid still in motion up and away from the target. This in effect closes the ellipse of the stain. The spines or spine present in these instances extend out beyond the rim and often spawn a satellite droplet. That is to say that at the end of each spine one will often observe a small developing droplet. Even at the end of the dispersion phase, surface tension is still a viable force seeking to maintain the connection between the main stain site spine and satellite droplet.

Retraction

The retraction phase is the final phase in the development of the stain. It appears to result from the effect of surface tension attempting to pull the fluid back into a single form. The inertial forces which caused the shifts in the droplet's mass are now either overcome by surface tension resulting in a

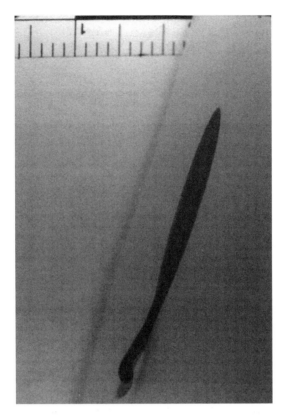

Figure 48 A classic wave cast-off developing during the dispersion phase of an acute angle impact.

complete retraction of the liquid, or these forces overcome the surface tension present in the spine resulting in the formation of spines and satellite spatter.

At the onset of the retraction phase, it appears that two forces attempt to counter one another. Inertia of the droplet developing at the end of the spine forces it away from the central stain; at the same time surface tension attempts to retract the liquid present in the spine. Particularly in acute-angle impacts, if the inertial forces are sufficient each spine will be stretched beyond the ability of surface tension to hold the fluid intact. Given these opposing forces, satellite droplets invariably detach. It is only at this point in the impact that the surface tension of the droplet is actually overcome (bursts), resulting in the creation of satellite spatter.

The blood retracted to the parent stain then coalesces and levels itself across the stain to some degree. A thick outer rim is still evident, both in the wet or dried stain. (See Figure 49.)

The impact angle has some effect on the stain in the retraction phase. For instance, in the 80° to 90° impact no part of the blossom's structure

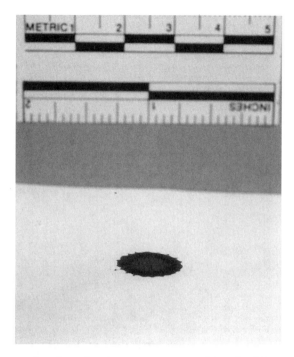

Figure 49   Retraction in a droplet impacting at 90°. The blossom we saw previously, retracts to the area defined in the displacement phase.

(excluding any spines) is responsible for the stain's ultimate length or width. The structure of the blossom completely retracts to the original boundary evident in displacement.

In the more acute-angle impacts, the majority of blood present in the spine retracts to the parent stain, but in many instances remnants of the spine simply fall to the target. The spines create the "tadpole tails" and "claws" we so often see in elliptical stains. Figure 50 shows an example of the retraction phase in an acute-angle impact.

Although roughness or irregularity of the target surface have little effect on the outcome of the stain during retraction, some target characteristics do matter. Of particular concern is whether the surface is of a wetting or non-wetting nature. In the situation of a nonwetting surface, the symmetry of the stain may be irregular as a result of irregular coalescing of the liquid stain. Absorbency of the target also plays a prominent role in affecting this symmetry.

In summing up our observations on the phases of impact, Figure 51 graphically depicts all four phases for varying impact angles. We recognize these observations will not change an analysis, but they do allow the analyst a better understanding of why the resulting stain looks as it does.

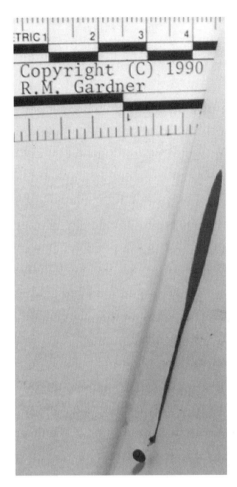

Figure 50 Retraction in an acute-angle impact. Inertia of the satellite droplet overcomes the surface tension in the connecting spine resulting in the complete detachment of the satellite. The spine simply falls to the target, creating a tail.

Liquid to Liquid Impacts

For the most part, considering liquid to liquid impacts serves little function in bloodstain pattern analysis. It may, however, assist the analyst in understanding the nature of stains such as drip patterns.

The four phases occur during liquid to liquid impacts but with differences. No major differences were noted for the contact/collapse phase. The droplet still collapses from the bottom up.

In the displacement phase, however, there appears to be more blood forced into the expanding rim. Blood present in the target flows into the rim

Impact Phases

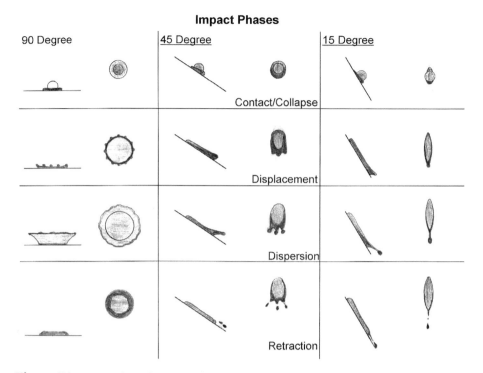

Figure 51 A graphic showing all four phases of impact as they occur in varying angles of impact. The drawing on the right side of each box depicts the view from the side; while the drawing on the left depicts the view from overhead. What is evident from this figure is that the collapse of the droplet is far from a simple "drop and burst" effect.

in addition to the blood from the droplet.[41] This is true both in instances where the impact occurs into a pool of blood or another drop of blood. Figure 52 shows an example of this abnormal blossom development.

As a result of the increased volume and lack of a solid target, we see a less-defined displacement phase and an early development of the dispersion phase. The blossom is far more pronounced and has been said to resemble a sea anemone.[42] The dimples are also more pronounced and always result in satellite spatter. In near 90° impacts, these spatter are thrown off in nearly every direction and seem to travel much farther. This result is quite evident in the classic drip pattern where the satellite spatter surrounding the pool extend out several inches from the central pattern.

In retraction, the only added result of a liquid to liquid impact is a rolling motion which develops in the pool. If other droplets impact the target while this motion is evident, the dispersion of the satellite spatter is even more random.

Figure 52 Dispersion in a liquid to liquid impact. The increased liquid in the rim often leads to an abnormal outflow of blood and an asymmetrical development of the blossom.

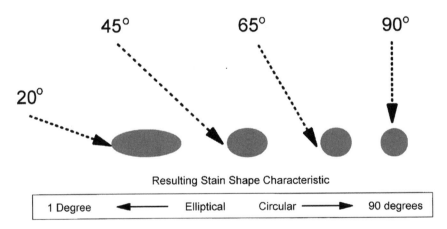

Figure 53 Stain shape and impact angle. The orderly collapse of the droplet onto the target produces characteristic shapes depending upon the angle of impact. The less acute the angle (e.g., 90°) the more circular the stain. The more acute the angle (e.g., 20°) the more elliptical the resulting stain.

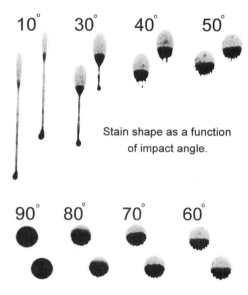

Figure 54   The resulting shapes evident from droplets impacting a target over a wide range of impact angles.

Stain Shape and Impact Angle Relationship

The prior discussion of the impact and collapse of the droplet leads us to a general understanding that as a droplet impacts any surface it collapses in an orderly fashion. This orderly nature, in combination with the angle at which the impact occurs, results in a very characteristic shape for the resulting stain. The specific shape (e.g., circular or elliptical) is dependent upon the angle of impact on the target. Droplets impacting at less acute angles (e.g., 80° to 90°) produce circular stains, while those impacting at more acute angles create elliptical stains. Figure 53 may assist the reader in understanding this relationship while Figure 54 shows examples of the range of droplet shapes possible.

The one exception to this relationship is, as Pizzola et al. discovered, a situation in which the target itself is in motion at the time of the droplet's collapse. In this situation the motion of the target creates a wave cast-off action in and of itself. As a result, a droplet impacting at 90° onto a moving target mimics a droplet striking a motionless target at a more acute angle (e.g., 20°).

As far as physical characteristics go, there are few differences between the two. One difference in the mimic stain is the lack of satellite spatter and spines. Although the mimic stain reflects an elliptical nature, it often does not exhibit spines or satellite spatter.

Summary

As we said in the beginning it is not absolutely necessary that an analyst understand the overall make-up of blood, the nature of the clotting process, or the manner in which a droplet collapses at impact. The analyst can easily conduct analysis without this specific knowledge. It is not our intent to overcomplicate the discipline, but we do feel this information can better prepare the analyst to conduct analysis.

Understanding the issues involved in blood loss or the manner in which a droplet collapses against a target can only aid analysts in their endeavors. It helps preclude analysts from making false cause and effect relationships with regard to stain characteristics they observe and the forces which caused those characteristics. Ultimately, this information assists analysts in understanding the bloodshed event.

References

1. Tortora, Gerad J. and Anagnostakos, Nickolas P., *Principles of Anatomy and Physiology*, 5th ed., Harper & Row, New York, 1987, pg. 440.
2. Strand, Fleur L., *Physiology: A Regulatory Systems Approach*, Macmillan, New York, 1978, pp. 239-241.
3. Tortora, Gerad J. and Anagnostakos, Nickolas P., *Principles of Anatomy and Physiology*, 5th ed., Harper & Row, New York, 1987, pg. 440.
4. Ibid.
5. Op. cit. pg. 441.
6. Op. cit. pg. 442
7. Op. cit. pg. 441.
8. Ibid.
9. Op. cit. pg. 449.
10. Ibid.
11. Op. cit. pp. 449-452.
12. Op. cit. pg. 490.
13. McDonald, James E., The Shape of Raindrops, *Scientific American*, Vol. 190, No. 2, February 1954.
14. Ibid.
15. Carter, A. L., Personal communications, July 1992.
16. Strand, Fleur L., *Physiology: A Regulatory Systems Approach*, Macmillan, New York, 1978, pp. 239-241.
17. Peterson, Ivars, Raindrop Oscillations — Raindrops Do More Than Just Fall; They Also Appear to Oscillate During Their Downward Plunge, *Science News*, Vol. 127, pp. 136-137.

18. Ryan, Robert T., The Behaviour of Large, Low-Surface-Tension Water Drops Falling at Terminal Velocity in Air, *Journal of Applied Meteorology*, Vol. 15, No. 2, Feb. 1976.

19. Ryan, Robert T., The Behaviour of Large, Low-Surface-Tension Water Drops Falling at Terminal Velocity in Air, *Journal of Applied Meteorology*, Vol. 15, No. 2, Feb. 1976.

20. Pizzola, P.A., et al., "Blood Dropplet Dynamics - I", *Journal of Forensic Sciences*, Vol. 31, No. 1, Jan. 1986, pg. 44.

21. MacDonell, Herbert L., *Bloodstain Pattern Interpretation*, Laboratory of Forensic Science, Corning NY, 1982, pg. 4.

22. MacDonell, Herbert L., *Bloodstain Patterns*, Laboratory of Forensic Science, Corning, NY, 1993, pg. 8.

23. Gardner, Ross M., "Deformation Levels of Blood Droplets Created by Impact," presented to the International Association of Bloodstain Pattern Analysts, Nov. 9, 1996, Albuquerque, NM.

24. Peterson, Ivars, Raindrop Oscillations — Raindrops Do More Than Just Fall; They Also Appear to Oscillate During Their Downward Plunge, *Science News*, Vol. 127, March 1985, pp. 136-137.

25. Beard, Kenneth V., Personal communications, Sept. 1989.

26. Gardner, Ross M., "Deformation Levels of Blood Droplets Created By Impact," presented to the International Association of Bloodstain Pattern Analysts, Nov. 9, 1996, Albuquerque, NM.

27. Raymond, Anthony, *Science and Justice*, July 1996.

28. Gardner, Ross M., "Deformation Levels of Blood Droplets Created By Impact," presented to the International Association of Bloodstain Pattern Analysts, Nov. 9, 1996, Albuquerque, NM.

29. Gardner, Ross M., "Deformation Levels of Blood Droplets Created By Impact," presented to the International Association of Bloodstain Pattern Analysts, Nov. 9, 1996, Albuquerque, NM.

30. Gardner, Ross M., "Deformation Levels of Blood Droplets Created By Impact," presented to the International Association of Bloodstain Pattern Analysts, Nov. 9, 1996, Albuquerque, NM.

31. TRACKS© is a copyright name of software created by Forensic Computing of Ottawa.

32. MacDonell, Herbert L., *Bloodstain Pattern Interpretation*, Laboratory of Forensic Science, Corning, NY, 1982, pg. 4.

33. Eckert, William G. and James, Stuart H., *Interpretation of Bloodstain Evidence At Crime Scenes*, Elsevier, New York, 1989, pg. 15.

34. Bevel, Tom and Gardner, Ross M., *Bloodstain Pattern Analysis: Theory and Practice — A Laboratory Manual*, TBI Inc., Oklahoma City, OK, 1990, pg. 9.

35. Gardner, Ross M., Bloodstain Droplet Dynamics and Oscillation Damping, presentation at the 76th Annu. Training Conf. Int. Assoc. of Identification, St Louis, MO, July 1991.

36. Pizzola, P. A. et al., Blood Droplet Dynamics — I, *Journal of Forensic Sciences,* Vol. 31, No. 1, pg. 44.

37. Baltzhazard, V. et al., Etude Des Goutes De Sang Projecte, Report presented to the 22nd Congress of Legal Medicine, Paris, Jun 5-7, 1939, pg. 17.

38. MacDonell, Herbert L., *Bloodstain Pattern Interpretation*, Laboratory of Forensic Science, Corning, NY, 1982, pg. 7.

39. Carter, Alfred and Podworny, Edward J., Computer Modelling of Trajectories of Blood Droplets and Bloodstain Pattern Analysis with a PC Computer, 2nd Annu. IABPA Training Conf., Dallas, TX, Dec. 1989.

40. MacDonell, Herbert L., *Bloodstain Patterns,* Golas Printing, Elmira Heights, NY, 1993, pp. 9-11.

41. Metropolitan Police Laboratory, Blood in Slow Motion, Droplet Dynamic Video, London, England, 1991.

42. Ibid.

Determining Motion and Directionality

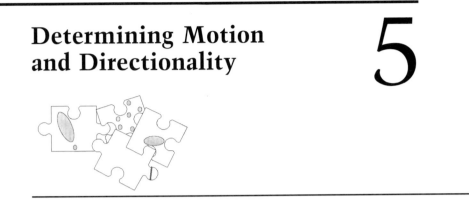

5

Establishing the motion involved in bloodshed events and specifically identifying directionality in blood droplets allows the investigator to more fully understand the specific events which occurred during the incident. The nature of this motion is threefold:

- General sequence of events — where did the event begin, where did it end?
- Droplet directionality — identifying the direction at which a given droplet struck a target.
- Recognition of blood trail motion — in which direction does a specific trail/stain lead?

General Sequence of Events

This first issue is one that may seem self evident, however, it is often misunderstood or misinterpreted. A rule exists in bloodstain pattern analysis which is reciprocal to a rule found in arson investigation. In an arson the investigator looks for the point where the fire caused the greatest damage. Typically, the point with the greatest damage is the point where the fire burned longest, which is likely to be the origin. In bloodstained scenes we apply this approach in reverse. The location where we find the greatest bloodshed is most likely the ending point of the incident. The location where we find the least blood (spatter and drips) is very likely at or near the point where the violence started.

Although a general rule, it exists for two reasons. As the attacker inflicts injuries the level of bleeding is likely to increase as greater damage and breaching of the circulatory system occurs. The resulting damage and shock decrease the victim's ability to escape and retain mobility. The end effect is an increase in bleeding volume at any given location in the latter stages of the event as compared to the earlier stages. Amazingly, analysts often overlook the second reason. Once breached, should death follow, nothing but body position prevents the victim from passively bleeding out the contents of the circulatory system. This rule is not to be taken as absolute, yet as we move through a given scene, those locations with only limited spatter or stains will likely lead to areas of greater spatter or stains. As the victim sustains different wounds the patterns may change, but the increase in bleeding should be apparent.

For example, if the first blows of an attack create a small laceration we may see evidence of drops falling as a result of venous bleeding. We may even find minor spatter on a wall or surrounding surface close to where the victim received the blow.

As the victim retreats to another area, the venous bleeding of the laceration continues. At the second location, the attacker strikes the victim again. Blood is present on the body from the first wound, thus the blow itself creates heavier spatter. These blows create a widening of the wound, which in turn increases the venous blood flow. Now attempting to defend against the blows rather than escape them, or perhaps dazed as a result of the blows, the progress of the victim may begin to slow. The volume of blood lost at any one point increases as the victim remains in that location longer. Throughout the events, the victim's hands and clothing become stained. In turn, these objects stain walls and surrounding items. The more blood, the more soaked the items; the more soaked the items, the more staining present. It is by viewing the stains in this fashion that we may discern a general flow of the overall incident and the events which define it.

Droplet Directionality

As discussed in Chapter 4, blood impacting a surface acts in a relatively defined fashion. Based upon this impact, one thing usually evident to the analyst is the directionality of a given droplet. The exceptions to determining directionality will generally be carpets and other highly absorbent or irregular surfaces.

As the liquid droplet contacts a surface, the droplet begins collapsing. Inertia keeps the mass of the droplet moving along the same path it was traveling before its encounter with the target. The blood present in the droplet flows outward to the edges of the stain during the collapse, creating either an elliptical or circular stain depending upon the angle of impact. Figure 55 details how this motion occurs. Whatever the shape, the resulting stain (unless impacting at 90°) will have both a major and minor axis.

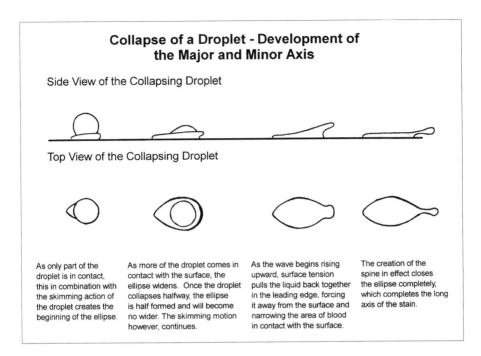

Collapse of a Droplet - Development of the Major and Minor Axis

Side View of the Collapsing Droplet

Top View of the Collapsing Droplet

As only part of the droplet is in contact, this in combination with the skimming action of the droplet creates the beginning of the ellipse.

As more of the droplet comes in contact with the surface, the ellipse widens. Once the droplet collapses halfway, the ellipse is half formed and will become no wider. The skimming motion however, continues.

As the wave begins rising upward, surface tension pulls the liquid back together in the leading edge, forcing it away from the surface and narrowing the area of blood in contact with the surface.

The creation of the spine in effect closes the ellipse completely, which completes the long axis of the stain.

Figure 55 A graphic of a collapsing droplet impacting at an acute angle. This demonstrates how the long axis of the ellipse develops and is oriented along the path of travel. Unless impacting at 90°, the axis associated with the direction of travel is always longer as a result of the skimming action of the droplet on the target.

It is the major (or long) axis of this circle or ellipse which begins our definition of the droplet's directionality. This axis defines a line with two possible droplet flight paths. (See Figure 56.) In viewing the stain, the analyst must seek information to eliminate one of the two. Satellite stains, scallops, or spines provide the analyst a means for making this elimination and identifying the direction of travel.

As the discussion of dispersion in Chapter 4 explained, when the droplet collapses a blossom effect begins. The exact nature of this blossom is defined by the angle of impact and the nature of the target surface. As this blossom develops, surface tension of the liquid pulls the blood into distinct dimples in the leading edge of the blossom structure. These dimples in many instances break from the blossom structure, creating satellite stains. Whether these dimples break completely free or simply form spines or scallops, their presence in relationship to the parent stain defines the motion of the droplet at impact.

Obviously, the path these spines and satellite droplets follow is defined by the redirection of the blood as it impacts. In instances of 75° to 90° impacts

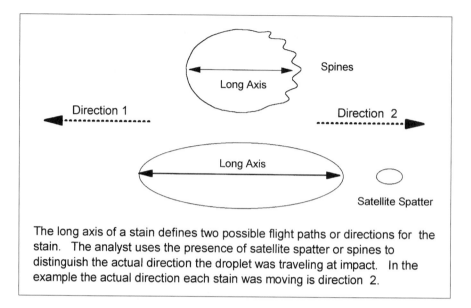

The long axis of a stain defines two possible flight paths or directions for the stain. The analyst uses the presence of satellite spatter or spines to distinguish the actual direction the droplet was traveling at impact. In the example the actual direction each stain was moving is direction 2.

Figure 56 The presence of spines, scallops, and satellite spatter all help the analyst identify the path the droplet was traveling at impact. The spines and satellite are found on the opposite side of the stain from which it originally impacts.

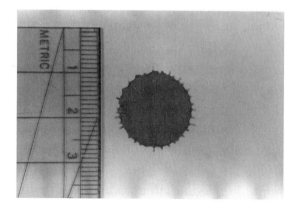

Figure 57 A 90° impact. Evident are small scallops which appear around the entire periphery of the stain.

(the more circular stains), spines and satellite stains may be evident all around the parent stain. As this angle decreases, however, one side will show greater evidence of both. (See Figures 57 and 58.) By considering the longest axis of the stain, the one with the presence of the higher number of satellite stains or spines on one side, the analyst can identify a general direction of travel for the droplet.

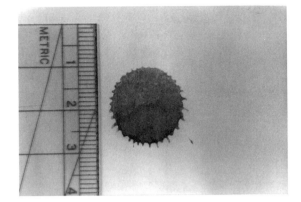

Figure 58 A 70° impact. Note that the larger scallops are evident primarily on one side of the stain. They point opposite to the droplet's origin thus detailing the direction of travel, which in this instance is from top to bottom.

Figure 59 A 45° impact. In this instance our scallops have all spawned a tadpole tail. Although the directionality of the droplet is not as specific as when we find a single tail, the analyst can still clearly define the droplet's directionality.

A measure of caution is always in order when considering 75° through 90° impacts. Surface disturbances or angles present in the target may lead to slight deviations in the outflow of blood. This can affect the resulting spines or satellite stains. Such deviations, combined with our ability to identify only a general direction in these instances, make the trustworthiness of the directionality much lower than those found in elliptically shaped stains.

Fortunately, clarity of this direction increases as the impact angle increases (e.g., moves towards a 10° impact). In droplet impacts between 40° and 70°, the nature of the outflow of blood is likely to create a number of spines and/or satellite spatter. The direction evident in the paths of such spines and satellite stains allows us to more accurately define the path of travel. (See Figure 59.)

In impacts beyond 40°, the resulting stains are much more elliptical. In such instances the outflow of blood travels almost exclusively along the leading edge of the collapsing droplet (much as in our drawing in Figure 55). Such an impact is likely to create a single satellite stain. (See Figure 60.) This

Figure 60 A 30° impact. This stain shows a specific tail and satellite. If we draw a line along the path indicated by the two, we have a clear specific indication of directionality of this droplet at impact.

Figure 61 A 30° impact without a satellite. Even without an accompanying satellite, the tadpole tail gives us a clear indication of the droplet's travel.

satellite stain when aligned with the major axis of the parent forms a very distinct alignment for the directionality.

In these elliptical stains, the direction of travel for the satellite stain almost always matches that of the parent stain. Minor redirection of the satellite may occur as a result of surface irregularities present on the target, but this is usually limited.

When considering satellite stains and their tails, parabola effects may also be evident. This is particularly true for stains impacting vertical targets. These effects may place the satellite somewhat off-line from its true path. This condition is easy to spot and will not distinctly challenge the analyst in determining the droplet's true directionality.

Even in cases where the satellite stain itself is not immediately evident (e.g., perhaps covered by surrounding bloodstains), the spine from which it was created will often be evident on the parent stain. (See Figure 61.)

If you will recall our discussion of parent and satellite stains in Chapter 3, we made it clear that it is important to differentiate between the two. As

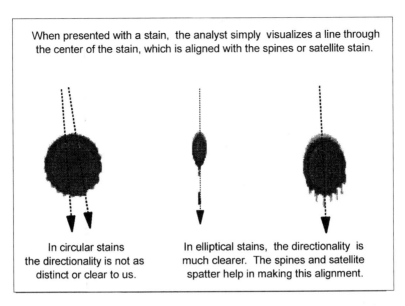

When presented with a stain, the analyst simply visualizes a line through the center of the stain, which is aligned with the spines or satellite stain.

In circular stains the directionality is not as distinct or clear to us.

In elliptical stains, the directionality is much clearer. The spines and satellite spatter help in making this alignment.

Figure 62   To visualize or demonstrate directionality in a droplet, the analyst simply draws a line down the long axis of the stain, splitting it into two equal parts. This line is oriented to the scallops, spines, or satellite stains.

evident in Figure 60, note that both the parent and satellite may have a tail. While the parent tail points in the direction of the droplet's travel, the satellite tail points 180° opposite to the droplet's direction of travel. If the analyst were to confuse a satellite for a parent, this would obviously confuse the investigative findings. In practice it is usually quite easy to identify a parent and satellite relationship, as their tails clearly align with one another.

So the presence of such satellite stains, scallops, and/or a spine help define the direction of travel for the parent stain. In practice it is simple for the analyst to visualize the directionality of any given droplet. The analyst simply draws a line down the center of the long axis of the stain (no matter what its shape), aligning it with any tail, scallops, or satellite. (See Figure 62.)

As should be evident, a rough target can impair our ability to read a stain; but rough or irregular surfaces alone, particularly in instances of the more elliptical stains, doesn't mean we can't define directionality. Consider a worst case, such as a stain found on asphalt. The resulting stain may well be disturbed (when compared to one impacting a smooth surface), but the directionality is still evident. The irregular outflow of blood in the parent stain during the displacement and dispersion phases is insufficient to mask the directionality entirely.*

* Color Plate 1 follows page 216.

Given our discussion, we can say the following:

- The more elliptical the stain, the more accurate the definition of directionality.
- Less elliptical stains demand a cautionary approach.
- The smoother the target, the less likely irregularities will occur which might mask the directionality.

A final word of concern regarding determining the directionality of a droplet. Directionality in relation to the source of the blood, although quite obvious, is not a certain conclusion for two reasons. First, when we speak of directionality we are discussing only the path a droplet was traveling at the time it impacted a given target. Although not common, it is possible to encounter ricochet situations in which a volume of blood strikes an interim target. This causes the blood to change its original path, impacting the target as evidenced by its final position. Ricochets are possible and must be considered in the overall analysis. Second, if the target itself is capable of motion at the time of bloodshed, consider the directionality and the angle of impact cautiously. Obviously, motion of a target makes it difficult at best to establish directionality in any fashion. If one cannot establish the target's exact position at the moment the droplet strikes, the stain itself tells the analyst little if anything.

Recognizing Blood-Trail Motion

Our previous consideration of stain directionality leads us to a major consideration: that of blood trails. As individuals become injured and move, or bloody items are moved within a scene, blood trails are likely to occur.

The drops which result from these dripping actions strike the surrounding floors and surfaces. As they break free, they are moving with the same momentum and in the same direction as the item from which they fell. The combination of gravity and this momentum cause the drops to impact the ground at varying angles. The resulting stains in the blood trail show evidence of this angle and its direction. (See Figure 63.) This directionality, in consideration of the repetitive nature of the blood trail, allows the investigator to determine which direction the trail leads. Figure 64 is a case example of a typical blood trail.

The faster the motion of the person or object from which the blood drops, the more momentum the falling droplet has. This forward momentum translates into a more acute angle of impact, which results in more elliptical stains within the pattern.

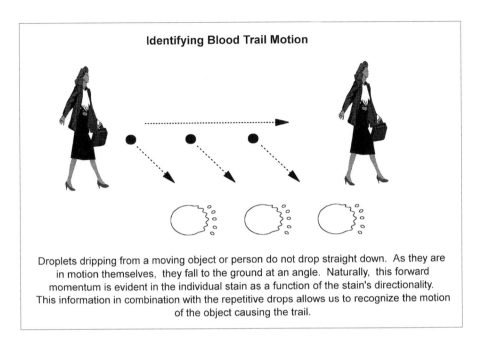

Identifying Blood Trail Motion

Droplets dripping from a moving object or person do not drop straight down. As they are in motion themselves, they fall to the ground at an angle. Naturally, this forward momentum is evident in the individual stain as a function of the stain's directionality. This information in combination with the repetitive drops allows us to recognize the motion of the object causing the trail.

Figure 63 Blood-trail motion is defined by considering the directionality of the individual droplets present in the blood trail pattern.

Determining Motion From Wipes and Swipes

Another consideration in determining motion are those stains which show evidence of a specific action of some nature. We defined wipes and swipes previously in Chapter 3. Both play a prominent role in defining motion.

As items become bloodied and stains are created, events at the scene may still be proceeding. These stains often become disturbed by other events, thus detailing specific motions for later evaluation. This motion is most obvious in instances of wipes, that is, when we have a preexisting stain. As an example, consider a blow which creates a spatter pattern. Subsequently, the spatter is brushed by an arm or hand. The spatter had specific boundaries to begin with. As the blood within the stain boundary is wiped through, it is moved in the same direction as the item disturbing it. In these instances the nature or direction of the motion which disturbed the pattern is clear and specific. (See Figure 65.)

In a situation involving a swipe, the direction may not be as evident. Depending upon how the bloody object comes in contact with the target, the leading and trailing boundaries for the stain may be similar or radically

Figure 64 A blood trail pattern. Although the photo doesn't show a close-up view, spines are still evident from which the directionality of the trail can be defined. In this instance the directionality indicates movement from the top of the photo down.

different. Generally, we seek to locate evidence of a thinning of the stain's appearance or color to define the motion. This thinning is typically a result of having a smaller volume of blood on the swiping object at the point where the contact ends. Imagine this thinning as the stroke of a paintbrush. The bloodied object typically has a limited source of blood, the majority of which is often consumed by the end of the contact. (See Figure 66.)

Besides a thinning of the color and consistency of the stain, we may also see trailers leading away from the main stain. These trailers are created when the bloody object loses contact with the target surface. Such trailers are also referred to as a feathering of the stain.

In this fashion wipes and swipes assist in defining motion, and may also help to identify the nature of the item which was in motion. We will discuss this latter aspect in greater detail in Chapter 8.

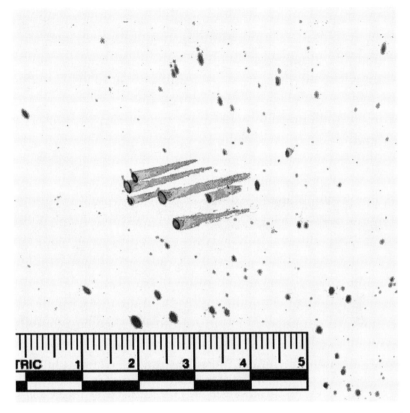

Figure 65 A spatter pattern that was wiped through after it was deposited. The wiping of the liquid blood from the spatter leaves obvious evidence of a left to right motion by whatever action caused the wipe.

Repetitive Pattern Transfers

Repetitive transfer patterns also define motion in the scene. A repetitive transfer pattern occurs when an item becomes bloodied and then comes in contact with a given target a number of times.

Repetitive transfer patterns occur as a result of any number of actions. Bloody hands, feet, shoes, and the like are frequently the major cause of such patterns. The item comes in contact with a blood source, as in the instance of a shod foot stepping into a puddle of blood. As the individual walks, blood is deposited each time the shoe contacts the target until it is depleted.

Defining this motion is based upon evaluating the dimming or diminishing of the pattern as the number of contacts increases. An analogy can be drawn to a parent following the muddy hand prints of a child through a

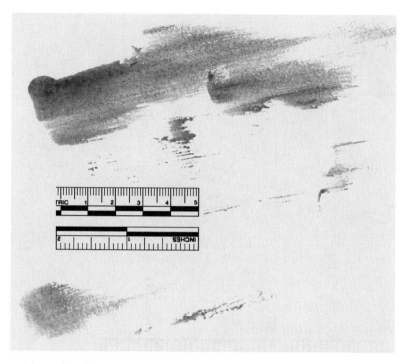

Figure 66   A hand swipe pattern. Note the feathering on the right edge of the pattern. Although not always as clear as a wipe pattern, this feathering also defines motion for the analyst. In this instance the motion was left to right and slightly upward.

home; following the direction evident in such a trail is not difficult. If all things are equal, the first contact leaves a greater volume than the next. Each subsequent contact depletes the available blood on the object, leaving less to make the next pattern transfer.

In considering the identification of patterns present in such trails to the object that created them, remember that the patterns made later in the series often hold greater detail. These stains are much more likely to have individual characteristics of use to the forensic examiner.

Flows

Blood flows also present critical information about motion. Obviously, blood flows will obey the laws of physical science, specifically gravity. Of concern to the analyst are flows which indicate body movement after the flow begins. Flows on the body which are irregular or defy expectations with regard to gravity, may point to earlier positions of the victim.

Another irregular flow which the analyst may encounter is due in part to capillary action. When an intervening object (quite often the body) is exposed to a large flow, or in some way dams a flow, the blood will tend to follow the contour of this object. If the object is later moved, the resulting flow pattern will likely appear abnormal or out of place. Patterns of this nature are discussed again in Chapter 8, along with a figure example.

Summary

Blood and bloodstains provide excellent indications to the analyst about motion and action. Understanding the minor nuances of directionality requires little effort because we observe liquid droplet behavior daily. Whether raindrops, bird droppings, or grease splashes, this concept is easily observed and recognized.

We also come to bloodstain pattern analysis with experience in swipe and wipe patterns. Whether paint, ink, or dirty mop water on a floor, the underlying motion or action is generally obvious to anyone.

General sequencing of events by following the blood volume may take a little more experience, nevertheless its basis is still simple.

We hope it is obvious to the reader that motion is truly the most basic consideration that bloodstains provide us at the crime scene. The amount of detail present in this type of evidence supports our ability to link and sequence the overall set of events defining any given incident.

Determining the Point of Convergence and the Point of Origin

6

Our prior discussion of directionality and the evaluation of the path a given droplet was traveling logically leads us to the next step: defining where the droplet came from and determining what common convergence point several spatters may or may not have.

We can determine the point of origin for several stains in three fashions. We may do this either by:

- Viewing the spatter from overhead to simply locate a point of convergence.
- Viewing the spatter both from overhead and from a side view to define point of origin.
- Viewing the spatter using either forensic software or the stringing technique.

Depending upon the specific questions raised about a given spatter pattern, the needs of the analyst may be different. Thus, an overhead point of convergence analysis may be sufficient for some circumstances. At other times the analyst may require more detailed information, demanding the use of the point of origin evaluation methods.

Determining Point of Convergence From Overhead

In each instance where we can define a stain's path, if we simply draw a reverse azimuth (that is, a line which extends backwards along the path the droplet was following), we can be reasonably sure the droplet originated somewhere along this avenue.

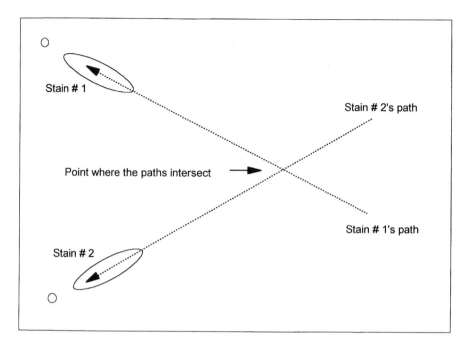

Figure 67   By following the reverse vector of each droplet to the point where they intersect, we can establish a probable point of convergence in two dimensions.

For the moment, lets limit our discussion to this single overhead viewpoint. Remember our perspective is a bird's eye view of the target on which we find the spatter. Once set in motion, assuming no ricochet event exists, a droplet will follow a straight path from its source to its destination. Gravity and air resistance will affect the droplet only in the path of its parabola.[1]

For instance, in Figure 67, stain #1 must originate somewhere along a reverse path as indicated by the directionality of the droplet. The only limits to the origin are the room's limitations or any intermediate obstacles. As an example, if the box for Figure 67 represented the room boundaries and the possible reverse path for stain #1 extends 13 ft, then the drop's origin may lie anywhere within those 13 ft. With only one stain, the resulting parameter of possible points of origin is very wide.

If we introduce a second stain, as in the figure, we can then look for a point where the two paths intersect. The process is no different from the technique known as resection in map reading. By taking two known points and applying reverse azimuths from each, we define an unknown point where the azimuths cross. In this instance the unknown point is the likely source for both stains.

By limiting ourselves to this overhead dimension, we certainly gain simplicity in the evaluation. We also gain an inherent difficulty. If our circumstances

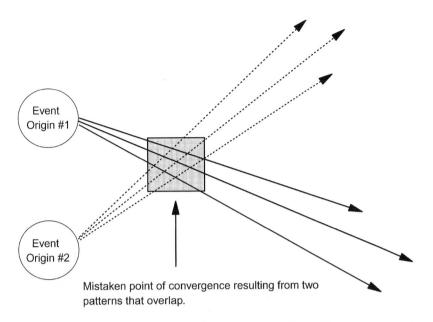

Figure 68   In addition to two stains having a coincidental intersecting point, it is also possible to have several patterns overlap. If this condition is not considered it might well result in a mistaken point of convergence.

limit us to only a few stains, it is always possible they are the result of more than one event. That is, an event created stain # 1, followed by another unrelated action that caused stain # 2. Given this situation, the points where their reverse paths cross is simply coincidental and has no investigative significance.

Widespread within a scene and showing no common convergence point, we would easily recognize such stains as separate actions. Found in proximity to each other, the likelihood increases of a coincidental convergence of the flight paths along their reverse paths. Unfortunately, we may choose to read this convergence as a single point of origin for both stains. With only a few stains to work with, it may be difficult to recognize such an error.

The same is certainly true when viewing two adjacent patterns. We may see a coincidental convergence area for two patterns and read this as the source for both. Figure 68 illustrates the possible error when viewing patterns from two closely located impacts.

As the number of evaluated stains available to us increases, so too increases our level of confidence. The more paths we find which intersect a given point, the more likely it is we have a true point of convergence. In circumstances of multiple events with the spatter intermixed, the primary convergence points should still be evident. In this situation, paths may cross at several locations, but those locations where we find clusters of intersecting paths will establish the primary convergence points of the spatter involved.

What this overhead method does not establish is the location above the point of convergence where the spatter originated. In an overhead approach we establish only the point of convergence on a single plane and accept that the flight paths originate somewhere above it. Once again, the possibility of multiple events always exists. The analyst may be viewing spatter from two or more events which originated at the same location in a room, but from different heights during different events.

The overhead technique, however, is still effective. Used in conjunction with Toby Wolson's[2] techniques of Roadmapping, which is discussed later in the book, it represents a graphic method of portraying the point within the scene from which the droplets originate. (See Figure 69.) We can also use this method in a limited fashion on vertical surfaces, but we must give obvious consideration to the droplet's parabola.

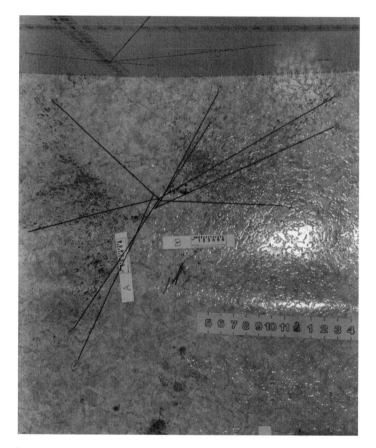

Figure 69   An example of using graphic tape to demonstrate a point of convergence in a spatter pattern.

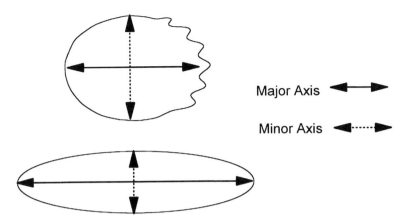

Figure 70   Our concept of a "well-formed" stain means simply that if we divide the stain along its major and minor axis, the opposite halves would be generally equal to each other.

To this point, we've narrowed our scope to finding the point of convergence along the paths of the stains of interest. The converging lines of these reverse vectors establish our point of convergence. To establish with a greater degree of accuracy a specific location above the point of convergence, we use a side-view approach of the target. This requires including the stain's impact angle in the analysis. Before we can consider this second method of defining the point of origin, we must define the individual droplet's impact angle.

Determining Impact Angles

We generally credit Dr. Victor Balthazard with having recognized that a relationship exists between the length and width of the resulting stain and the angle at which the droplet impacts. MacDonell later refined this concept applying the length/width ratio in conjunction with specific math functions (e.g., sine). This allows the analyst to use straight line geometry in defining the bloodstain event.[3]

Given a well-formed stain where we can accurately measure the width and length, we can easily establish the impact angle using Dr. Balthazard's concept.[4] A well-formed stain is one which, if divided along the major or minor axis, the two halves of the stain would be approximately equal to each other. (See Figure 70.)

To apply the impact angle formula it is important to understand that in right triangles certain relationships exist between the angles of the triangle and the length of its sides. These relationships are trigonometric functions such as the sine, cosine, and tangent. These relationships are in no way

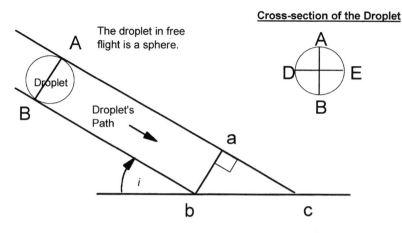

Figure 71 The relationship of the droplet to an imagined right triangle. Using the sine function and this relationship, the analyst can establish the angle of *i*. This is the droplet's impact angle.*

dependent upon the factors found at the crime scene; they are mathematical in nature. What we do is make an analogy to our scene using these relationships.

Imagine a right triangle formed between the droplet and the target surface as the droplet strikes. Figure 71 outlines how this triangle might look. A blood droplet in flight is in the shape of a sphere. Therefore, in viewing Figure 71, Line DE (the width) can be considered equal to Line AB (the height) of the sphere. An analogy can then be drawn between Line ab and bc and the width and length of the resulting stain. (See Figure 72.) Based on the analogy, Line ab is represented by Line ML of the stain and Line bc is represented by Line JK of the stain.

As a result of this analogy we have two known quantities from our crime scene which we can apply to a formula. By measuring the stain's length and width and applying them to the following formula, the droplet's impact angle becomes evident:

$$\text{Sine } i = \text{Width (ab)/Length (bc)} \tag{1}$$

$$\text{Inverse Sine (ASN) } i = \text{Impact Angle} \tag{2}$$

---

* Although one might infer from the drawing that a 1:1 relationship exists between the size of the droplet and the size of the resulting stain (e.g., AB = ab). This is not the case. As the droplet collapses there is a lateral spread of the liquid. We do not yet fully understand this lateral spread and resulting ratio; however, it has no apparent effect on the actual application of the process.

Example:

Width = 3 mm
Length = 5 mm
0.6 (Sine i) = 3/5 (Width/Length)
Inverse Sine i (0.6) = 36.8
Impact angle = 36–37°

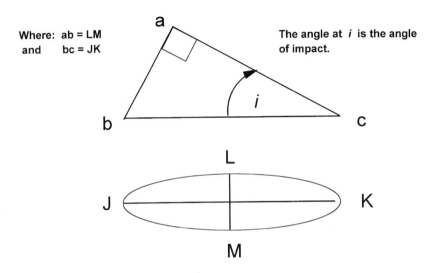

Where: ab = LM
and   bc = JK

The angle at i is the angle of impact.

Figure 72 We can draw an analogy between the right triangle formed in Figure 71 and our bloodstain. Line ab is analogous to line LM as is bc to JK. Thus the length and width of the stain are quantities we can apply using the laws of sines to determine the impact angle (i).

It is important to recognize that the formula provides the analyst with an estimate of the impact angle. The precision of the math should not be construed to mean a similar precision in the definition of the angle. Issues related to ballistics and oscillations in the droplet preclude us from accepting this angle as absolute. As a general rule the angle indicated is probably accurate to within 5° to 7°.

In addition to using a calculator with a sine function, there are two other related methods for determining impact angle. The first involves the length/width ratio chart. (See Figure 73.) The analyst divides the measured length of the stain by the width, resulting in a number greater than 1. If the result is less than one, you've reversed the length and width in the formula. Using the result, the analyst locates the corresponding number on the vertical axis of the L/W ratio chart. Where the line intersects this point, one simply reads the angle listed on the lower axis.

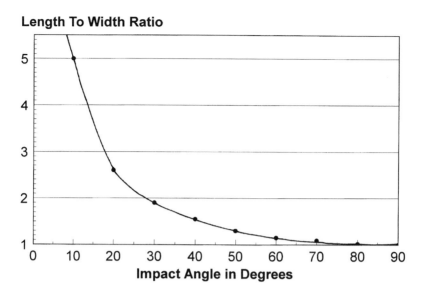

Figure 73 A length-to-width ratio chart. By dividing the length of the stain by the width, we generate a number which is always greater than 1. The analyst first finds this number on the vertical axis, then reading to the right locates the corresponding point where the graph line intersects. The angle listed below this point is the approximate impact angle. For example, a L/W ratio of 1.9 equates to an impact angle of 30°.

The second method involves dividing the width of the stain by the length and comparing this number to a sine function table. (See Figure 74.) In this instance the result will be less than 1. The analyst finds the corresponding number on the sine function table to determine the angle. A sine table simply eliminates the need for a calculator.

Stain Measurement

Measuring the stain is obviously critical, as this provides the analyst with a length and width. In considering the measurement, the analyst measures only the main body of the stain. This measurement must exclude any portion of the satellite and spine present in the stain. To accomplish this, one might simply envision a perfect ellipse superimposed on the stain. By choosing a point on the stain which naturally completes the ellipse, the remaining tail portions are not subjectively drawn into the calculation. (See Figure 75.)

It's important to understand that the inclusion of any excess scallop or portion of the spine will change the overall length to width ratio. For example, consider a stain with an actual 5 mm length, a 4 mm width, and a 0.5 mm scalloped tail. Given such a stain, the following is possible:

Degrees	Sine	Degrees	Sine	Degrees	Sine	Degrees	Sine
1	0.0175	26	0.4384	51	0.7771	76	0.9703
2	0.0349	27	0.454	52	0.788	77	0.9744
3	0.0523	28	0.4695	53	0.7986	78	0.9781
4	0.0698	29	0.4848	54	0.809	79	0.9816
5	0.0872	30	0.5	55	0.8192	80	0.9848
6	0.1045	31	0.515	56	0.829	81	0.9877
7	0.1219	32	0.5299	57	0.8387	82	0.9903
8	0.1392	33	0.5446	58	0.848	83	0.9925
9	0.1564	34	0.5592	59	0.8572	84	0.9945
10	0.1736	35	0.5736	60	0.866	85	0.9962
11	0.1908	36	0.5878	61	0.8746	86	0.9976
12	0.2079	37	0.6018	62	0.8829	87	0.9986
13	0.225	38	0.6157	63	0.891	88	0.9994
14	0.2419	39	0.6293	64	0.8988	89	0.9998
15	0.2588	40	0.6428	65	0.9063		
16	0.2756	41	0.6561	66	0.9135		
17	0.2924	42	0.6691	67	0.9205		
18	0.309	43	0.682	68	0.9272		
19	0.3256	44	0.6947	69	0.9336		
20	0.342	45	0.7071	70	0.9397		
21	0.3584	46	0.7193	71	0.9455		
22	0.3746	47	0.7314	72	0.9511		
23	0.3907	48	0.7431	73	0.9563		
24	0.4067	49	0.7547	74	0.9613		
25	0.4226	50	0.766	75	0.9659		

Figure 74   An abbreviated sine function table. In this method we divide the width by the length, which always generates a number less than 1. The analyst then looks for the closest corresponding number under the sine column of the chart. The number adjacent to this lists the degrees of the impact angle. For example, a 0.5 W/L ratio equates to a 30° impact angle.

Correct Measurement and Evaluation
   Length: 5 mm
   Width: 4 mm
   Impact Angle: 53°

Incorrect Measurement and Skewed Evaluation
    Length   5 mm plus 0.5 mm scallop
    Width: 4 mm
    Impact Angle: 46°

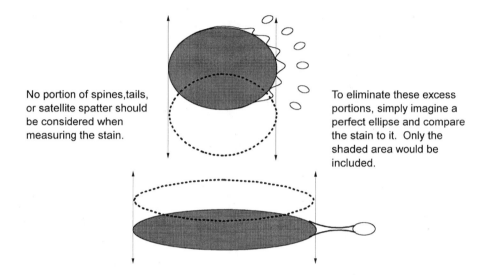

No portion of spines,tails, or satellite spatter should be considered when measuring the stain.

To eliminate these excess portions, simply imagine a perfect ellipse and compare the stain to it. Only the shaded area would be included.

Figure 75 By comparing the stain to an imagined ellipse, one can generally distinguish those portions of the stain to disregard during the measurement process. Including the spines, scallops, and satellite spatter in the measurement will result in a skewed estimate of the impact angle.

In the example, the small excess scallop adds an error of 7° to what we already accept as an *estimation* of the impact angle. Obviously, by including these excess portions the analyst can change the calculated impact angle significantly. Unfortunately there are no absolute rules for closing out the ellipse. The analyst must judge each stain individually and make an attempt to eliminate these scalloped edges and tail portions from the measurement. Figures 76 and 77 show examples of that portions of the stain the analyst should include and exclude.

The methods most often used to measure a stain include measurement with a ruler alone, measurement using a drafting compass and ruler, measurement with a micrometer, or the use of a scaled photographic loupe. Any one of the methods is adequate as long as the analyst is cautious in the approach.

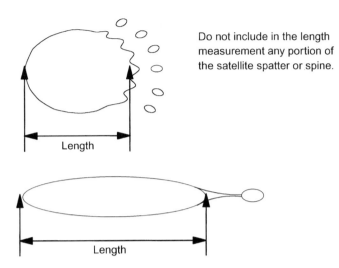

Do not include in the length
measurement any portion of
the satellite spatter or spine.

Figure 76   The length of a stain is measured along its major axis. Once again, the analyst must exclude from the measurement any portion of the spines, scallops, or satellite stains that may be present.

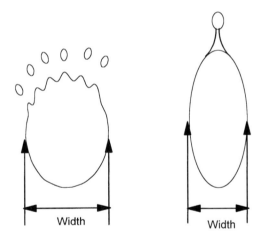

Once again, no portion of spine or satellite should be included
in the width measurement.

Figure 77   The width is measured along the minor axis of the stain. Although satellite spatter are less a concern when measuring this axis, scallops along the outer edges of the stain are often encountered. Do not include the scallop in the measurement.

Determining Point of Origin Using Both Side and Overhead Views

Having learned to determine the impact angle, lets combine the convergence point (the overhead view) and the impact angle (the side view) techniques. For the sake of simplicity, in the following example we will leave all stains on a single surface, such as a floor.

Consider Figure 78. In this instance we have three stains of concern. Their flight paths appear to have a common convergence point in the scene. Assuming our three stains are "well-formed", the analyst measures each and applies the sine formula, identifying each stain's impact angle.

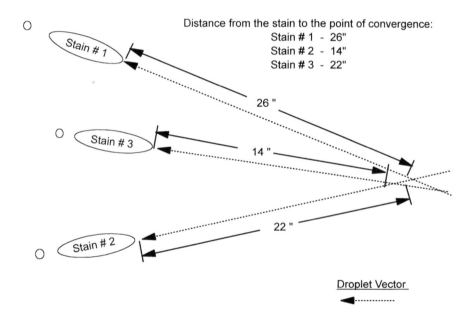

Figure 78 Another example of using point of convergence evaluations. In this instance we have three stains with a common point of convergence and we wish to determine if they share a common point of origin. We measure the distance from the base of each stain to the convergence point. We then combine this information with the impact angle in a graph (Figure 79), which allows the analyst to visualize the point of origin of the spatter.

Although Figure 78 depicts elliptical stains, accept for the example, that based on the width/length ratio the three stains impacted as follows:

- Stain # 1   30°
- Stain # 2   35°
- Stain # 3   46°

For purposes of the example, imagine that the analyst then measures the distance from the convergence point to the rear edge of each stain. In this instance the analyst found:

- Stain # 1 is 26 in. from the convergence
- Stain # 2 is 22 in.
- Stain # 3 is 14 in.

Graphing Points of Origin

One method of combining this impact angle and convergence point information is to use a graph. To do so, the analyst draws a graph with a positive X and positive Z axis. The Z axis represents the point of convergence; it graphs the height above the target involved. The X axis represents the target plane; it graphs the distance of the stain from the point of convergence. The two axes are scaled the same, with whatever scale we choose.

The analyst begins by placing a mark for each stain along the X axis at the appropriate distance (e.g., 14 in.). From this point, using a protractor, a line is drawn along the indicated angle of impact extending it to the Z axis. The analyst repeats this process for each of the stains involved. The resulting graph would look like that in Figure 79. The point where the lines converge on the Z-axis scale establishes the probable point of origin for the spatter above the convergence point on the target.

As we draw the lines along the angle of impact for each stain a common point of origin on the vertical Z axis should become evident, assuming of course a true common origin exists. If the spatters evaluated are the result of two or more different events which occurred at different heights, that too would become evident. Figure 80 is an example of what one would expect to see in a situation involving two impacts at different heights over the same location. Remember the Z axis represents the area above a single point of convergence on the target. When viewed from above, all the paths for the stains involved cross at this point. Viewed only from an overhead perspective, one might choose to believe they originated from a single event.

By considering the impact angles in conjunction with the overhead view for Figure 80, a distinct grouping becomes evident with a common origin close to the target's surface. Another group is also evident with an origin higher than the first. This tends to indicate two different spatter-producing impacts at that convergence point.

Defining Point of Origin With the Tangent Function

Using a scientific calculator, it is possible to forego the graphing process and simply calculate this distance above the point of convergence for each stain.

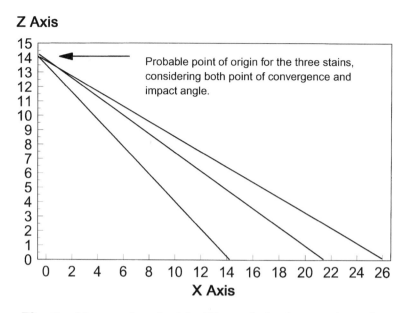

Figure 79   Graphing a point of origin. We mark the distance from the convergence point on the X axis and then draw a line to the Z axis at the indicated impact angle. Where this line intersects the Z axis is the probable point of origin (the height above the target) for that particular stain. In this instance, the three stains appear to have a common point of origin at about 14 to 15 in. above the target.

The analyst does this using another relationship related to right triangles. Figure 81 shows the relationships of the scene to this imagined triangle.

The first step in making this determination is to identify stains which appear to have a common convergence. As in the graphing method, the analyst measures the distance from these stains back to the point where the stains have a common intersection. The analyst also determines the impact angle of each stain.

To determine point of origin, the analyst uses the following formula:

$$\text{TAN } i = \text{H/D} \qquad\qquad (3)$$

where i equals the known impact angle, D equals the distance to the convergence point, and H equals the unknown distance above the target surface. (See Figure 82.) For example:

$$i = 19°$$

$$\text{D} = 25 \text{ in.}$$

$$\text{TAN } 19 = .344$$

$$0.344 \star 25 = 8$$

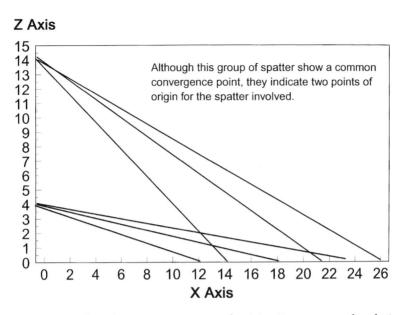

Figure 80   A graph indicating two points of origin. From an overhead view, all six stains would appear to share a common convergence point The inclusion of the impact angle information adds an additional dimension making it apparent that two separate groups are present, indicating two separate events.

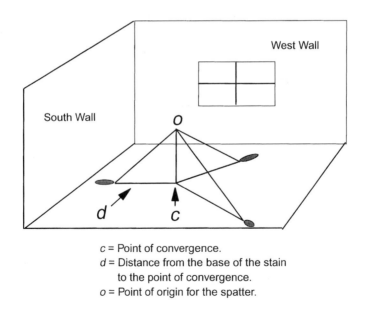

c = Point of convergence.
d = Distance from the base of the stain
     to the point of convergence.
o = Point of origin for the spatter.

Figure 81   The base of each stain's present position, the point in two-dimensional space where their paths converge (c), and their point of origin (o), define another right triangle.

To solve for H we simply balanced the equation by multiplying Tan *i* by D, giving H = 8.66 in. This procedure is convenient and provides immediate feedback at the scene. Once again, the analyst requires a calculator with trigonometric functions to use this method.

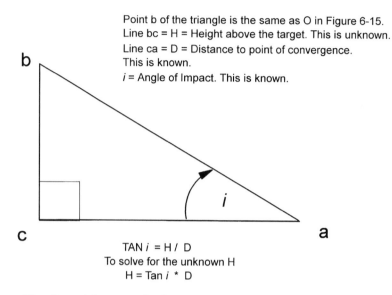

Point b of the triangle is the same as O in Figure 6-15.
Line bc = H = Height above the target. This is unknown.
Line ca = D = Distance to point of convergence.
This is known.
i = Angle of Impact. This is known.

TAN *i* = H / D
To solve for the unknown H
H = Tan *i* * D

Figure 82   Our right triangle from Figure 81, further defined. We know the distance from the stain to the point of convergence (ac) and we can establish the impact angle (*i*). Using this information in the formula TAN *i* = H/D, we simply balance the equation and solve for the unknown H. Thus H = TAN *i* * D.

Limitations in Point of Origin Evaluations

Using straight-line geometry and trigonometric functions, both the graph and tangent approach allow the analyst to identify the probable point of origin for our stains. Although generally accurate, it should be evident to the reader that both methods make a major assumption. Both assume the droplets involved travel in straight-line trajectories. Unfortunately this isn't true, as both gravity and air resistance affect the droplet, creating distinct arched parabolas.

As long as the analyst recognizes this inherent limitation, the two methods are both functional and useful. They do not define the droplet's flight paths absolutely. They do, however, place specific limits on that path. Consider Figure 83. The impact angle for each droplet in effect sets a limit of possible and impossible flight paths.

For example, a droplet traveling downwards towards the wall at an angle of 60° may have originated at some point behind the indicated angle of impact. That is, it may have been projected out towards the wall at 80°. As the droplet slows in flight its parabola angles downward into the ground, eventually striking the target at the indicated 60°. What cannot happen, however, is for the droplet to gain momentum on its own. Having been projected towards the target at 40°, the droplet cannot strike at a less acute angle (e.g., 60°). Obviously, this effect is relative to the plane of the target.

What this limitation tells us is that we must always use caution in considering the results of the point of origin evaluations. This is particularly true for those situations involving dual impacts, like those expressed in Figure 80. The indicated point of origin sets an absolute upper limit for the event, but cannot always exclude the event from having occurred at a point beneath the indicated point of origin. The ability to make such an exclusion is situation driven, depending upon the number of stains available and the nature and dispersion of the stains.

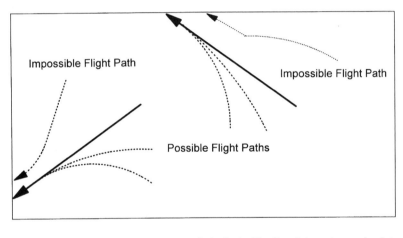

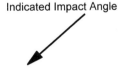

Indicated Impact Angle   The impact angle indicated by the stain, sets an absolute limit for possible and impossible flight paths. Although a droplet may originate from a point below the indicated angle, unless acted on by an outside force its source cannot be above the impact angle.

Figure 83 The angle of impact establishes an absolute limit for the droplet's origin. For instance, a droplet can originate at some point under the angle of impact. As it follows the parabola, gravity affects its path. As the droplet's path becomes steeper it angles downward and eventually strikes the target at the indicated impact angle. What cannot happen is for the droplet to alter its parabola on its own, defying gravity's effect, thus striking the target from a point above the indicated impact angle.

Three-Dimensional Evaluations of Point of Origin

A final manner of evaluating point of origin is in a graphic three-dimensional fashion. This is possible both in a physical sense, using the "stringing" technique or by using computer-aided analysis tools.

Stringing Scenes

For many years stringing was a basic method taught to bloodstain analysts, but its place in on-scene analysis is slipping into the past. It is still useful, however, as a visual aid to help explain "point of origin" to both juries and students. (See Figure 84.) The true origin of stringing is somewhat in question. Herb MacDonell is the first person to describe the process itself, yet we usually credit Balthazard et al. for developing the foundation of stringing.[5]

Whoever the actual originator, the process is simply a physical extension of what we've described to this point. Stains from the pattern are chosen and impact angles determined. Based on directionality and convergence points, thread or string is taped in place at the base of the actual stain. This base is the point on the long axis of the stain, opposite the scallops, tail, or satellite stains. (The reader may wish to refer back to Chapter 5 for a discussion of droplet directionality.) The string is then extended back along the indicated path and angle. The point in space where the strings from several stains produce a generalized convergence point indicates the probable point of origin.

Stringing as a technique has several drawbacks which owe to its demise. First, it requires the expenditure of immense effort. Placing the strings into the scene and finding objects to attach them to is a chore. The analyst ends up interjecting tripods, or extending strings across rooms to opposite walls. This of course produces clutter, which the analyst must move around while completing the stringing process. A second and perhaps more dangerous flaw of stringing is the error evident in the process. Placing the strings at accurate angles and precisely along the indicated path is difficult at best.

Whenever reviewing the results of a stringing technique, if the analyst should "pinpoint" a position using more than three or four stains, that should raise an immediate red flag. The likelihood of obtaining a pinpoint position with strings is low to begin with. As we increase the number of stains and strings considered, that possibility decreases dramatically.

Forensic Software Applications

Computer software advancements over the past ten years suggest that we replace stringing in its entirety. These programs offer the analyst an efficient

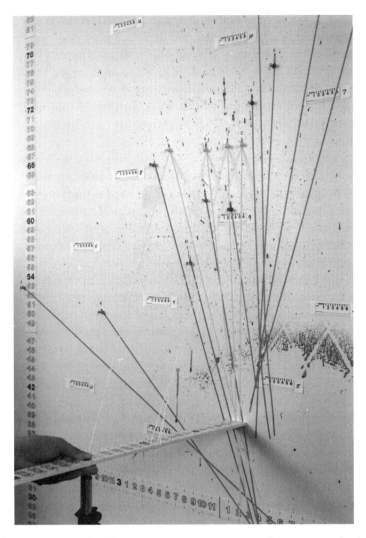

Figure 84 An example of on-scene stringing in combination with the use of graphic tape. The graphic tape demonstrates the point of convergence, while the strings demonstrate the point of origin. (Photograph courtesy of Toby Wolsen, MS, Metro Dade Police Department.)

and relatively effective method of analyzing spatter patterns for point of origin information. A program called *Trajectories* was one of the first true "analysis" programs. Developed by Dr. Alfred Carter of Carleton University in 1987, it allowed the analyst to evaluate point of origin using crime scene data.

Dr. Carter improved upon *Trajectories* and eventually released it through Forensic Computing of Ottawa (FCO) as *BackTrack*®, a full-function program which allows for point of origin calculations on vertical surfaces.[6] *BackTrack*® employs actual flight path (parabola) calculations, which incorporates estimates of blood droplet volume, and gravity and air resistance factors.

Shortly after *BackTrack's* release, FCO released another program, *Back-Track/Strings*®.[7] FCO scaled down this version somewhat, changing the manner in which it handles the point of origin algorithm. It has all the primary functions of *BackTrack*®, but utilizes a strings approach in determining flight paths in lieu of the parabola approach.

In running *BackTrack/Strings*®, the analyst measures the stains present at the crime scene. This includes identifying the stain's coordinate position, width and length, and the glancing angle (a term synonymous with directional angle). Once entered for each stain, the analyst moves to a top view and chooses paths that converge. The chosen lines of convergence provide the computer with an averaged CPx and CPy (an overhead convergence point in the X and Y plane).

The analyst then moves to the side view and, again considering the paths, chooses an appropriate CPz. Generally, the analyst does this by lowering the cursor and choosing a point below the paths of the computer's virtual strings. Once chosen, the analyst saves these convergence points and the software creates a graphical representation of the probable point of origin.

Another software program for computer-aided point of origin analysis is *No More Strings*®.[8] Developed by Miller Forensic Software of San Jose, CA, *No More Strings*® offers the analyst a viable method of documenting, analyzing, and presenting bloodstain information. Richard and Victoria Miller began *No More Strings*® in 1990, recognizing the need for an easier method than working with physical strings.

No More Strings® accepts data from the analyst, who provides impact angle measurements, coordinate information, and the angle of travel. This angle of travel is synonymous with Dr. Carter's glancing angle, but measured in a slightly different fashion. The program draws straight-line paths for each bloodstain, then using vector analysis finds the point of closest approach for each path.

After providing stain data, the general approach to analysis with *No More Strings*® is to move to the graphical view of the stains. To conduct vector analysis the program compares each stain and its path against every other stain and path. This results in a series of colored dots, which represent the point of origin for each droplet.[9]

In this graphical view, dots widely off-line or out of range with the main cluster may indicate errors or stains unrelated to the specific event being examined. The program backs up the graphical evaluation with two data analysis functions. Through these functions, the analyst attempts to optimize the location of the point of origin of the stains by tightening the cluster of dots.

Automation Efficiency or Precision — An Important Distinction

We hope it is evident that both *No More Strings*® and *BackTrack*® allow the analyst to more efficiently locate the point of origin of a given event. The computer handles the data and calculations in a precise manner, eliminating human math errors and some of the subjectivity inherent in the stringing and stubby pencil routines. What is not evident is whether a more efficient mathematical process means a more precise definition of the true point of origin. Your authors would argue that it does not.

In a classic stringing technique, one usually limits the point of origin to a 10- or 12-in. area in which the strings appear to cross each other. Rarely has the need existed to define this location further, particularly by trying to define an absolute point. Using the graphing technique described, one also identifies a generalized area in which the various stain paths appear to converge. This limitation in precision really doesn't matter because the nature of events that create spatter are themselves dynamic and probably cannot be pinpointed in 99% of all situations. They occur over a given area involved in the event.

Granted, in some instances the movement involved may only be a few inches in area, but that is distinct when compared to a precise point in space. Events rarely, if ever, occur at a precise XYZ coordinate point. Additionally, one must consider that wounds are often jagged and are certainly not defined by precise points. Thus trying to define an absolute XYZ coordinate as a point of origin is really a moot issue. For the analyst to state that an event occurred at a precise point in space is almost ludicrous.

Unlike the old stringing technique, however, the computer provides us with a very precise point in three-dimensional space. Both *BackTrack*® and *No More Strings*® graphically depict this point and then give an absolute XYZ point in text. Having failed to read the software documentation and lacking an understanding of basic blood droplet dynamics, someone evaluating this information could easily assume the computer had narrowed the event down to this absolute location. As analysts, we recognize these points as idealized and based on the averages contained in the data. They do not place the event in an absolute location with absolute precision.

Can we more easily compute point of origin using computers? Yes. Are computers more absolute in their accuracy of defining the event? No. Mere placement of a decimal point in a mathematical calculation will not eliminate the level of uncertainty that will always exist in these situations.

Summary

Having defined the point at which a group of stains converge or originate from, how does the analyst use this information? Lacking specific knowledge of the crime, this process helps identify the general location at which some type of blow or impact occurred. This is particularly useful in placing the subject or victim at specific locations within the scene. By differentiating two distinct points of origin from what appears to be a single spatter pattern, it also identifies an additional blow or impact that was not otherwise evident.

Primarily, we will use this information to refute or corroborate claims by those involved in the incident. Imagine a situation in which a subject claims self defense and that all blows delivered to the victim were struck as the victim made a standing attack against the subject. In evaluating the point of origin, let us assume we find evidence of blows delivered from a point low on the ground. Finding this, we have physical proof with which to dismiss, at least in part, the subject's statement.

Point of origin determinations are not always necessary, but they can be very illuminating. As discussed, the analyst can choose to view the stains considering only directionality. This simply identifies a point of convergence on a single plane.

A second more functional approach demands the analyst determine the impact angles of the individual droplets involved. This angle is determined using the ratio of the length of a stain to its width. The impact angle, when combined with point of convergence, better defines the point in space from which the droplets originated.

In the past, we generally used the stringing or graphing methods to identify this point. Recent automation advances now allow us to complete the analysis in a more refined and efficient fashion. Even with such advancements, the analyst still recognizes that any point of origin estimation is exactly that — *an estimation*.

References

1. Carter, Alfred, BackTrack/Strings User Manual, Forensic Computing of Ottawa, 1992, pg. 17.

2. Wolson, Toby, Documentation of Bloodstain Patterns, presentation to the Int. Assoc. Bloodstain Pattern Analysts (IABPA), Colorado Springs, CO, 25 Sept. 1992.

3. MacDonell, Herbert L., *Bloodstain Pattern Interpretation*, Laboratory of Forensic Science, Corning, NY, 1982.

4. Balthazard, Victor, Piedelievre, R., Desoille, Henri, and Derobert, L., *Etude Des Gouttes De Sang Projecte*, XXII Congres De Medicine Legale, Paris, France, June 1939, pg. 25.

5. MacDonell, Herbert L., Baltzhazard Was Great But He Didn't String Us Along, *Int. Assoc. Bloodstain Pattern Analysts*, Vol. 11, No. 1, March 1995, pg.10

6. Registered Trademark of Forensic Computing of Ottawa, Ottawa, Canada.

7. Registered Trademark of Forensic Computing of Ottawa, Ottawa, Canada.

8. Registered Trademark of Miller Forensic Software, San Jose, CA.

9. Anon., *How to Use the No More Strings Demo Disk*, Miller Forensic Software, San Jose, CA, pg. 5.

Evaluating Impact
Spatter Bloodstains

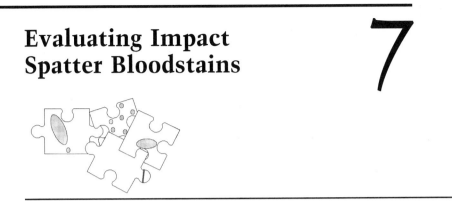

7

One of the primary functions of the analyst is to define or categorize the specific stains and patterns found. Once categorized, the analyst then attempts to identify the underlying nature of the event causing the pattern. An important pattern found at many crime scenes is the spatter pattern. As defined in Chapter 3, spatter is a stain resulting from some application of force or energy to a blood source. As definitive as this is, unfortunately there is little agreement on how to differentiate spatter. What is generally agreed upon is that spatter patterns often help us identify the nature of the force involved in the event.

Methods of Description

The first concern with the pattern is to categorize or describe it. What does it look like? What criteria does it meet? These are the questions most commonly asked. Analysts base one approach to categorizing spatter on impact velocities. As a result of early references in bloodstain analysis, bloodstains routinely became categorized into three velocity groupings. These categories refer to the nature of the impact or force causing the stain and are called Low, Medium, and High.[1] Not everyone agrees with this grouping, but used as intended the categories were and are adequate.

In a descriptive sense low-velocity stains are those of relatively large size. The limited amount of energy applied to the blood precludes the drop from breaking up. Such stains are not true spatter and generally are at least 4 mm or larger in diameter.

Low-velocity stains are said to result from normal gravitational forces or actions up to a force or energy of 5 ft/s. These stains are typical of venous bleeding in which the individual is injured and natural blood flow subsequently falls to the floor. The category of low-velocity stains now includes many different types of stains. Generally, analysts include any nonspatter stain in this classification. As a result, the category is so broad it does little to define the specific character of the stain in question.

Medium-velocity spatter are patterns in which the preponderant stain size is generally 1 to 4 mm in diameter, and which are created as a result of some application of force.[2] Historically, they are considered the result of forces or energy of up to 25 ft/s. The spatter is smaller than that found in low-velocity stains, and results from the increase in the energy applied to the event. Figures 85 and 86 depict two medium-velocity spatter patterns.

High-velocity spatter are patterns in which the preponderant stain size is 1 mm or less in diameter. Such stains are associated with a force or energy in excess of 100 ft/s.[3] Descriptively, the stains are mist-like. (See Figure 87.)

The problem with the "velocity" method of description is most evident when discussing stains among analysts. Quite often when using a velocity label as a description, others assume it to mean a definition of the event. That is, by classifying something as a high-velocity incident, they believe the analyst means the underlying event must be a gunshot.

Besides assigning event status to the stain, many analysts also tend to set absolute ranges for the so-called low-, medium-, and high-velocity spatter patterns. Analysts generally quote the work of MacDonell and Bialousz as a basis for such ranges.* In fact there are no absolute size ranges evident in the writings of either MacDonell or Bialousz. Nor is it clear if they intended that absolute parameters were in force based on their experiments.

It is also evident that they did not intend to assign event status to "medium velocity" or "high velocity" labels, but as a result of their work analysts often make such associations. For instance, we generally associate medium-velocity spatter with blunt trauma events, but these patterns are not in and of themselves defined as being "ONLY" the result of such events. MacDonell and Bialousz simply provided a basic method of definition or description for spatter patterns, and associated certain events with the patterns.

What remains evident in their work is the correlation that as we increase the amount of energy applied to the blood source, we see a corresponding decrease in spatter size. It is this particular characteristic which often allows us to differentiate the spatter of one event from another.

There is one important note regarding the velocity label. Remember that the speed (i.e., 5 and 25 ft/s) refers to the velocity of the wounding agent (the force applied) and not to the velocity of the blood in flight. This issue is often confused.

---

* The authors (Bevel and Gardner) as well as others, are guilty of this latter action.[4,5]

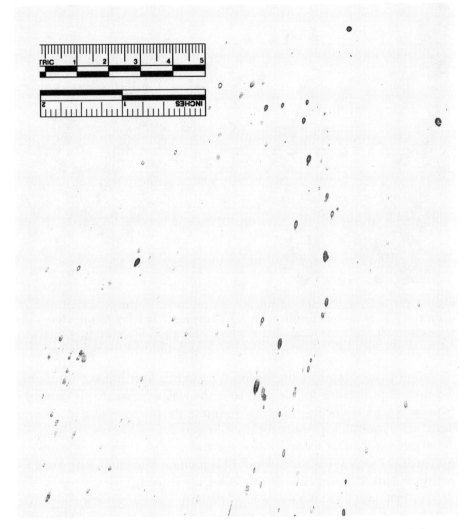

Figure 85   An example of a stain meeting the "medium velocity" definition. This pattern was produced by a blunt force impact to a blood source.

Contrasting the velocity label approach is the descriptive label. As a result of their observations, Parker et al. chose to refer to spatter patterns based on descriptive labels. Their intent was to describe the stain based purely on the physical characteristics the analyst observed. Parker et al. classified these groupings as either "fine" or "coarse".[6] Their fine category included spatter with diameters of 3 mm or less, while coarse spatter were those stains with diameters of over 3 mm.[7] The approach was not radically different from MacDonell's; it simply didn't consider the underlying event.

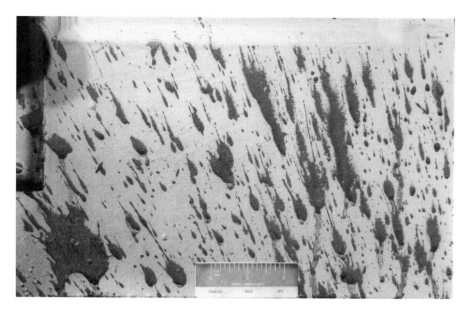

Figure 86 A case example of impact spatter meeting the "medium velocity" definition. These stains resulted from a blunt force beating to the victim. The stains were then altered somewhat by a fire set to conceal the crime. (Photograph courtesy of Donald R. Schuessler, Eugene Oregon Department of Public Safety.)

Another advocate of a descriptive approach is Judy Bunker. Ms. Bunker did not adopt Parker's terminology, but she teaches students to identify all patterns present, documenting each with a detailed physical description based on observable characteristics. This purely descriptive approach has definite merit. Bunker's intent is that the analyst first observe the stains, and make conclusions about them later.[8] This method also eliminates some disparity evident with velocity labeling as we use it today.

For instance, there is a category of pattern typically associated with low velocity in which the force fails to meet the criteria of the associated category. The pattern involved is the spatter caused when blood simply drips into liquid blood. We know, based on experimentation by MacDonell, that the terminal velocity of blood appears to be about 25 ft/s.[9] Other work in the area of fluid dynamics certainly supports MacDonell's figure.[10] Based on terminal velocity, we know the force active in creating satellite spatter when drops simply fall can't be higher. The satellite stains found around a pool of blood result singularly from this application of gravity and the shifts it causes in the mass of the blood drop.

Nevertheless, satellite stains in these patterns usually range between 1.5 to 2 mm in diameter, so in this instance we have a clear example of spatter from a "low"-velocity incident, which meets the "medium"-velocity range. This begs the question, should we relabel our definition of what gravitational

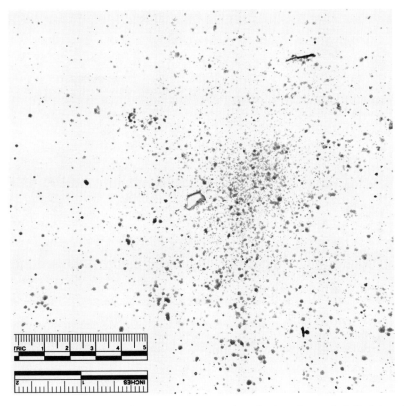

Figure 87 An example of a stain meeting the "high velocity" definition. This pattern was produced by a .22 caliber gunshot through a bloody sponge.

forces are or simply associate the stain group with the medium-velocity category?

It is not the intent of your authors to attack the velocity description — it simply has limitations. When used to describe and categorize spatter of specific sizes it works fine in most instances. Its limitations come from assigning absolute demarcation points (e.g., 5 to 25 ft/s) for which known exceptions exist, from associating the label to specific events to the exclusion of others, and from the broad categories it establishes.

Whatever method of description one chooses to use, the analyst's first concern is in realizing that descriptions of patterns should be nothing more than descriptions. Any description should define only the observable characteristics evident in the pattern. As Ms. Bunker aptly points out: save the conclusions to the end.

Having said this, we can still make some general statements regarding the events that are typically associated with spatter. Medium-velocity or coarse spatter is typical of situations in which blunt trauma is the cause of the bleeding injuries. High-velocity or fine spatter is more typical of gunshot

Figure 88 The pattern produced when a "flash-bang" device was activated next to a small pool of blood. The target was in a vertical position, representing a wall. (Photograph courtesy of Tom J. Griffin.)

injuries. Although not common to most crime scenes, examples of high-velocity spatter are also found in circumstances involving explosive force. (See Figure 88.) The reader should consider these statements as a general guideline and nothing more.

Understanding the Concept of Preponderant Stain Size

Whether using the velocity label or the descriptive label, at some point the analyst must evaluate a given impact pattern and categorize it. As discussed, we generally categorize a pattern by looking at the size of the stains present in the pattern. Unfortunately, within any given pattern there may be a wide range of individual spatter sizes.

Imagine a pattern of 15 individual spatter stains with the following sizes:

Individual Stain Size	# of Stains
0.25–1 mm	3
1.1–4 mm	10
4.1–6 mm	2

If the analyst chose to use the smallest stain (e.g., 0.25 mm) the pattern might be categorized as high velocity. On the other hand, if the analyst chose to use the largest stain present (e.g., 6 mm) the stain might be categorized as low velocity.

To properly categorize a pattern, the analyst looks at the preponderant individual stain size within it. In this instance that happens to be the 1 to 4 mm size (i.e., 66% of the pattern fits this range). Using a velocity label, that would identify the pattern as "medium velocity".

It is important to understand when making this decision that "perfect" impacts don't exist. There are no perfect patterns. The size range evident in any pattern is often great. There simply are no absolute demarcations within the pattern that will correlate to either our velocity or descriptive label.

This lack of a demarcation is the result of the dynamic nature of the impact itself. We know a single impact will act upon a blood source in different fashions during the milliseconds in which the event occurs. As the action unfolds the force is applied, the energy or pressure exerted by the force builds, it reaches a peak, it then declines. There is rarely a perfect impact in which force is applied cleanly, evenly, and in the same fashion across the entire blood source. Across the continuum of time it takes the event to occur, the blood may be acted on quite differently. (See Figure 89.)

Droplets created when the force is at its predominant level, the shadowed area of Figure 89, represent the vast majority of droplets created by the action. These stains will likely reflect the "preponderant" stain size of the pattern and establish a macro view of the event or action. Stains created at the onset or end of the action may well be larger. Just the same, we may also find spatters much smaller than our preponderant stain size that were created when the force was at its absolute peak.

In some fashion the analyst must decide which size of stain is the preponderant stain in the pattern. Most often when deciding the nature of this preponderant stain size, analysts use an eyeball method. They simply evaluate the stain and pick the size which appears to be the most prevalent. We caution you to use care with such "eyeball" examinations. The process is not always accurate. This is particularly true when evaluating stains which contain hundreds of spatter.

In one instance known to us, an analyst claimed that a spatter pattern could neither be included or excluded as resulting from backspatter. He naturally labeled backspatter as high velocity, but then claimed the pattern in question matched a slap-type event.* He chose to label this slap as a medium-velocity event. Remember, the velocity label describes the size of the stain and nothing more.

---

* An event in which a small volume of blood was slapped by several fingers.

The pattern in question included 160 individual stains which were evaluated and ranged in size as follows:

Individual Stain Size	#/% of Stains
0.25–0.49 mm	67 (41%)
0.5–0.99 mm	70 (45%)
1 mm or greater	23 (14%)

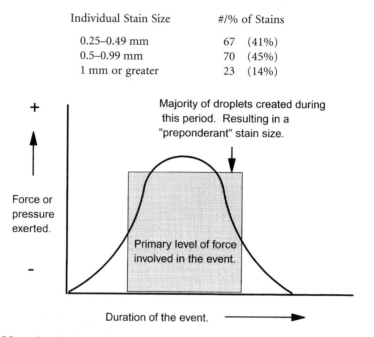

Figure 89   The shadowed box represents the level of force most evident in the event. The predominant spatter present in the pattern will result from this level, but as the force builds, peaks and then wanes spatter will also be produced. Thus smaller and larger spatter may be present within the pattern as well.

For comparison, slap-drop standards were created under the conditions claimed by the other analyst. The two patterns (the scene pattern and slap-drop standard) evaluated using only the eyeball examination appeared quite similar, but when evaluated in depth showed marked differences. The "medium-velocity" slap actually created a preponderant stain size much smaller than that found in the questioned pattern or a backspatter standard. (See Figure 90.)

This example demonstrates some of the difficulties encountered when categorizing spatter patterns. The slap pattern was not consistent with the questioned pattern, yet based on a limited eyeball examination it appeared to be consistent. Additionally, categorization of a stain as medium velocity, 86% of which is under 1 mm in size, fails to consider either the whole pattern concept or rewrites the underlying definition. Such contradictory issues are probably more common than we might imagine. They demand we carefully consider what specific characteristics lead us to our spatter pattern conclusions.

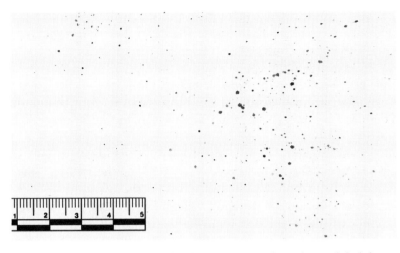

Figure 90   An example of the difficulty present in the velocity label description. This spatter resulted from a slap, which we would generally define as blunt trauma. It produces, however, a fine spatter which is well within the parameters of the "high velocity" definition. Velocity definitions should always be attributed to the pattern based on stain characteristics and not the event.

This is not to say that the analyst must measure each and every stain to make a call on a pattern, but they must ensure the sampling used for categorization is sufficient. Once again, we would prefer the decision to include or exclude a pattern as being consistent with something be based on a clear, specific, and verifiable characteristic.

Distinguishing Spatter From Contact Stains

Given the prior discussion in Chapter 4 of blood's adhesive quality, it should not surprise us to find bloodstains on those who discover victims of crime. Such witnesses may touch, cradle, or move the victim in some fashion, which in turn will result in the transfer of blood onto clothing and skin. The likelihood of such transfers is not lost on the perpetrators; they too may claim incidental contact transfers as the source of stains found on their clothing.

Situations of this nature require the analyst to attempt to distinguish the difference between spatter created by violent dynamic events and stains created by mere incidental contact. When found as a whole pattern or large stain, the differences between the two are easy to distinguish. Often, however, the nature of these stains are quite small and their true source may not be immediately evident.

But even when presented with only limited staining, the analyst can often make this distinction. This is particularly true when the stain is present on fabric. Remember, the two stains result from distinctly different actions. One is projected onto the target, while the second merely makes contact with the target.

When viewing the contact stain under low magnification, the analyst will observe blood traces on the upper weave of the fabric. As the stain is generally the result of a wipe or swipe (with lateral motion), the deeper areas of the weave are often left untouched by the blood source. Even in situations in which there is a compression contact, areas within the weave may still be free of blood.

On the other hand, when spatter strikes the clothing it does so in a projected fashion. The small droplets impact into the weave, rather than brushing against it. When viewing a spatter stain, the lower levels of the weave are likely to exhibit staining. Pex and Vaughan found this type of examination particularly useful in situations involving gunshots.[11] In their efforts to distinguish between contact staining and backspatter situations, they found that small backspatter droplets were often evident deep in the weave of a fabric.

Thus some level of discrimination by the analyst is possible. This allows the analyst to distinguish projected spatter stains from those caused by contact. The reader may recall Dr. Ziemke's reminder about the necessity of recovering the clothing of those who discover the victims of beatings and shootings. This concern is still true today, since the analyst can often corroborate or disprove statements of such individuals using the bloodstains present on their clothing.

Impact Droplet Size

As discussed to this point, the size of a spatter stain is a basic consideration, which at least points us in the general direction of defining the nature of the force involved in creating the stain. The volume of blood present in a droplet is the primary determining factor for the subsequent stain size. What forces are required to cause subdivision of a blood source to create droplets? As MacDonell, Parker, and most other researchers discovered, blood and blood droplets do not spontaneously degenerate from one volume to another.

It is the application of force or energy transferred from the impact to the mass of blood that causes the blood source to become droplets. This is also true of droplets in free flight. To further divide and become smaller droplets, some force must act on them. This force creates oscillations within the mass of blood which may overcome the cohesive forces (e.g., surface tension, viscosity) working to hold the original structure intact.

Once set in motion by an impact, no spontaneous subdivision will occur as it is unlikely droplets will collide in flight.[12] The force of impact almost singularly defines the drop size which establishes the stain size we ultimately see.

As one might expect, based on the size of impact spatter stains, impacts result in significantly smaller droplets than those resulting from drips and similar actions. We have found impact droplet diameters of 2 mm and smaller.[13] Remember, these are the actual droplets in flight and not the resulting stains. Droplets this size have volumes of 5 µl or less.

This issue of the droplet's size is significant in our consideration of impact spatter for one reason. As we examined in Chapter 4, the smaller the droplet the quicker it attains and holds a true spherical shape. As a result of the very small droplet diameters found in impact spatter events, considerations in determining impact angles and defining the point where the impact occurred appear generally reliable. At the source of the impact we may see major droplet oscillations or unstable spine and sheet-like structures, but these effects dissipate in less than 0.01 s. Away from the source of impact, the shape of droplets in flight is not distinctly affected by other extraneous forces (e.g., wind or air currents) and they travel as near-perfect spheres.

Pattern Configuration and Dispersion in Impacts

Patterns associated with impact spatter as a general rule have a radiating effect. (See Figure 91.) The center of this radiating pattern, as one would imagine, is the point where the impact occurred to the blood source. The nature of how the pattern and individual stains within the pattern manifest themselves is dependent upon the relationship of the target with regard to the impact site.

For targets that lie parallel to the primary direction of force in the impact, we are likely to see elliptical stains within the pattern. On targets that lie perpendicular to the force, we will see the more spherical stains. Figure 92 provides a basic understanding of this relationship. The reader might also refer back to Chapter 4 for a discussion of how angle of impact affects the resulting stain shape.

As the patterns disperse or radiate out, it should also be evident that the closer a given target is to the impact site the more stains one will find per square inch. As the droplets travel outward from the impact site, the distance between stains increases as they follow their given paths.

This is best understood if we limit our discussion to stains in a single dimension. Using Figure 93, imagine an impact creating droplets. These droplets travel along a single plane, as represented in the figure. Based on this radiating effect, the droplets passing the cross section labeled A are closer together than when passing B.

If we replace the cross section with a vertical target and include a three-dimensional droplet pattern originating from the impact, the resulting stains

Figure 91   An example of a radiating effect in spatter patterns. The origin of the spatter is a point about 40 cm from the floor; note how the pattern expands outward the farther from this point it is deposited. This particular pattern was the result of a stomping death. (Photograph courtesy of Lt. William Gifford, Anchorage Police Department, Alaska.)

would reflect this dispersion. Figures 94 and 95 show examples of this effect. The two patterns, produced by similar gunshot events, were each at different distances from the event. As a result, the closer target (Figure 94) shows a level of dispersion lower than that evident in the distant target (Figure 95).

This dispersion effect is also true for lateral distance. In viewing Figure 93 note that those stains found in the center of cross section B are closer together than those found at either end of the cross section.

Of course, this is not the only factor affecting the dispersion of droplets and their resulting stains. You will recall that air resistance has an inverse effect on droplets based on their size. Figure 96, a *Tracks* model, demonstrates how droplet size can distinctly affect the distance it travels. All of the droplets in the model were projected at the same speed and along the same initial path. As a result of their sizes they followed distinctly different parabolas. Smaller droplets simply do not carry as far as larger droplets. This issue is also a consideration when viewing the dispersion of patterns, particularly those found in "high-velocity" impacts.

Other factors affecting the overall pattern shape and dispersion are the manner in which the weapon contacts the impact site and the shape of the

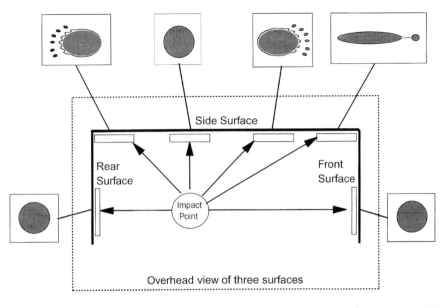

Figure 92   Stain shape and the relationship of the target to the impact. The stains we find in any given event may exist on any number of target surfaces. Thus, the position of the target in relation to the impact point will produce any number of different impact angles. By considering the resulting stain shapes, the stain positions, and the overall pattern configuration, we can distinguish the probable impact point.

weapon. These factors may limit how the blood actually ejects from the impact site. The angle at which the weapon strikes or the surfaces on the weapon may preclude blood ejecting in a symmetrical fashion.

The analyst should never accept, as it is not evident based on empirical data, that a given weapon will produce a singularly distinctive pattern each and every time it is used. Minor variations in the weapon's contact or application may result in significantly different effects when recreating the stain.

In some instances this difference may provide the analyst with a better understanding of "how" the weapon was used. If the weapon creates a distinctive pattern when used one way and another pattern when used some other way, this may become evident during recreation attempts. If present, such evidence factually defines the specific application of the weapon.

Dispersion characteristics also relate to our consideration of the presence of spatter on the subject. It is not an absolute fact that a subject involved in a spatter-producing event will have spatter on his person.[14] This lack of spatter may result from being behind the radiating pattern, where the level of dispersion is often quite small. Additionally, the manner in which the event takes place may limit the spatter dispersion in some manner, such as in the

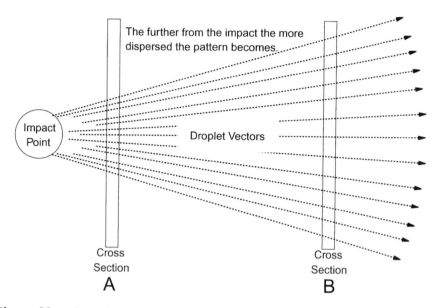

Figure 93   The radiating effect of a spatter pattern results in a higher level of dispersion in the stains farthest from the impact point. The figure is idealized and does not consider the effects of air resistance and/or individual droplet parabola. These factors also play a role in the apparent dispersion present in a pattern.

case of intervening clothing or bedding. Lack of spatter alone does not prove lack of participation in the event.

Dispersion characteristics of a stain often provide the analyst with information regarding the general distance the spattered target was from the impact. They also verify that a given item was in proximity to the event in the first place. The pattern's configuration helps establish the relationship a given target had with regard to the impact. All of this, as Eckert and James explained, "... [helps] determine the relative position of the assailant and victim at the time the blows were delivered."[15]

Spatter Resulting From Gunshots

Gunshot Spatter — Forward Spatter and Backspatter

Impact spatter very often results from gunshot injuries. When a projectile strikes a target, sufficient force is transferred to the wound or bloody surface to create spatter in the form of a fine aerosol of blood droplets. As MacDonell illustrated, the droplets resulting from such an impact radiate out in a three-dimensional pattern which we refer to as a cone.[16]

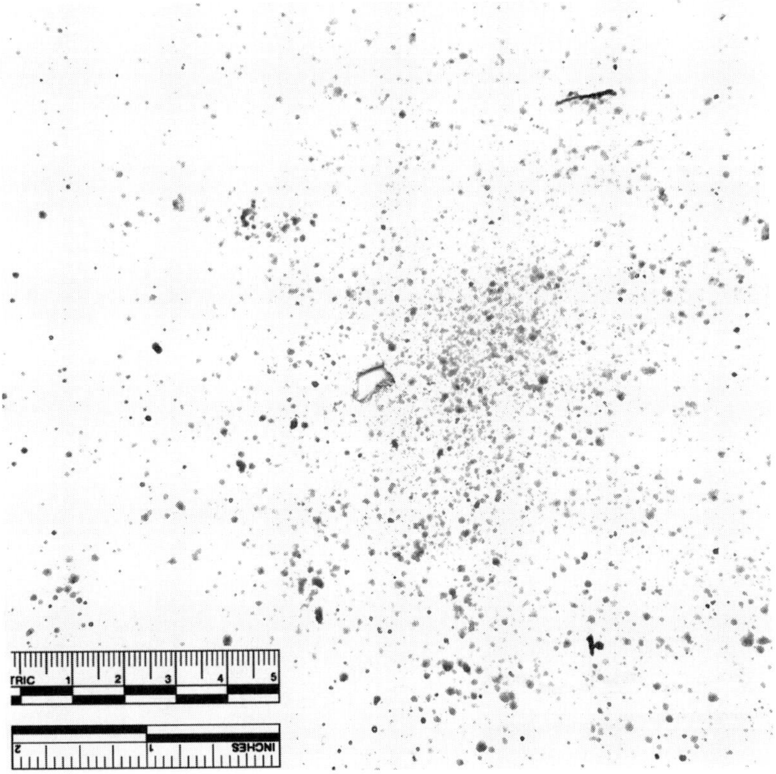

Figure 94 This pattern shows the level of dispersion in a gunshot event when the target was at a 6-in. distance from the blood source. Note the misting effect and the high number of stains present in the central area of the pattern. Compare this to the dispersion in Figure 95.

This spatter not only follows a cone-shaped pattern in the original direction of the projectile, but may also create a backspatter effect. (See Figure 97.) Obviously, forward spatter patterns in gunshot occur only when an exit wound of some nature occurs, while backspatter is always possible. Figure 98 graphically depicts the development of the cone of forward and backspatter as a bullet passes through a bloody target. In addition to spatter, the force of the projectile may drive tissue and bone out of the wound. These bloody particles can create stains of their own.

With regard to the conical shape in both forward and backspatter patterns, considerations on dispersion hold true here also. The closer to the target, the more spatter we are likely to find. In spatter patterns found very close to the target, the lack of dispersion combined with the size of the droplets involved (e.g., the atomized or mist-like stains) may produce a fine spray-paint effect. The area contained within the pattern will appear as if someone used a spray can to create it. Further away, the pattern becomes

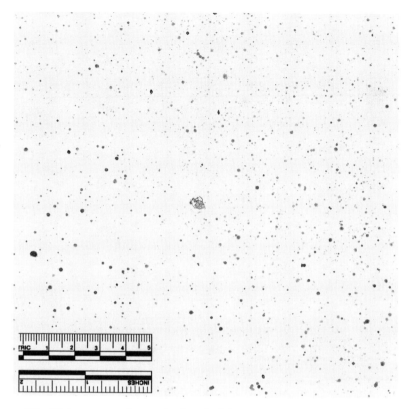

Figure 95   This pattern shows the level of dispersion present in a gunshot event when the target was 18 in. from the blood source. The pattern has a more dispersed nature with less of a misting effect.

more dispersed with fewer mist-like stains, eliminating this effect. Refer back to Figure 94, which shows this mist-like pattern. In Figure 95, the stains are more dispersed as a result of being further from the blood source.

Size Ranges of Gunshot Spatter

MacDonell and Bialousz in their original work, clearly made the point that gunshot spatter included larger stains beyond the aerosol or atomized stains. They stated:

> "In addition to the fine particles, larger droplets, but essentially all under 1/8 in. diameter, will also be produced."[17]

Laber and Epstein placed the size of the mist stains as 0.2 mm or less, adding that "Beyond this, the size of spatter produced by gunshot overlaps many other impact spatter patterns."[18]

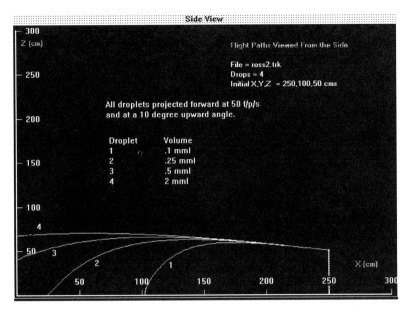

Figure 96 This Tracks model shows four droplets projected along the same initial path at the same speed. Note that all four follow different parabolas, with the smallest (droplet #1) traveling the shortest distance. This is the result of the effect of air resistance on the droplet, which is inversely proportional to the size of the droplet.

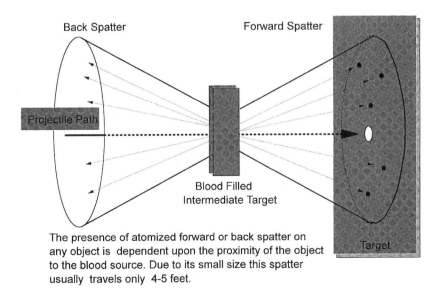

Figure 97 Spatter resulting from a perforating gunshot produces both forward spatter and backspatter. The spatters project out from the source (e.g., a body) in a cone-shaped pattern, but most do not travel far as they are quite small.

Figure 98 In this stop-motion photograph we see the development of the cone of spatter after a bullet passes through a bloody sponge. The bullet is traveling right to left. There is a distinct development of fine droplets of blood in the forward spatter, but those projected to the rear are far fewer in number.

Anyone conducting similar experiments will routinely find spatter from gunshot with 1 to 2 mm diameter stains intermixed among the mist-like stains. Once again the presence of a wide range of spatter size in any pattern, including those created by gunshot, should not surprise the analyst.

Kinetic Energy, Wound Cavitation and the Creation of Gunshot Spatter

In reading current references, it is apparent there is lack of agreement on what forces cause spatter during a gunshot injury. There seem to be many beliefs regarding the creation of gunshot spatter.[19,20]

Dr. Martin Fackler, through his efforts to understand missle-caused wounds disputes portions of these beliefs, or at least some of the misconceptions that are often attributed to them. First, Dr. Fackler points to collapse of the temporary wound cavity as the probable source of most gunshot-oriented spatter, both forward or back.[21] Second, he established that kinetic energy potential does not define wound cavitation, nor is spatter produced by the sonic shock wave which precedes the projectile. In his experiments Dr. Fackler discharged his weapons from 9 to 25 m from their targets, thus eliminating "hot gasses" as the source of such wound cavitation.[22] This is not to say that in instances of close or contact wounds, hot gasses do not play a role in adding to tissue disruption. Yet, as Dr. Fackler points out, it does not cause an increase in wound cavitation itself.[23]

Dr. Fackler defines temporary wound cavity disruption by saying, "After passage of the projectile, the walls of the permanent [wound] cavity are temporarily stretched radically outward."[24] He likens the disruption process to that of a splash being made in mud. The potential for tissue disruption depends upon both the projectile mass and projectile velocity, while the utilization of this potential is based on construction, shape, and its interaction with tissue.[25] Dr. Fackler's findings dispute the widely held belief that a higher-velocity projectile always produces a larger temporary wound cavity. Dr. Fackler also established that a bullet creates both the entrance and exit wounds milliseconds before the highest level of temporary cavity occurs.[26]

What we are left to consider, based on this information, is that the permanent wound cavity created by the physical crushing of tissue as the projectile passes through also causes a temporary wound cavitation. This temporary stretching of the surrounding tissue, then collapses back to the final defect size. This collapse of the temporary wound cavity often occurs after both the entrance and exit of the projectile, leaving two holes from which blood may be ejected by the force of the collapse.

An interesting effect related to gunshot spatter and this squeezing action, is when two or more successive shots occur. The first wound usually bleeds during the intervening period between shots. When a second shot impacts the body, the tissues surrounding the first wound compress, causing the blood-filled wound to "squirt" out its contents. The resulting spatter is much heavier than that normally associated with a single gunshot. The closer the location of the wounds are to each other, the more dramatic the effect. This condition certainly indicates that the mere compression of a wound track by the energy of a passing projectile is sufficient to eject spatter from a wound opening.*

Gunshot Pattern Shapes and Dispersion

In considering gunshot spatter pattern shapes, forward spatter patterns tend to be more symmetrical when compared to backspatter patterns. This is probably due to the primary force of the impact being transmitted in the direction of the projectile. Backspatter patterns as a whole tend to be less defined.

Of particular note to the analyst, the presence of backspatter on the subject or weapon is in part dependent upon the manner and distance at which the weapon is held. Due to their small mass, these droplets will carry only 4 to 5 ft. Air resistance, if you will recall, is inversely proportional to droplet size. No matter how fast they are moving, the droplets rapidly lose

* Color Plates 2 and 3 folow page 216.

Figure 99 An example of backspatter found on the inside facing of a crossbow. The owner was shot in the head while holding the bow in a firing position and pointing it at a police officer. The officer fired his weapon and struck the subject in the forehead. The presence of the backspatter supports the officer's contention that the victim was aiming the bow at the time he was shot. (Photograph courtesy of Lt. Johnny Kuhlman, Oklahoma City Police Department.)

speed and drop. There are also indications that in some instances these small droplets of blood dry almost instantly while suspended in air. This too may be a factor in the lack of staining on surrounding objects. The small dried specks simply fall to the ground and fail to adhere to any surfaces.

It is also possible that while suspended in the air these droplets may move on air currents, which may result in deposits farther than 4 ft. This demands that an active air current of some kind is moving in the scene. In this instance, the droplets would "rain" down and be found only on the top of horizontal sections.

Nevertheless, up to the 4 ft range, a gunshot event may deposit small stains on the weapon, shooter's body, or clothing. Figures 99 and 100 depict backspatter on the inside surface of a crossbow, while Figure 101 shows backspatter on the hand of a suicide victim. The size of such stains, combined with their highly dispersed nature, can make them easily overlooked both by the shooter when cleaning up and by the investigator during subsequent contact. Backspatter may also be evident on the inside of the weapon's muzzle.

Expiratory Blood

In instances in which a victim receives bleeding injuries to the mouth, nose, throat, or lungs, and continues to breath; spatter may also be present. Spatter

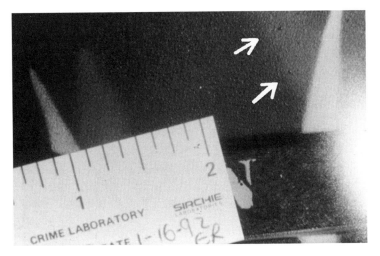

Figure 100 A second photograph of the crossbow, with a scale of reference. Several more small spatter stains are evident to the right side of the photograph.

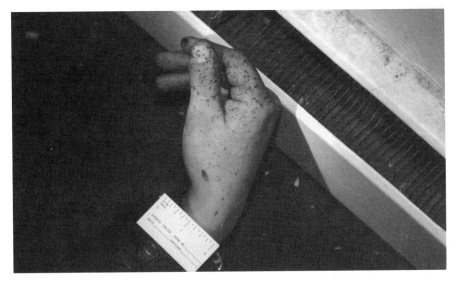

Figure 101 Backspatter present on the hand of a suicide victim. Note also the larger elliptical stain at the base of the wrist. This is a good example of why targets which are capable of motion during the event represent a poor medium in terms of directionality of stains. This stain cannot be reconciled as being from the initial deposit of backspatter itself as it shows an opposite directionality. This deposit occurred after the wrist rotated away from the body. (Photograph courtesy of John Graham, Arvada Police Department.)

Figure 102 An example of expiratory blood. In this instance the subject was wearing these cutoff jeans as he stood over a victim whose throat was cut. Stains are evident on both the inside and outside of the pant leg. (Photograph courtesy of Donald R. Schuessler, Eugene Oregon Department of Public Safety.)

resulting from expiratory blood may range from heavy large stains to light mist-like stains comparable to those found in gunshot situations. (See Figure 102.) At times these stains can mislead the analyst, and their similarities demand proper evaluation.

Oftentimes, expiratory blood that mimics gunshot spatter is less vivid in its coloration. It may give an indication of being watered down and very likely will exhibit a focused direction for the pattern. There may also be evidence of air bubbles in the pattern, or traces of popped air bubbles. Expiratory blood is most often recognized by correlating the position of the spatter with bleeding injuries observed on the nose, mouth, or airway.

Fly Spots

Although not true spatter, another pattern often confused with spatter is the "fly speck" or "fly spot" pattern. Flies present within the scene will feed on blood found there. This blood is both tracked about and regurgitated by the flies. In the instance of the tracking pattern, the marks are extremely small but a pattern may be evident on close examination.

In the case of regurgitation, the specks are remarkably symmetrical. (See Figure 103.) Most often, the analyst finds these patterns in warm areas where the flies rest, such as high in window corners or along walls where the sun

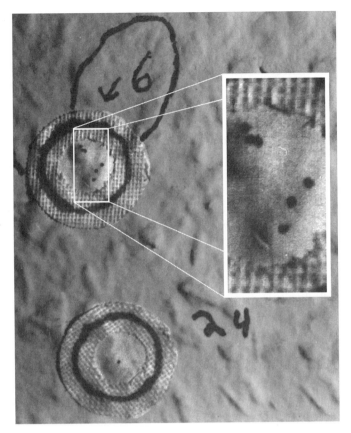

Figure 103 An example of fly spots. The small circular stains found within the gummed reinforcements were initially thought to be related to a gunshot event. The insert demonstrates just how symmetrical the spots are. Only after considering position, time, and the entire scene did it become evident they were not spatter.

strikes. Such stains will usually test positive for blood with a presumptive test. Obviously, care should be exercised in evaluating any abnormal patterns which meet these criteria.

Summary

We encounter impact spatter patterns frequently at crime scenes. The analyst's first issue is to properly describe and categorize them. Whatever method one chooses to use, its focus should be in describing those characteristics observed by the analyst. Differentiating spatter patterns based on the preponderant size of the stains is the most common method employed by the analyst.

In considering patterns the analyst must recognize that spatter sizes range widely from event to event. Overlap in stain size is often encountered. This demands a cautionary approach by the analyst in evaluating any spatter pattern. Any decision to identify a pattern as "consistent with" or "inconsistent with" should be based on specific characteristics present in the stain.

A major point of concern when considering a spatter pattern, as MacDonell put it, is "a few bloodstains do not a pattern make."[27] Whichever stains are chosen for evaluation, the analyst should be confident that they have a relationship to one another.

The radiating effect of the spatter pattern certainly helps the analyst recognize this relationship, particularly in instances of blunt trauma. Considering the dispersion found on an item can also help establish relationships with the scene. Spatter dispersion increases the farther away from the target the item is.

Unfortunately, the spatter pattern is impossible to predict in all instances. The presence of hair, clothing, bedding, and other items, or the characteristics of the weapon and how it was used, may affect the deposit of the spatter in the overall pattern. As such, a lack of spatter in and of itself does not establish the innocence of an accused.

In situations of gunshot, spatter may form both as forward spatter, which is projected outward in the direction of the bullet, and backspatter which is projected back towards the weapon. This condition often results in deposits of spatter on the subject or other parties present near the assault. When attempting to distinguish forward from backspatter, the analyst may look for a less symmetrical pattern and fewer stains in the latter. Beyond that, little distinction is evident based on the stains themselves.

Backspatter patterns in gunshot situations may effectively place the individuals at or near the victim. These stains rarely travel beyond 4 ft from their source. When found on someone's clothing, it is difficult to refute that person's presence near the event.

Mimic stains may cloud the analysts observation. Both expiratory blood and flies can produce patterns that an analyst can misidentify as either gunshot or impact spatter. The analyst, if knowledgeable of such stains when considering the full context of the scene, is less likely to make such a mistake.

Given the discussion of patterns and a knowledge of defining the point of origin, analysts have tools with which they may define clear information relevant to where in the scene these spatter events occur and distinguish one event's spatter from another.

References

1. MacDonell, H. and Bialousz, Lorraine F., Flight Characteristics and Stain Patterns of Human Blood, National Institute of Law Enforcement and Criminal Justice, LEAA Report PR -71, U.S. Government Printing Office, Washington, D.C., Nov. 1971, pp. 20-21.

2. Op. cit., pg. 20.

3. Op. cit., pg. 21.

4. Bevel, Tom and Gardner, Ross M., *Bloodstain Pattern Analysis Theory and Practice, A Laboratory Manual*, TBI Inc., Oklahoma City, OK, 1990, pg. 18.

5. Parker, N. Leroy, et al., Summary report of the Bloodstain Analysis Research Group, Florida Department of Law Enforcement, Tallahassee, pg. 65.

6. Op. cit., pg. 66.

7. Op. cit., pg. 57 and 66.

8. Bunker, Judy, Presentation to the Rocky Mountain Association of Bloodstain Pattern Analysts, 22 Apr. 1991.

9. MacDonell, H., *Bloodstain Pattern Interpretation*, Laboratory of Forensic Science, Corning, NY, 1982, pg. 3.

10. Ryan, Robert T., The Behaviour of Large, Low-Surface-Tension Water Drops Falling at Terminal Velocity in Air, *J. Appl. Meteorol.*, Vol. 15, No. 2, Feb. 1976.

11. Pex, James O. and Vaughan, Charles H., Observations of High Velocity Bloodspatter on Adjacent Objects, *J. Forensic Sci.*, Vol. 32, No. 6, Nov. 1987, pp. 1587-1594.

12. Beard, Kenneth V., Personal communication, Sept. 1989.

13. Gardner, Ross M., Oscillation Damping in Spatter Created by Impact, Unpublished.

14. MacDonell, Herbert, L., *Bloodstain Patterns*, Golas Printing, Elmira Heights, NY, 1993, pg. 61.

15. Eckert, William G. and James, Stuart H., *Interpretation of Bloodstain Evidence at Crime Scenes*, Elsevier, New York, 1989, pg. 55.

16. MacDonell, H., *Bloodstain Pattern Interpretation*, Laboratory of Forensic Science, Corning, NY, 1982, pg. 70.

17. MacDonell, H. and Bialousz, Lorraine F., Flight Characteristics and Stain Patterns of Human Blood, National Institute of Law Enforcement and Criminal Justice, LEAA Report PR -71, U.S. Government Printing Office, Washington, D.C., Nov. 1971, pg. 21.

18. Laber, Terry L. and Epstein, Baton P., Experiments and Practical Exercises in Bloodstain Pattern Analysis, Minnesota B.C.A. Forensic Science Laboratory, St. Paul, MN, Nov. 1983, pg. 38.

19. Laber, Terry L. and Epstein, Baton P., Experiments and Practical Exercises in Bloodstain Pattern Analysis, Minnesota B.C.A. Forensic Science Laboratory, St. Paul, MN, Nov. 1983, pg. 38.

20. PEX, James O. and Vaughn, Charles H., Observations of High Velocity Bloodspatter on Adjacent Object, *J. Forensic Sci.*, Vol. 32, No. 6, pg. 1588, 1987.

21. Fackler, Martin L., Col (Ret) M.D., Presentation to the Int. Assoc. Bloodstain Pattern Analysts, Colorado Springs, CO, Sept. 24, 1992.

22. Fackler, Martin L., Col (Ret) M.D. et al., Emergency War Surgery, U.S. Government Printing Office, Washington, D.C., 1988, pp. 13-32.

23. Fackler, Martin L., Personal communications, August 1995.

24. Fackler, Martin L., Col (Ret) M.D. et al., Emergency War Surgery, U.S. Government Printing Office, Washington, D.C., 1988, pg. 17.

25. Fackler, Martin L., Col (Ret) M.D., Presentation to the Int. Assoc. Bloodstain Pattern Analysts, Colorado Springs, CO, Sept. 24, 1992.

26. Fackler, Martin L., Col (Ret) M.D., Presentation to the Int. Assoc. Bloodstain Pattern Analysts, Colorado Springs, CO, Sept. 24, 1992.

27. MacDonell, Herbert, L., *Bloodstain Patterns*, Golas Printing, Elmira Heights, NY, 1993, pg. 64.

Characteristic Patterns of Blood Which Aid in Analysis

8

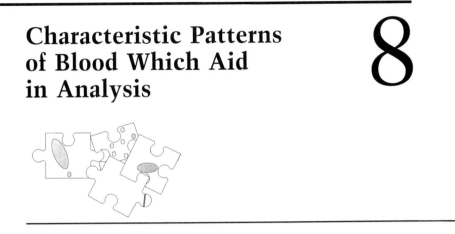

This chapter deals with some of the more common patterns the analyst may encounter. The reader will find definitions of "what" these stains are in Chapter 3, but here we discuss some of the ways they assist in reconstructing the events in question.

Cast-Off Stains

Cast-off stains occur from two actions: both from centrifugal force as a bloody object is swung in an arc and from inertia at the cessation of the swing. These stains generally have a linear patterned feature which make them easily recognized. This linear feature doesn't mean they must all line up along a single line. The nature of the arc, the width of the item from which they were cast off, and the volume of blood available all play a part in the resulting pattern.

Cast-off patterns are important to analysis in that they identify at least a minimum number of blows struck during the event. By considering directionality of the individual stains in the pattern, the forward and backward swings of the arc become evident to the analyst. As such, the analyst can group them, defining from this the number of blows evident in the pattern. Quite often analysts take this number and add an additional blow, assuming that the first blow struck by the assailant will have produced insufficient blood to cause a cast-off.

What this information cannot tell us is the total number of blows delivered during the event. That number may always be higher than the number of blows evident in the cast-off pattern. The subject, however, cannot refute this minimum number of blows. In some fashion the subject's story must account for the information evident in the pattern.

Additionally, cast-off stains may give indications as to the nature of the blow; that is, was the blow left to right or right to left. This orients any blows to the scene and may also indicate which hand the individual created them with. This indication of handedness does not define the subject as either "right-handed" or left-handed" in and of itself. There are some distinctions evident between a cast-off created by a person's strong hand as compared to the weak hand. The strong hand cast-off is likely to be more fluid with a smooth arc. The weak hand, since it is not usually involved in such forceful blows, may show indications of a jerky nature which will translate into a less smooth arc in the pattern. Normally, such observations are evident only under lab conditions and the analyst may never actually observe them in the field. This type of evidence and any decision made in this regard are subjective and should be considered cautiously.

Given several targets (walls and floors) on which a cast-off pattern is found, we can often orient the position of the individual swinging the item. At the onset of the swing, droplets are cast off which strike the adjacent wall at 90°. As droplets are cast off farther into the swing, they strike at more acute angles creating elliptical stains. When the relative position of the target changes, as in the juncture of a wall and ceiling, so too does the angle of impact. The analyst is likely to find 90° impact droplets both on the wall and the ceiling. Correlating the two in relation to each other allows some indication as to the general pivot point of whatever item was involved. (See Figure 104.)

We may also consider cast-off trails and their respective change on the surface involved. Remember, the source of the blood in our cast-off pattern is invariably the victim's. The analyst may see the start of the first cast-off high on the wall, with the second one lower, and a third almost at the base. This indicates the victim's position changed as the subject delivered the blows. One caution in considering cast-off patterns — they may result from actions by either the subject or victim. The victim can also produce such patterns while swinging bloody appendages.

In situations involving exaggerated swings, it is not uncommon to discover small cast-off stains on the back surfaces of the subject's body and clothing. The cessation action at the terminus of the backswing may cast small droplets onto the shoulders, back, and legs. (See Figures 105 and 106.)

This condition is dependent upon the nature of the swing and the position of the subject's body. For example, when kneeling we might expect the subject to have such spatter on the back surfaces of the lower pant leg. The analyst can then correlate these spatter with soaked blood traces on the fabric in the knee area. Such evidence would certainly provide solid information regarding the subject's position during the attack.

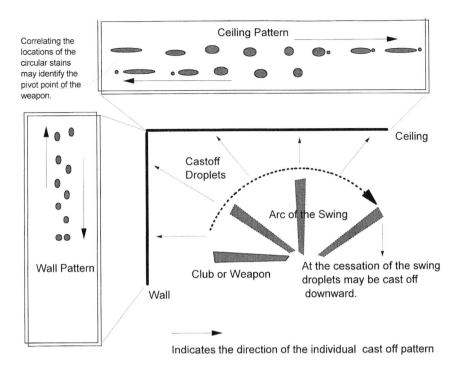

Figure 104 Cast-off patterns. Droplets flung from a bloody weapon impact surrounding surfaces at varying angles, but in a generally linear pattern. By considering the directionality evident in these stains, we can easily distinguish forward from backward swings. Consideration of the points on the varying surfaces where we discover rounded stains may also identify the probable pivot point of the weapon involved.

Pattern Transfers

Pattern transfers are probably the most overlooked evidence within any given scene. As discussed, blood is extremely adhesive in nature. Once a small amount contaminates some object, that object will then contaminate others. A little blood goes a long way.

Any comparison of a pattern transfer to the item we believe created it is likely to be limited to a finding of "consistent with" or "inconsistent with". Granted, the analyst would prefer to make "identifications" based upon individual characteristics, but that doesn't happen in every case. Nevertheless, toolmark and fingerprint examiners should be given every opportunity to consider such evidence in the hopes of making an actual identification.

Consider Figure 107. Present on the pant leg is a large stain which also holds an area where a small unstained section is evident. This unstained section exhibits a distinctly curved edge. Figure 108 is the weapon which

Figure 105   A student involved in a cast-off pattern experiment. Note the presence of droplets on his back. (Photograph courtesy of Jouni Kiviranta, National Bureau of Investigation, Helsinki, Finland.)

created the pattern. At the point where the tool head and shaft join, the reader will note a beveled edge, the outline of which corresponds to the curved feature evident in the unstained area. Through simple recreations, the analyst can easily correlate the class characteristics of the tool to those present in the stain. It is just as possible that a toolmark examiner may match individual characteristics caused by accidental marks or flaws on the tool.

Even if lacking such individual characteristics, class characteristics in the pattern are still strong evidence. They often point the analyst to objects within the scene. The nature of these characteristics are unlimited. Such patterns include any number of swipes and wipes or compression contacts, all of which help the analyst understand what weapons or other items were in use.

In deciding if an object is or is not consistent with a pattern, experimentation by the analyst is necessary. Such experimentation occurs only after all other forensic examinations are complete. If comparing only the class characteristics of the item, the analyst may choose to use an item of similar construction. Do not, however, expect to make a Xerox copy of a scene pattern

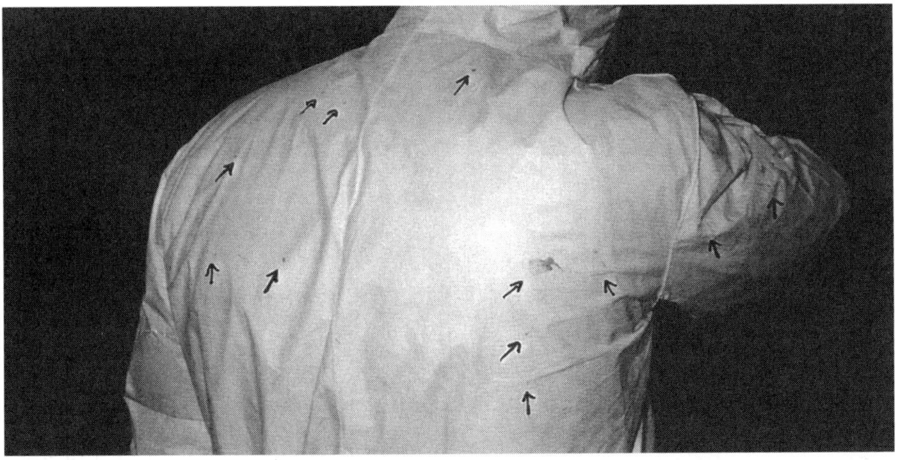

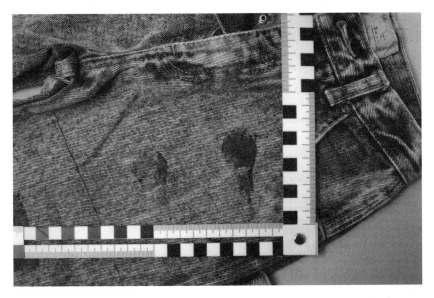

Figure 106   A close-up view of the student's back. Each arrow points to spatter and other stains. In this instance, the spatter may be the result of both the cessation action in the backswing and droplets thrown off the weapon in high overhead parabolic arcs. (Photograph courtesy of Jouni Kiviranta, National Bureau of Investigation, Helsinki, Finland.)

Figure 107   A pattern transfer on a fabric in which the general characteristics of the object are evident. Note the distinct elliptical voided area in the lower third of the pattern. (Photograph courtesy of Jouni Kiviranta, National Bureau of Investigation, Helsinki, Finland.)

Figure 108   The tool which created the stain in Figure 107. Note the beveled edge where the tool head and shaft come together. This characteristic is clearly evident in Figure 107 as the elliptical area void of blood. (Photograph courtesy of Jouni Kiviranta, National Bureau of Investigation, Helsinki, Finland.)

in every circumstance. Remember, the dynamics of how much blood was involved, how the object came in contact with the surface, and the surface characteristics all affect the resulting stain. The analyst is not often presented with situations which allow reproduction of the original events in absolute detail.

There are two basic approaches to evaluating pattern transfers. The first considers looking for a unique pattern within the questioned stain and comparing that defect to the standard, while the second starts with characteristics in the standard and looks for similar ones in the questioned stain.

Don Coffey offers this approach to the first method:

- Seek a landmark in the questioned stain, some pattern or defect which is distinct.
- Compare this characteristic against the class characteristics found in the standard. Expect a class match at best; but always seek an individualized match.
- As a result of the complexity or dynamic manner in which the questioned stain may have been created, do not expect an exact match. Creation of the standards must also be a dynamic process.
- Consider the use of "screen positives" to compare a questioned with a standard.
- The more eyes viewing the stain the better, as this eliminates tunnel vision on the part of the analyst.[1]

The second method of comparing pattern transfers begins with the standard. Our initial evaluation of the scene pattern may direct us toward some object or group of objects. Using these, we create standards and look for specific class characteristics. We then compare these characteristics with the questioned pattern.

It might seem that the two methods are distinguished by mere semantics, but in fact both change the perspective the analyst uses in viewing the stain. The utilization of both methods may be of value to the analyst.

In considering patterns and the dynamic nature of their creation, the manner of how the target surface and item come together can make a drastic difference in recognizing the resulting stain. Recreations in which we simply change the items orientation to the target often result in radically different patterns.

For instance, consider the classic butterfly pattern caused when a bloody knife is wiped with a fabric. If the cloth is folded over and the knife wiped close to the fold, the classic pattern will occur. If the cloth is folded and the knife wiped further away from the fold, the analyst ends up with each half of the butterfly in two widely separated locations on the cloth. Whenever the analyst produces standards for comparison, a major consideration is the orientation of the tool or object to the target. Never assume that the way you put the two together is the only way to put them together. Minor differences in this orientation can result in drastically different patterns.

The classic butterfly pattern, associated with edged weapons, often provides very distinct information regarding the features of the weapon creating it. For instance, Figure 109 shows an example of slightly separated butterfly pattern. Within the pattern is a clear representation of one side of the blade. The edge of the backstrap and the blade are quite distinct. Measured at a point about 30 cm from the apparent tip, the width of the pattern is 17 mm. Figure 110 is the weapon which created the pattern, a measurement of the blade at the same point shows the width to be 17 mm. In case examples, however, the amount of blood evident in the pattern is often less than that found in a lab-produced example. Figure 111 shows a case example of the butterfly effect.

Knives are not the only item capable of creating a distinct pattern; Figure 112 is an interesting example of a peculiar pattern. This pattern transfer on cloth showed two linear features that were almost at a 90° angle to one another. When measured, however, the angle was actually 88°. A long gun used in this incident had a barrel which the owner shortened. The angle at which the barrel was cut was consistent with the angle in the pattern. During recreation attempts, this particular weapon was bloodied and tossed down onto a similar surface (a pillow) resulting in a pattern nearly identical to that found at the scene.

Figure 109 A butterfly pattern transfer created by the wiping of an edged weapon. Characteristics evident in the pattern include the backstrap of the blade and the general blade dimensions. The backstrap width (the thickness of the blade) is often the most evident characteristic in the butterfly pattern. Very few things interrupt the creation of this dual linear mark found in the central portion of the stain between the two "wings". (Photograph courtesy of Jouni Kiviranta, National Bureau of Investigation, Helsinki, Finland.)

Figure 110 The knife that caused the pattern in Figure 109. Although there are no individual characteristics evident, we can still compare general dimensions (e.g., blade width and backstrap width) with those found in the pattern. Such an examination will allow at least a "consistent with" or "inconsistent with" finding. (Photograph courtesy of Jouni Kiviranta, National Bureau of Investigation, Helsinki, Finland.)

Figure 111   An example of a knife pattern transfer in which the knife has been placed directly over the pattern. Case examples often exhibit far less blood in the pattern than those created under lab conditions. Nevertheless, distinct features are often evident. Note the "L"-shaped feature in this pattern that matches with the base and tang of the pocket knife.

The use of "screen positives" as a means of comparison is based on the work of Peter McDonald, which is found in his book *Tire Imprint Evidence.* Mr. McDonald stresses that "screen positives are the most effective way of making visual comparisons…"[2] The method involves making clear transparencies of the standard and questioned stain and then evaluating them with the use of a light box. This method is best suited for circumstances in which the pattern transfer is on a rigid substrate. Don Coffey uses this technique effectively in considering many types of pattern transfers. He cautions the analyst by stating that the method is both expensive and limited, since point-to-point comparison is not always possible.[3]

In the crime scene, the most often-encountered pattern transfers are fingerprints, handprints, and foot or footwear prints. All of these help the analyst detail motion in the scene. Combining the information present in the pattern with the concept of a repetitive pattern transfer, the analyst can often detail specific actions by the involved individuals.

Another classic pattern transfer is the hair swipe. These patterns often show characteristic bifurcated endings. (See Figure 113.)

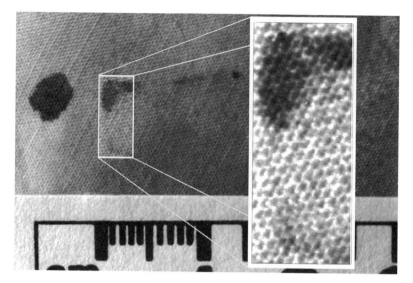

Figure 112   Oftentimes a pattern transfer is anything but specific and therefore not considered of value. In this instance, we have a simple stain that suggests the dimensions of the corner of some item that caused it. On closer examination it became evident that the two stain edges were not at a right angle to each other, but rather at an 88° angle. A weapon bloodied during this event also had a distinct cut which formed an 88° angle. During recreation attempts, the examiner was able to recreate this pattern using the cut area of the weapon.

One major caution is in order when considering pattern transfers. Whenever possible, evaluate them on-scene or through photographs exposed early in the scene processing. Post-incident pattern transfers occur as a matter of routine. Police, medical, and coroner personnel often create post-incident pattern transfers by moving items during scene processing. If an object is still wet and then moved it is likely to cause a transfer. Additionally, these same personnel are themselves moving in the scene and may end up tracking blood.

Finally, while placing the victim into a body bag extraneous blood will often flow, this can destroy existing patterns and create post-incident patterns. If the victim's clothing has spatter or stains of significance noted at the scene, it's best to consider removing the items there. This will preclude marring the patterns. Of course, any decision to do so must be considered in light of all investigative issues and approved by the appropriate coroner or medical examiner.

Projected Blood

Projected blood patterns are characterized by two things: volume and spines. The most typical naturally occurring projected patterns are the arterial gushes

Figure 113 A classic hair swipe pattern transfer. Note the many small bifurcations evident in the pattern. These are very specific and define the object that created the pattern as being hair or a hair-like substance. (Photograph courtesy of Jouni Kiviranta, National Bureau of Investigation, Helsinki, Finland.)

or spurts. They are recognized by the spines present in individual stains, which reflect both the presence of force behind the projection and the volume of blood projected. As MacDonell illustrated, such patterns as a whole may look quite different, depending upon the location of the artery breached.[4] Yet, the pattern will in some fashion reflect the spines. These spines indicate the blood struck the target with force. Many times these patterns will show the pressure fluctuations of the circulatory system, with peaks and valleys being evident in the overall pattern. Figure 114 depicts an arterial gush, while Figure 115 shows an arterial spurt pattern resulting from a severed carotid artery.

An important correlation for arterial spurts and gushes is the condition of the victim. Given a breached artery and a live victim, some evidence of the projected blood will be found. Lacking such stains, one would surely

Figure 114 An arterial gush. The pattern on the sidewalk resulted from a wound to the heart. As with most projected blood patterns, both volume and spines are evident throughout the pattern.

question whether the victim's heart was beating at the time the artery was breached. Again, volume and projection are the characteristics the analyst looks for. Passive flows and drips will not suffice to explain the lack of these gushes. It is possible that clothing or other items over the wound may block the overall development of the pattern, but if the victim was alive there will usually be evidence of the arterial wound.

Flow Patterns

In considering flows found in the scene, the primary issue for the analyst is to distinguish passive from active. Passive flows occur as a result of gravity

Figure 115   The patterns present on the drywall resulted from a severed carotid artery. Note their appearance — as if squirted onto the wall with a small hose or hypodermic. (Photograph courtesy of T. Daniel Gilliam, Larimer County Sheriff's Department.)

and body position. They have limited investigative importance, other than pointing to movement of the body after death. Active flows, on the other hand, occur while the victim is alive. They result from bleeding and assist the analyst in positioning the victim at different locations in the scene during the event.

With regard to positioning, consider an example in which we find a flow pattern on the face of a victim. The victim is found flat on his back in the scene, but the flow runs up the nose, not down. This gives the analyst a clear indication of a change in the victim's final position. At some point the victim must have been positioned with the head slightly downwards. Recognition of such an abnormal blood flow provides the analyst with specific indications of the victim's position. Blood flows will always obey gravity.

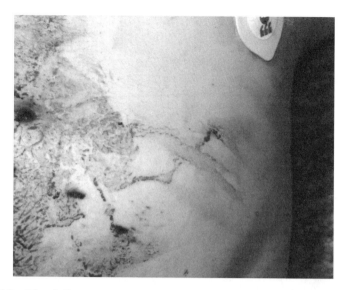

Figure 116 Blood flow inconsistencies. Note the two small flows evident on the torso that create an "X". This pattern could not be reconciled with the subject's story. The subject claimed the victim was sitting when they occurred, but the flow, which makes a distinct dogleg, (the lower portion of the X), is actually flowing up towards the victim's armpit.

For example, in Figure 116 the reader will observe two minor flows which create an "X". One is disturbed, while the other shows a distinct dogleg, with motion towards the upper right-hand corner of the picture. In this instance the subject claimed the victim was sitting upright when these two flows occurred. Unfortunately, the dogleg flows from the victim's stomach upward towards the victim's armpit. Given the direction of the flow and the congealed blood at the end of the flow, one cannot reconcile the subject's claim as to the positioning of the victim. Figure 117 is another example of an abnormal flow. By considering the effect of capillary action in relation to the flow pattern's position, it is evident that the victim was moved at some point following the creation of the flow.

Additionally, the interruption of flow patterns may assist the investigation. The point of interruption will often show pattern transfers of the object causing the interruption. Stoppage of the flow (congealing of the blood) may also indicate sequencing and passage of time between the flow, the interruption, and the subsequent removal of the interruption. (See Figure 118.)

Voids and Ghosting Patterns

Voids are typical of spatter pattern situations. Between the impact point and the location where we find the spatter pattern (the primary target) it is always

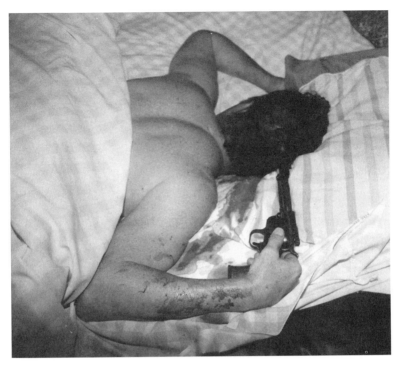

Figure 117   An abnormal flow pattern in a murder scene which was staged to look like a suicide. The blood present on and around the arm is obviously inconsistent with a final position of the victim. The flow from the wound fails to follow the line of the victim's current body position (capillary action) and indicates some motion of the body following the flow. (Photograph courtesy of Barie Goetz and Charles Green.)

possible that some secondary target was present or intervened. This will result in a lack of spatter in a specific area of the pattern on the primary target.

This effect, sometimes referred to as ghosting, may indicate the nature or shape of the secondary object. If this object is known, it may help identify specific movements, or lack thereof of these objects in the scene. As an example, consider Figure 119. A spatter-producing event below and to the right of the picture frame resulted in distinct demarcation lines where the frame interrupted the pattern's development. One demarcation is evident on the right side of the frame while a second is evident above the frame.

It is important to caveat the consideration of voids by saying there is a big difference between a spatter pattern which is interrupted and then continues as compared to a pattern that simply stops. (See Figures 120 and 121.)

Voids may occur in either instance, but in the latter instance the analyst may be less confident about viewing an actual void. If the pattern ends abruptly with a distinct linear demarcation it is more probable the pattern

Figure 118 An area of congealed blood which holds a child's hand print. As the flow occurred, the blood congealed while the hand was present in it. The hand was then removed. This type of pattern defines evidence which points both to the nature of the object that caused it and to issues relating to timing and sequencing aspects. (Photograph courtesy of Edmond Police Department, Edmond, OK.)

represents a true void. If no true demarcation is present it may simply be the natural end of the pattern.

Voids are often functional for establishing body position of the victim or assailant at the time of a spatter event. For example, voids on the clothing may establish that a hand or arm was up or extended. In such instances, arms and legs may shield the clothing and skin behind them from the spatter event. The resulting voided areas may provide the analyst with a clearer picture of the individual's body position.

Pools and Standing Blood

The analyst will also find many instances of pools or standing blood within the scene. By considering the drying time of blood, the clotting time, and by estimating the amount of bloodshed the analyst can detail information about the overall incident.

Drying time and skeletonization are both important. Like any fluid, when shed blood reacts to its environment, the manner in which it reacts points the analyst to the passage of time within the scene. Of particular concern is the drying time of both droplets and larger volumes of blood. Pex and Hurley established that a ring always appears on the edge of a blood stain within

Figure 119   This photograph demonstrates the nature of the demarcation typically found in voids. Note the absence of spatter along the right edge and top of the picture frame. (Photograph courtesy of Detective Mark Nelson, Springdale, Arkansas Police Department.)

50 sec after being exposed.[5] In some instances this ring may appear earlier. This effect is referred to as skeletonization. The dried outer ring evident in the stain does not wipe away even in situations where the stain is vigorously wiped. Depending upon environmental factors and the surface on which we find the blood, a droplet may take more than 20 min to dry completely. The skeletonization effect, however, consistently occurs not later than 50 sec after initial bloodshed. (See Figure 122.)

To establish actual drying times of droplets the analyst must consider the scene's environmental conditions. By experimentation, the analyst may define with some level of confidence the drying times of stains of different sizes. Even if lacking this knowledge, the skeletonization effect by itself defines

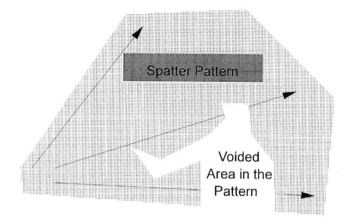

Figure 120   Interrupted pattern with an obvious void. Voids of this nature are easy to identify as the pattern clearly continues beyond the limits of the voided area. Often, the shape of the void will assist the analyst in identifying the object that intercepted the spatter.

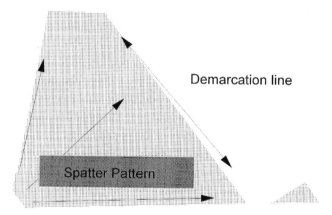

Figure 121   A less evident void. In this instance we may still be viewing a void (e.g., the area to the right of the distinct demarcation line), but it is also possible we are simply viewing the natural termination of the spatter pattern. In a pattern of this nature, decisions relating to whether this is or is not a void require a level of caution.

whether a specific pattern or stain was or was not disturbed immediately after its creation.

Clotting also gives the analyst an indication of the time that passed between bloodshed and the observation of clotting. Anita Wonder defined three stages for clotting. She referred to these as: clot initiation, clot firmation, and clot retraction.

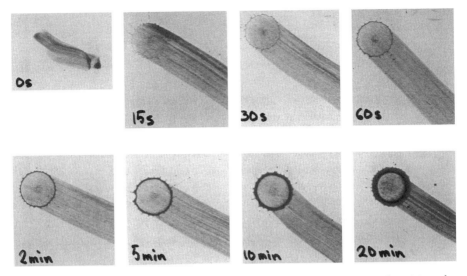

Figure 122 The skeletonization effect in a blood droplet. Note that 30 s after creation, a ring begins to develop on the outside boundary of the stain. At 60 s· this ring is readily apparent. This effect is referred to as skeletonization and allows us to distinguish if a droplet or pattern was disturbed immediately after creation. The time necessary for a droplet to dry completely is dependent upon the environmental factors found at the scene. (Photograph courtesy of Jouni Kiviranta, National Bureau of Investigation, Helsinki, Finland.)

According to Wonder, initiation starts between 10 sec and 1.5 min after bloodshed. This is a natural result of the blood's exposure to the outside environment. Wonder described clot firmation as the point where, if disturbed, no flow-back will occur. This begins anywhere from 5 to 20 min after bloodshed. Clot retraction, which Wonder defined as serum separation from the fibrin mass, begins anywhere from 30 min to 1.5 h after bloodshed.[6]

Obviously, categorizing the stage of clotting is a parameter decision. We strongly caveat the times involved, because that time is affected by issues of temperature, humidity, and the surface on which the blood was shed. Laber and Epstein found similar clotting times ranging from 5 to 40 min. The primary environmental factors they consider related to the clotting process include surface of the target and temperature.[7]

As well as considering the passage of time since the bloodshed, another issue often raised about blood pools is the total volume represented by the pool. This is particularly true in instances where no body is present. At issue is whether the wounded individual could survive the wounds indicated by the volume. There are instances in which cases were adjudicated without a body, in part because the blood volume made it clear the individual was dead.

Such estimations are exactly that — estimations. Any attempt to define this volume must consider the surface characteristics, including its absorbency, the depth of the clot or congealed blood on the surface, and the leveled nature of the surface. Such estimations require corroboration using experimental methods which consider all the factors listed above. Hopefully, any result would include a level of confidence on the total blood volume developed through some type of statistical analysis.

Lee and co-workers developed four methods of considering this estimation. All of the methods are based on the dry weight of bloodstains. They established a dry weight constant (0.4167 ml/mg) which they simply multiplied by the weight of the dry blood crust present in the stain. The most difficult part of their process is eliminating the weight of any substrate the dried crust may be present on. Three of their four methods included:

- Removing and weighing the actual blood crust present on nonabsorbent surfaces and multiplying that number by the constant.
- Weighing the substrate and blood crust, determining a weight, of the substrate alone, subtracting this weight, and then multiplying the remainder by the constant.
- Determining the area of substrate covered by the blood, weighing a single unit (e.g., a square centimeter), multiplying by both the constant and the total area.[8]

Another method for estimating blood volume is a wet volume estimate in which the analyst attempts to create a similar-sized pool or stain. The first step is to measure the overall dimensions of the stain in question and define the total area within the stain. (See Figure 123.) Using a similar substrate, the analyst then pours whole blood onto the surface in a slow and methodical fashion such as in Figure 124, all the while monitoring the overall stain size as it develops. The analyst then measures the test stains (several tests may be necessary) to include defining their total area. (See Figure 125.) This comparison of the area encompassing the standards may indicate to the analyst a rough estimate of the volume of blood present in the questioned stain. Although certainly not absolute, these estimations of blood volume, wet or dry, do at times serve the investigative process.

Blood Dripping Into Blood

The characteristic pattern of blood dripping into pooled blood is at times significant. These patterns occur when a blood source (typically a bleeding person) remains in place long enough for dripping to occur. The pattern has two distinct features — the random satellite spatter surrounding the pool and the inverted fan shape evident on adjacent vertical surfaces, if present.

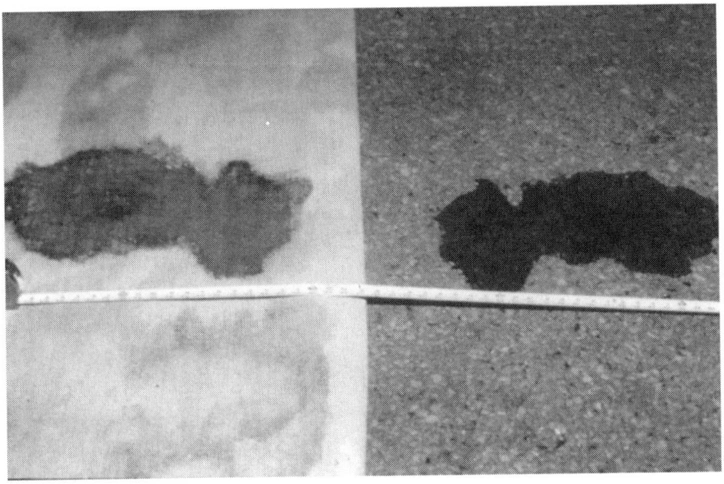

Figure 123 Estimating blood volume using a wet stain method. In this first photograph the questioned stain is shown. This stain must be measured completely and its total area defined.

Blood droplets as they impact into a liquid pool form the large blossom structures discussed in Chapter 4. The satellite spatter which detach from the blossoms are projected outward from the pool. They create small (1 to 2 mm spatters) which will show evidence of varying angles of impact. These spatter may radiate out from the pool for several feet. As a result of the rolling motion which may occur in the liquid pool (resulting from the droplet impacting the liquid) such satellite spatter are projected out from the pool in random directions. The resulting stains will show this random directionality. This type of pattern often mars other patterns of interest, particularly spatter patterns. Based on their small size, the analyst may confuse drip pattern spatter as impact spatter.

If an adjacent vertical surface is near the pool and drip, a very distinct pattern often occurs on the vertical surface. As the droplets detach from the blossom structure they follow varying parabolas which the vertical surface will interrupt. (See Figure 126.) Obviously, the closer the vertical surface is to the pool the earlier in the parabola the interruption will occur. Thus the pattern evident on the vertical surface will show a voided area which resembles an inverted fan or "V" shape. (See Figure 127.) The bottom of the "V" will be the point where the surface was closest to the dripping action. Figure 128 is an example of a typical drip pattern.

Drip patterns may suggest the presence of a bleeding individual at a specific location for a few moments. Although it is difficult to estimate how long this period was, the delay at that point will be evident. This contrasts a moving drip pattern such as that found in a blood trail, which is evidence

Figure 124 The next step is to create a similar-sized stain on a similar surface. Blood is added slowly and the size of the stain is monitored by the analyst. This is done in order to match the general dimensions of the questioned stain as closely as possible.

of continuous motion. One caution, however, is that the item dripping (depending upon the level of dripping evident) may be either a bloodied object or the subject. Care is certainly in order in trying to establish a specific source of the drip pattern.

Summary

The patterns included in this chapter are not meant to be inclusive of all those possible, but they do represent some of the more common patterns evaluated by the analyst. Recognition of the pattern is not enough, the analyst must consider what information these patterns illuminate regarding case specifics.

Figure 125   The analyst then measures the total area evident in the standards. This figure is compared to the area in the questioned stain. This comparison in correlation to the known volume used to create the standards allows the analyst to roughly estimate the volume of the questioned stain.

Cast-off patterns are extremely effective for defining events involving blunt trauma. They not only place people in the scene, they also allow the analyst to refute claims like "I only hit him once!" Pattern transfers document movement and contact of various articles and persons throughout the scene. They truly are the most widely encountered pattern found in bloody scenes. Unfortunately, far too often analysts don't take the time to consider them in detail. Lacking an immediate pattern, analysts assume they hold no clues and are just smudges or smears.

Projected bloodstains like the arterial spurt help establish the condition of the victim. They often graphically depict the victim's subsequent movement in the scene. Flow patterns assist the analyst in positioning the victim or in recognizing some interruption of the flow. Voids not only assist the analyst in positioning, but also point to the nature of the object which caused the void.

Finally, blood pools and blood droplets, when considered with both drying and clotting times, provide information on the passage of time and sequencing of events within the scene. They can clearly refute statements of individuals who claim to have found the victim after the crime occurred. Drip patterns surrounding pools may also establish a delay, indicating the presence of an individual at a location for some period.

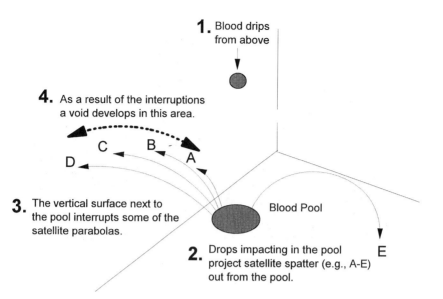

Figure 126 Drip pattern development on an adjacent vertical surface. (1) Blood dripping from a source impacts a static pool of blood. (2) The impact causes satellite spatter to be projected out from the pool in every direction. Allowed to follow a natural parabola, the spatter will project out away from the pool (E). (3) The droplets that strike the adjacent vertical target have their individual parabolas interrupted. (4) The closer the vertical target, the sooner the parabola is interrupted (A-B). Droplets impacting the wall at more acute angles travel farther and thus attain a greater height before they impact (C-D). This causes a distinct arced demarcation line in the pattern.

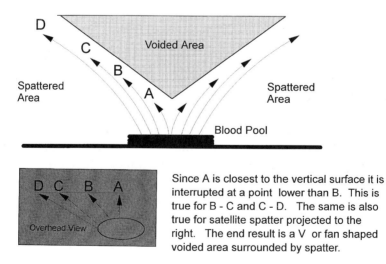

Since A is closest to the vertical surface it is interrupted at a point lower than B. This is true for B - C and C - D. The same is also true for satellite spatter projected to the right. The end result is a V or fan shaped voided area surrounded by spatter.

Figure 127 As a result of these interrupted parabolas, the spatter pattern that results will resemble a "V" or "U" shape, with a voided area in the center.

Figure 128   An example of a drip pattern on both the vertical and horizontal targets. On the vertical target a V-shaped void results near the pooled blood. All about the pool on the horizontal target are small random spatter.

References

1. Coffey, Donald, Personal communications, December 1993.

2. McDonald, Peter, *Tire Imprint Evidence*, Elsevier, New York, 1989, pg. 61.

3. Coffey, Donald, Personal communications, December 1993.

4. MacDonell, Herbert L., *Bloodstain Patterns*, Golas Printing, Elmira, NY, 1993, pp. 47-55.

5. Pex, O.J. and Hurley, N.M., Sequencing of Bloody Shoe Impressions by Blood Spatter and droplet Drying Times, Presentation to the Int. Assoc. Bloodstain Pattern Analysts, 1990 Training Conference, Reno, NV, Nov. 1990.

6. Wonder, Anita K., What is Blood, *International Association of Bloodstain Pattern Analysts News*, Vol. 2, No. 2, May 28, 1985.

7. Laber, Terry L. and Epstein, Barton P., Preliminary Results — Clotting Time Studies, Unpublished, Undated.

8. Lee, Henry C., Gaensslen, R.E., and Pagliaro, Elaine M., Bloodstain Volume Estimation, *International Association of Bloodstain Pattern Analysts News*, Vol. 3, No. 2, October 1986, pp. 47-55.

Documenting Bloodstains 9

There is a saying used in the Army CID regarding documentation: "If it's not written down, it didn't happen." Analysis and reconstruction demand this type of thinking whenever possible. No matter how good the evaluation and subsequent reconstruction, without documentation that allows us to share those efforts the evaluation may be for naught.

The Function of Documentation

Documentation serves several functions. These include:

- Verification of scene integrity.
- Providing a quality court presentation.
- Allowing outside analysis.
- Providing for independent defense evaluation.

The most important function of documentation is simply maintaining a record of the scene integrity as the analyst finds it. We want to be able to state with some authority the condition in which we found the evidence and how that evidence relates to other items. The court expects and demands this of the crime scene technician.

Good scene documentation precludes investigators from including post-incident artifacts in the analysis. It ensures the inclusion of evidence which may not survive the processing attempts and provides sterling proof to the court of the scene condition. To this end, documentation cannot be haphazard.

To properly understand issues of maintaining scene and evidence integrity demands an understanding of crime scene processing as a whole. This book is not an appropriate vehicle for teaching all-encompassing crime scene processing techniques. For that reason we'll offer this one comment: if the reader has not been exposed to training and experience in proper crime scene processing, that deficiency should be corrected before attempting to conduct a bloodstain pattern analysis or crime scene reconstruction.

Eventually the court will need to know what the analyst knows. For court presentations, good documentation allows the analyst to clearly present the sometimes complicated information in a fashion understandable to the audience. This is particularly critical when considering presentations to the jury. In order to believe the reconstruction, the jury must understand the reasoning and evidence which supports it.

Outside analysis is not that uncommon either. If a given department has no specific training in bloodstain pattern analysis or crime scene reconstruction, they may choose to bring in outside assistance. The outside analyst is limited by the documentation efforts of those who process the scene. Good documentation makes the outside analyst's job easier.

The final function of documentation — that of supporting defense evaluations — is also important. No matter what others may say, police agencies serve but one master — the truth! Therefore, the analyst should have little concern over defense analysis of their work. If we expect others to discover the same truths we found, they must certainly have access to the same information we had. If the analysts applied themselves appropriately, then any analysis or reconstruction will stand the test of scrutiny.

Granted, with regard to defense evaluations its easily argued that little in the legal profession deals with truth. Defense attorneys or prosecutors will raise odd and curious questions; certainly they will not limit themselves to attacking only the evidence. Nevertheless, such attempts to muddy the water will be less successful if good documentation exists. Ours is an adversary system in which defendants should and do have the right to their own impartial evaluation. Good documentation simply affirms the investigator's neutrality.

Given these concerns for scene and evidence integrity we will consider the following areas which define proper documentation:

- Collection and detection of bloodstains and traces.
- Photography of bloodstains, including video tape recordings.
- Sketching techniques.
- Written reports for bloodstain documentation.

Collection

It's not enough that the analyst recognize a pattern as defining some specific action. Without knowing "who" was involved, this knowledge does little in defining a reconstruction. Bloodstain evidence does not stand alone; in particular, serology evaluations are critical to understanding the relationship of bloodstains to the crime.

The vast majority of jurisdictions now utilize DNA analysis for determining whether a given sample from the scene is consistent with a particular individual. Forensic laboratories use both Restriction Fragment Length Polymorphism (RFLP) or Polymerase Chain Reaction preparation techniques (PCR). Both methods require a level of care in collecting and storing the specimen in order for it to be of later value.

Beyond documenting the stain's location, as a general rule the analyst should be concerned with five issues in collecting stains for subsequent serology analysis. These are:

- Proper discrimination between stains.
- Sufficient identification of samples to patterns.
- Sufficient collection of samples.
- Precluding cross contamination of samples.
- Sample collection prior to destructive testing.

The first concern is really the investigative benchmark. Failing to discriminate if a given stain belongs to a specific pattern will cause the serology information to be useless to the analyst. In approaching each pattern for collection of samples, the analyst needs to be confident that the stains selected are representative of that pattern and only that pattern. If several spatter patterns intermix in a given area, one cannot arbitrarily select stains from the conglomerate. Always choose the stains carefully, to preclude later confusion.

In addition to having confidence that the analyst is collecting stains from a single pattern, the recovered samples must be marked in a fashion that will guarantee relating it back to that pattern. Ensure that the evidence collection notes and report have a clear correlating label which identifies the stain group involved. One of the authors (Gardner) prefers establishing a number for each stain group early in the scene processing. Any subsequent mention of the pattern includes a reference to this number. This number is also listed on the evidence collection forms, along with other standard data. The following examples contrast this information with and without the use of the identifying pattern number.

Inappropriate Evidence Collection Example:

Item #	Description
1	Stain, red in color, dried. Approximately dimensions 2 mm × 2 mm. Found on the west wall, about 2 ft from the floor. Stain scraped into pharmacist's fold and sealed. Fold marked RMG 1200 2 OCT 95.

This description certainly tells where the item was found and the analyst can later identify the stain using the evidence mark (initials, time, and date), but it fails to associate the stain to a specific pattern or group.

Appropriate Evidence Collection Example

Item #	Description
1	Stain, red in color, dried. Approximately dimensions 2 mm × 2 mm. From Stain Group 2. Found on the west wall, about 2 ft from the floor. Stain scraped into pharmacist's fold and sealed. Fold marked RMG 1200 2 OCT 95.

This description provides all of the previous information but adds a ready reference to the stain group the analyst identified in the crime scene documentation as Group 2. This simple addition to the documentation effort can eliminate subsequent controversy regarding whose blood is involved in which patterns.

Sufficient collection of blood samples is also an important issue. Remember that no single person's efforts help the bloodstain analyst more than those of the serologist. Don't hamstring that effort. Cutting corners while collecting samples at the crime scene may save a few moments, but it will prove costly in the end. Take the time to provide the lab personnel with sufficient samples to do their job.

The authors asked a group of practicing forensic technicians and scientists to comment on methods of collecting bloodstain samples.* We felt we could obtain a consensus of opinion on the "best" method for collection. Unfortunately, there was no true consensus. From organization to organization the methods of collection differed. Some experts believed liquid blood should never be collected from the scene, while others felt it an appropriate response. Some felt scraping dried stains was a good method while others felt swabbing was more effective. Since there is no consensus for the collection of samples, it is imperative that the individual analyst coordinate their specific collection techniques with their own crime laboratory. This will ensure that whatever method is used, it meets the needs of the supporting serology department.

No matter what method is used, collection techniques should preclude cross-contamination and depending upon the advice of the serology department, may need to consider the collection of substrate control and blank control samples. Substrate and blank controls are still considered applicable to DNA analysis, as they allow the serologist to recognize when contamination is present which may interrupt the analysis.

Whatever method is used, it is probably insufficient to collect a single sample from any given pattern. No matter what the size, issues of contamination or simply a degraded sample can result in an inconclusive serology

* The question was posed to the members of the FORENS-L Newsgroup on the Internet.

report. The analyst should collect a fair sampling of stains (a minimum of two or three) from the pattern.

To prevent issues of cross contamination the analyst should exercise specific care in the collection process, following these general guidelines. First, use only new gloves and change gloves between patterns. Don't use standard "crime scene kit" tools for collection. Instead, use either disposable scalpels or single-edge razor blades for scraping, sterile swabs, or disposable pipettes and syringes for collecting liquid samples. **ALWAYS** change the scalpel or pipette when moving from one stain to another.

Once recovered, the analyst must properly containerize the sample. Dried stains are best packages in a druggist's fold, which is then sealed in another wrapping such as an envelope. Don't use the adhesive of the envelope unless forced to and in those instances, wet the adhesive with sterile water. Never lick it! The adhesive alone will not seal the package completely. If the sample subsequently escapes the druggist's fold it may be lost from the envelope as well. Wetting the adhesive with other than water (e.g., saliva) opens opportunities for cross contamination. A preferred method to using the adhesive is to seal the outer container completely with adhesive tape on all openings.

If liquid samples are collected from the scene, the vials or tubes need to be enclosed in a second container. Heat-sealed bags work well for this purpose. Should the tube be breached through spillage or accidental breakage, the heat-sealed bag may preclude the loss and degradation of the sample.

Items stained with blood, such as clothing, should be thoroughly dried. Once dry, individually wrap them in clean butcher paper. Use enough paper to encapsulate the entire item. If possible do not fold the item directly over onto itself. It may be important to determine not only whose blood is on a particular item of clothing, but also where the blood is found on the item. Place an intervening piece of paper between the surfaces when the item is folded. This precludes the possibility of creating inappropriate pattern transfers and eliminates a source of cross contamination if multiple DNA samples are present. Do not simply toss items of clothing into a bag or container and certainly never toss multiple items of clothing into the same container.

Just as the analyst prefers that the actions of those processing the scene will not disturb the physical stains, so too the serologist prefers that the analyst not destroy the samples. The destruction of serology specimens occurs as a result of many factors, several of which the analyst can't control. It only makes sense that we eliminate sources of degraded samples whenever possible. The use of many chemical enhancement methods, which we'll discuss in this chapter, represent a major source for such degradation. Dr. Lee demonstrated that many of these chemicals degrade standard ABO and enzyme serology tests. Although his research is not all-encompassing with regard to their effect on DNA, it certainly indicates a major concern.[1] Never arbitrarily spray enhancement chemical on any item of evidence until after the collection of proper serology specimens. If any questions exist on how to proceed, consult the supporting crime laboratory before acting.

Detection of Blood

At the scene the issue will often arise: What is this stain? Is it blood? Several methods of detection are applicable to the bloodstain pattern analyst. They include presumptive tests and enhancement techniques.

Presumptive Tests

Presumptive testing methods include: Hemastix®, o-tolidine, phenolphthalein, and leucomalachite green. Their function is simply to demonstrate with some level of confidence that the stain in question is worth the efforts of the analyst; if a stain isn't blood it doesn't make much sense to conduct a bloodstain pattern analysis. These detection tools, however, are presumptive; as such, confirmation testing by a serology lab should follow them.

Hemastix® is a simple presumptive test. Designed for hospital use, the item comes prepared as a short stick. The reagent present on the end of the stick is touched to a swab of the stain in question. The analyst then adds a drop of sterile water, and an immediate green color reaction will occur in the presence of blood. Given a sufficient blood sample in the questioned stain, Hemastix® strips work well.

If working with trace amounts of a suspected bloodstain, the other reagent tests are probably best. In these instances the analyst folds a small section of clean filter paper, creating an edge or point. This point is rubbed against the stain or area in question. An alternative approach is to moisten this edge or point with saline solution, particularly in instances of very dry stains, and then rub the moistened area against the stain. The analyst then applies the particular reagent as required.

In the U.S. the orthotolidine test, a derivative test of benzidine, is still in use. It, too, is widely accepted and easily completed.[2] The analyst prepares the mixture of orthotolidine, ethanol, glacial acetic acid, and distilled water. Several drops of the mixture are used, followed by several drops of hydrogen peroxide. A positive test results in an instantaneous blue-green reaction.

Phenolphthalein solution is another standard approach. The analyst requires the active reagent, ethanol, and hydrogen peroxide. After sampling the stain, the filter paper is dampened with a drop of phenolphthalein. The analyst then adds a drop of ethanol, followed by a drop of hydrogen peroxide. An immediate purple-pink color reaction will occur in the presence of blood.

Leucomalachite green acts both as a presumptive test and as an enhancement tool. Used as a presumptive test the reagent includes a mixture of sodium perborate, leucomalachite green, glacial acetic acid, and water. As with the other tests, several drops are applied to the test swab or filter paper, followed by a few drops of hydrogen peroxide. A positive test results in an instantaneous blue-green color.

All of these chemicals may represent health risks. Before using any method, the analyst should seek and receive instruction in their usage from the supporting crime laboratory.

Enhancement Techniques

The specific enhancement techniques we will discuss include Luminol and leucomalachite green. Other enhancement methods available to the analyst include amido black, DAB, and TMB. All of these chemicals allow for better visualization of the bloodstain not only for the bloodstain pattern analyst, but also the fingerprint and toolmark examiner. If lacking experience in the use of these techniques, check with a local crime laboratory. They are likely to have considerable experience in preparing and safely using any of these chemicals.

These chemicals react to peroxidase activity in the heme of the red blood cell.[3] Unfortunately they also react to other peroxidation changes in many substances. These substances include vegetable matter and phosphates present in detergents, bleach, and other common household chemicals. Before accepting the enhancement product, the analyst must consider any enhancement reaction within the context of the entire scene and all evidence.

Luminol enhances our ability to see what are oftentimes invisible traces of blood. In that regard, it is a valuable tool. The overall recipe for a Luminol solution includes sodium perborate, sodium carbonate, 3-aminophthalhydrazide, and distilled water. The ratios for the mixture are, respectively, 0.7, 5, and 0.1 g dissolved in 100 ml of water.[4] Commercially prepared kits are available, but for the sake of economy most crime laboratories create their own.

Luminol reacts to the hemoglobin which is present in the red blood cells.[5] The result is a chemiluminescence, or creation of light, which appears blue-green. This is an important factor to consider: that which the analyst observes is a light source. Obviously, light sources have boundaries which are measurable, but it is unlikely that clear specific boundaries exist (e.g., sufficient to define an individual spatter stain's impact angle). Overall dispersion and general dimensions of patterns and smears will be obvious, beyond that evaluations are speculative.

Since the reaction is light producing, the analyst must observe the area or object of concern in darkness. Outdoors, Luminol works effectively at night; inside the analyst can darken the room by turning off light sources and covering all windows.

Some of the benefits of Luminol include:

- It is applied easily.
- It's noncorrosive and nonstaining.
- It's relatively nondestructive to blood with regard to ABO typing.
- Methods exist to photograph the reaction.[6]

Luminol's disadvantages are:

- It reacts to some metals, vegetable peroxidases, and chemicals including bleach.
- The method demands darkness.
- Interpretations are limited.[7]

The following examples illustrate the possible uses of Luminol:

- Depicting or discovering light smears or wipes present on floors and walls.
- Following bloody trails from the scene of a murder to indicate direction of flight by the murderer.
- Enhancing patterns present on clothing.
- Checking scenes of suspicious disappearances, even years later, for indications of invisible blood traces left by clean-up actions.

Although Luminol reacts to many things, Doug Perkins, a criminalist with the Oklahoma State Bureau of Investigation, offers the advice that with sufficient practice and experimentation the analyst can often identify such false-positive reactions. Perkins looks at three areas when evaluating a Luminol reaction: color, intensity, and duration.[8] He then compares each with his knowledge of the reaction evident in known blood samples.

To this issue, Bevel also feels that Luminol is an outstanding investigative aid; however, it is one which is often misused by those with an insufficient training foundation. Before attempting to use Luminol in a case circumstance, the analyst should experiment with it and become familiar with the ranges possible in the reaction.

Another concern for the analyst is documenting the Luminol reaction. In the late 1980s Gary Reni and Fred Gimeno perfected methods of photographing Luminol reactions. Prior to their efforts, generally all Luminol photographs were exposed in completely darkened rooms. The result was good luminescence but no frame of reference for the viewer. One could not tell exactly where the reaction occurred on the evidence. By using paint-with-flash techniques similar to those used in spelunking and outdoor crime scene photography, Reni and Gimeno produced images which include both the luminescence and the evidence item. Their efforts are documented in two articles published in the *Journal of Forensic Identification*.[9,10]

Ray Clark of the Oklahoma City Police Department uses similar time exposure techniques and a flashlight as a light source to effectively document Luminol reactions. Clark usually starts with a 5-min time exposure, but may expose the negatives for as long as 15 min depending upon the strength of the reaction. At the end of the exposure, Clark uses the paint-with-light technique to add detail of the surrounding scene. This is done with a standard flashlight. The beam is turned on momentarily and reflected off various walls and surfaces surrounding the area in question.* Color Plates 4 through 7 are examples of Luminol photography using this technique. Color Plate 8 is an additional technique developed by the Larimer County Colorado Sheriff's Department, which uses luminous tape and a clear ruler to ensure a scale is evident in the photograph.

Leucomalachite green offers an advantage over Luminol, since it gives a color reaction. The results are observed, measured, and documented more easily than Luminol reactions. It is prepared in a solution and sprayed on the surfaces in question. Stains that react to the solution discolor green, allowing better visualization.

Whenever working with chemical enhancement tools, the analyst must consider proper safeguards. Disposable protective clothing and breathing protection are all necessary when spraying chemicals in any location. Remember: many of these chemicals are carcinogenic or suspected to be carcinogenic.

Bloodstain Pattern Photography

Far too often crime scene photographs of bloodstain evidence is meager, insufficient in detail, and generally lacking. Simply put, photographers shoot from afar never filling their film plane with the image of concern. Unfortunately, most of the analysis process and certainly outside analysis requires detailed photographs. The information in this section is important not only to the bloodstain pattern analyst, but also crime scene technicians and investigators.

---

* Color Plates 4, 5, 6, 7, and 8 follow page 216.

The problem with bloodstain photography is recognizing the level of detail that is necessary. The technicians responsible for the scene photography may not understand the nuances of bloodstain pattern analysis. Unfortunately, their efforts at the scene can easily determine if any conclusion is possible at all. At times they document too much of the wrong thing, or worse yet, far too little of anything.

It's important to understand that not every drop of blood shed needs to be photographed. This approach is both time intensive and expensive. Common sense and good judgment are the best guides in making such determinations. If a stain naturally causes questions in the technician's mind, it may be of importance in the ultimate analysis. If in doubt, however, take a photograph.

We offer the following guidelines as the minimum photography documentation requirements:

- Document the entire scene *in situ*. Include overall photographs.
- Photograph evident pattern transfers, flows, and other fragile patterns early.
- Document all identified pattern groups or stains using evidence establishing shots.
- Take macro photographs of all stains of interest: include a reference scale in each.
- In instances of spatter patterns, where point of origin determinations are made, document some of the individual spatter used in the determination.
- Use Toby Wolson's *Roadmapping* method or a similar procedure.[11]

Documenting the scene is important no matter what the nature of the crime. Whether bloodstains are involved or not, the crime scene technician should photograph the scene immediately upon arrival. As a general rule these photographs include overall or 360° photos of each room to include the ceiling and floor. The technician, using a wide-angle lens (e.g., 28-mm), shoots across the room from each of the four corners or from any other configuration that captures the condition of the entire scene. All photographs of this nature should have some level of overlap with the next photograph.

Overall photos serve little function in the courtroom. The wide-angle lens causes obvious perspective distortion. Nevertheless, these photos are immensely helpful to the analyst and investigator, particularly when trying to verify where some item was at the time the processing began. As every crime scene technician knows, a primary goal is to document the scene as found and eliminate the destruction, addition, loss, or movement of items within the scene.

Figure 129   An overall photograph which establishes the presence of an arterial spurt intermixed with other stains on a bathroom wall. The specific stain of interest is evident, but not clear in this photograph. The photo, however, shows the stain in question with regard to the rest of the scene and will use an intermediate landmark (the large smeared area) to help orient the location of the stain in question. (See Figure 130.) (Photograph courtesy of Tom J. Griffin, Bruce Goodman, and Ken VanCleave, Louisville Colorado Police Dept.)

Questions regarding such actions will arise. Was the Styrofoam cup present originally, or was it added by the Chief? Was the bloody smudge on the wall caused by Officer Smith or the suspect? Was the chair in that corner, or by the table? Overall photos help eliminate some of this confusion, which can plague the analysis or reconstruction attempt.

After taking the 360° or overall photos, the technician takes an evidence establishing shot and close-ups of all obvious items of evidence. Establishing shots serve the function of identifying where in the scene a particular item is and any relationships it may have to other items of evidence. For example, Figures 129 through 131 take the viewer from an overall perspective to a close-up view of the evidence of concern. In the end, the viewer realizes where the arterial spurt in question is in relationship to the bathroom wall. Again, this process should be done upon arrival. The photographer carefully moves through the scene, documenting the condition of all obvious items of evidence before anyone can disturb them.

As the analyst continues to process the scene using a standard processing model, photographs are made of all newly discovered evidence. The analyst can also take more controlled close-up photos as the item is actually collected. This helps document the item's complete condition.

Having discussed the general requirements for photography, let's turn our attention to the specifics of photographing bloodstains. Pattern transfers

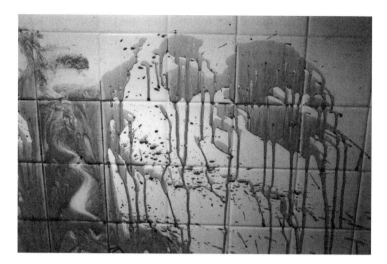

Figure 130 An evidence establishing shot. This photograph shows a closer view of the bathroom wall using the large wipe and swipe as a landmark. The viewer of the photograph can also see more clearly the location of the arterial spurt to the right of the smeared area, but not in sufficient detail. An evidence close-up photograph is still necessary. (See Figure 131.) (Photograph courtesy of Tom J. Griffin, Bruce Goodman, and Ken VanCleave, Louisville Colorado Police Dept.)

Figure 131 An evidence close-up photograph without a scale. Individual stains present in the arterial spurt are now much clearer. Directionality of the stains is evident, and given a scale, measurements could be made and impact angles computed. Additionally the closer view allows us to see the small remnants of air bubbles in the stains, an important feature which indicates the arterial spurt originated from a lung or airway injury. (Photograph courtesy of Tom J. Griffin, Bruce Goodman, and Ken VanCleave, Louisville Colorado Police Dept.)

in the scene and flow patterns are perhaps the most likely stains to fall into a "fragile" evidence category. Actions in the scene during processing can mar or obliterate them completely. Document these stains as soon as possible with close-up photography. Afterwards take any and all steps to protect the pattern from physical damage.

If the analyst follows our previous documentation advice, then all major pattern groups in the scene will have some identifiable number or letter. The next step of photography is to document these major patterns. The photographs should include an evidence-establishing shot. This photograph has some identifying marker so that similar-looking patterns can be distinguished from each other. The establishing photo clearly places the item or pattern in relation to some other identifiable object in the scene. In dealing with small spatter stains and other small bloodstains, it may be necessary to use several establishing shots — each successively closer to the stain. Without this photo, patterns lose relevance particularly when viewed by others later on in the investigation. Consider Figures 132 and 133. Without the establishing shot (Figure 132) the evidence close-up photograph (Figure 133) tells the viewer little with regard to where in the scene the item actually is. The same is certainly true for close-up photographs exposed after collection of the evidence. The pattern evident in Figure 134 means little to the viewer without the accompanying photograph, Figure 135, that shows its location on the murder weapon.

The next step is to photograph the individual stains of interest. This means taking macro photographs in which the film frame is filled with the detail present in the stain. Pattern transfers or swipes and wipes are all examples of stains which might be of interest.

Macro photographs or evidence close-up photographs are taken with the lens inches away from the stain, not feet away. The close-up photograph of a pattern should have as much detail as possible, while still including the entire pattern. Camera orientation is critical in the close-up. Forget the fashion photography technique where the camera is shot at every conceivable angle. Place the film plane parallel with the plane you are photographing. Once that's done, fill the viewfinder with the subject. Both of these concerns are imperative if the analyst wants clear, undistorted images of the patterns and stains.

If the scene involves spatter patterns and point of origin (PO) determinations are necessary, then photograph some of the individual stains used to make that determination. Again, this photo is taken with the lens inches away from the individual stain. Using this photograph, another analyst can measure the stain and verify its impact angle. This will effectively preclude any major challenge to the PO determination.

Evidence close-up photographs should be exposed both with and without a scale of reference in the photographs. When using the scale (e.g., when

Figure 132 Another example of an establishing shot. In this instance we can read the label of the stain in question (Stain 3A) and we see its position near the door above the table.

documenting spatter or droplets) it's best to align this scale along the length and width of the stain. This makes it easier to verify the dimensions from the photograph. To this end, Gardner developed the bloodstain photographic template. (See Figures 133, 136 and 137.)

The template has scales along two axes and a reference section that allows the analyst to identify each stain. A box is provided to align the template with either "North" or "Up", which is necessary if the analyst chooses to align the template scale with the droplet's axis. These templates work well in conjunction with the roadmapping method.

Roadmapping is the most effective method of completing photography documentation of bloodstains. It developed out of the efforts of Toby Wolson, a criminalist with the Metro-Dade Police Department, Miami, Florida. Although effective, it's also intrusive. To properly map the scene, the analyst must insert many "road signs" and scales for reference. For this reason, the analyst usually waits until the completion of the scene processing to complete this roadmap. Roadmapping is effective for documenting both still and video images.

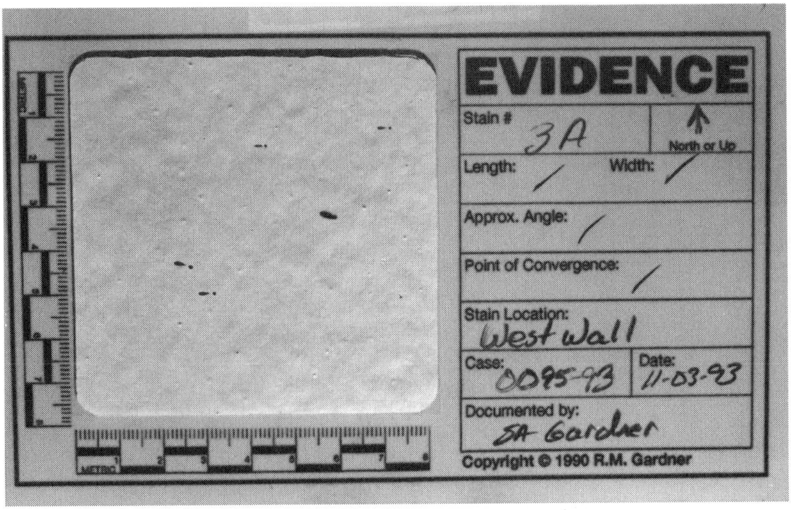

Figure 133   A close-up photograph of the stain in Figure 132. Once again, without the accompanying establishing photograph, it is difficult for the viewer to understand this spatter's relationship to the scene.

When using Roadmapping, each major stain group is identified with a label, either a letter or number (e.g., Stain Group A). (See Figures 136 and 138.) Individual stains or smaller patterns of interest within this larger pattern are given an additional identifier such a A-1 or A-2. Labels are taped or placed by each stain, using large lettering that allows them to be read from several feet away.

Adjacent to the pattern, the analyst introduces large reference scales to the surface involved. These scales are commercially available from forensic sources. For instance, on a wall the analyst places them along the side of the wall and above or below the stains. If possible, the pattern should be outlined by the scales.

Once in place, the analyst photographs the overall surface including the scales. The stain labels should be readable in these shots. The analyst then moves in and photographs the individual patterns. Finally, the individual stains of interest within the patterns are photographed. In any given photograph, the scales and labels should make it evident where on the wall or surface the analyst is looking. These labels are the "signs" on our roadmap. They preclude us from being lost. (See Figure 139.) To be effective, each photo should include at a minimum the individual stain label. Establishing shots are more effective if they show several of the surrounding labels. Figures 140 and 141 document the spatter observed in Figure 139, using the Roadmapping method.

Figure 134 An interesting pattern resulting from a beating death. The scale indicates the size of the stains, but where were they found and what relationship to the scene do they hold? Without the accompanying photograph, Figure 135, the viewer has little with which to judge the significance of the pattern. (Photograph courtesy of Donald R. Schuessler, Eugene, Oregon Department of Public Safety.)

The analyst can also use graphic tape in addition to these labels to show indications of motions in swipes or wipes, or to show points of convergence of spatter and other information that they felt is important. Figures 142 and 143 are examples of the inclusion of graphic tape in the roadmapping process.

We cannot overemphasize how effective this method is for conducting subsequent analysis. Too often, the relationship of one stain to another is anything but evident in crime scene photographs. Roadmapping takes the viewer from an overall view, to the pattern, then to the individual stains. Every photo graphically exhibits its relationship to other stains. It eliminates much of the viewer's confusion and also makes for outstanding case documentation. Roadmapping works not only for the scene but for later documentation of individual items of evidence. For instance, Figures 144 through 146 show documentation of a bloodstained shirt using this method.

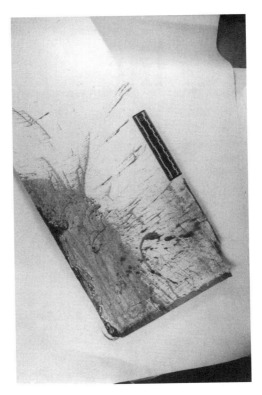

Figure 135 An establishing shot for the pattern in Figure 134. We now recognize the pattern as being present on the murder weapon, a shelf from a kitchen cabinet. The weapon was used to inflict blunt trauma to the head of the victim. (Photograph courtesy of Donald R. Schuessler, Eugene, Oregon Department of Public Safety.)

Another method used for photographic documentation of small spatter stains is the introduction of hole reinforcements into the picture. After making standard evidence establishing and evidence close-up photographs, self-adhesive reinforcements are placed around individual spatter. Then another evidence close-up photo is taken. The reinforcements make each stain more obvious in the photograph. (See Figure 147.)

As a final consideration in still photography, the analyst can't always count on the photos coming out. Mistakes occur and accidents do happen. For that reason an instant camera on scene is also beneficial. Specific stains of obvious interest are documented with the instant camera before leaving the scene. This precludes the possibility of not having **ANY** photos of a critical stain. Instant photography cannot replace 35 mm or large format film photography, but it does supplement it. Figure 148 is an example of a stain documented using an instant camera that comes with an easy to use 1:1 copy stand.

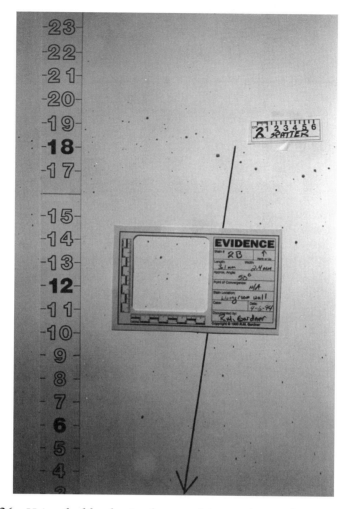

Figure 136 Using the bloodstain photographic template to document evidence. In this instance the photograph is that of an intermediate establishing shot. When used to shoot evidence close-up photographs, such as Figure 137, the template is a subtle reminder to the analyst to fill the frame of the lens with the image. It also allows for administrative data to be included in the photo with the stain.

Our consideration of photography is also incomplete without discussing video. The video camera can be extremely useful in documenting a blood-stained scene. It serves as a functional method for documenting the scene *in situ*. A quick nonintrusive walk-through of the scene can be invaluable later when the analyst is trying to verify the original condition of the scene. In combination with the initial scene photographs, video often clears up specific concerns regarding scene integrity issues.

EVIDENCE

Stain # 2B   ↑ North or Up

Length: 3.1 mm   Width: 2.4 mm

Approx. Angle: 50°

Point of Convergence: N/A

Stain Location: Living room wall

Case: Date: 4-6-94

Documented by: R.M. Gardner

Copyright © 1990 R.M. Gardner

Figure 137 A close-up photograph of the spatter from Figure 136. In this instance we include measurements of an individual spatter stain, which was circled, and indicate its apparent impact angle.

Figure 138 The roadmapping technique. In this instance we have an intermediate evidence-establishing shot, the intent of which is to show the relationship of stains D, E, and F to each other. The large yellow scale lets the viewer know that the stains are some 36 in. from a wall or similar juncture. Of course, this photograph would also require an accompanying photograph which would show the stains and scale at a greater distance and in relationship to the overall scene.

Figure 139   The typical close-up photograph found in most documentation files. Although the analyst should expose photos without a scale of reference, such photos by themselves do little to define the scene or identify the stain in question. In this instance we have a spatter pattern, but no evident landmark. The viewer is in effect "lost" in the scene with no means by which to associate the picture to its origin. (Photograph courtesy of Toby Wolson, M.S., Metro Dade Police Department, Miami, Florida.)

After completing the scene processing the video camera is also effective for overall documentation purposes. Using Toby Wolson's roadmapping techniques, the scales and "signs" are already in place. The analyst merely "walks" the viewer through the scene, showing the relationship of the specific stains to other items of interest. Combined with the roadmapping process, this video can bring immense clarity to the situation. It provides the viewer a far better context in which to consider the scene. The use of video in analysis has a bright future. There are current software packages available which allow the capture of video images of spatter to be introduced and evaluated by computer. These programs allow the analyst to obtain measurements and impact angles from the video image alone.

One caution is appropriate to video camera usage at the scene. During the video taping, the analyst should limit narration to a description of the stains observed. Pursuing the "analysis" too soon in a taped medium may come back to haunt the analyst at a later date.

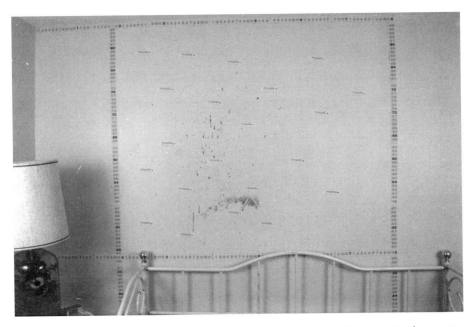

Figure 140   A Roadmapping example. Using the stain in Figure 139, this series demonstrates the function and utility of roadmapping. In this photo, the photographer provides us with an overall perspective which includes scales of reference, furniture items, and roadmap labels. Although perhaps difficult to read in this reproduction, the individual stain labels are readable. In this type of situation, a second or intermediate establishing shot would be helpful. (Photograph courtesy of Toby Wolson, M.S., Metro Dade Police Department. From *J. Forensic Identification*, Vol. 45, No. 4, Aug. 95.)

Scene and Pattern Sketches

Crime scene sketches are and will remain an integral part of scene documentation. They allow the viewer to "see" the relationship of where items of evidence were, where certain actions occurred, and help the trier of fact to understand the overall circumstances of the crime.

All major stain patterns should be included in the crime scene sketch. They allow an individual who has never visited the scene to see relationships of one stain to another or correlate a stain to its physical surroundings. The level of detail necessary for bloodstains in a sketch is entirely dependent upon the needs and desires of the analyst. We feel that all major patterns should be addressed in some fashion. This may only require the inclusion of the pattern label (e.g., Stain A) at the general location in which the pattern was found. This concept does not preclude the analyst from sketching any stain of significance into the drawing itself.

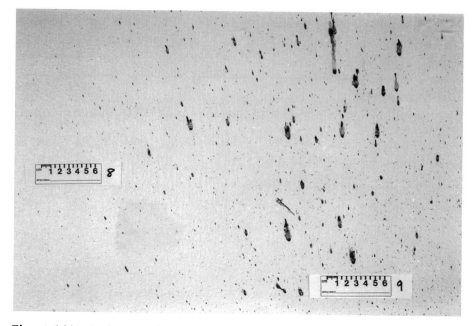

Figure 141 A close-up photograph of the spatter in Figure 139. Using the two labels (numbers 8 and 9) in conjunction with Figure 140, the viewer is able to recognize where in the scene the spatter is actually located. Roadmapping as a method moves the viewer from an overall perspective to the pattern, and then to the detail of the individual stains of concern. (Photograph courtesy of Toby Wolson, M.S., Metro-Dade Police Department. From *J. Forensic Identification*, Vol. 45, No. 4, Aug. 95.)

Oftentimes when considering a bloodstained scene a cross projection sketch is necessary to fully document the scene. In the cross projection sketch, the analyst simply "lays" the surrounding walls down and appropriate stains and evidence are drawn onto them. This serves the function of relating one stain pattern to the location of another. (See Figure 149.)

As indicated, the analyst may choose to include only the labels of the stains present in the overall crime scene sketch. To provide greater detail, in addition to photographs the analyst may wish to create individual sketches of stains of importance. Such sketches can include freehand drawings of patterns, patterns on clothing, or tracings of a given pattern.

Freehand drawings may or may not be to scale, depending upon the needs of the analyst. The analyst should highlight all observable characteristics evident. *In situ* evaluations are truly the best evaluation circumstance, while making the sketch the analyst may see detail that is not discernible in the crime scene photographs. For this reason Epstein favors the use of detailed drawings when evaluating clothing. He feels this forces the analyst to look

Plate 1 Despite an extremely rough and irregular surface, this photograph demonstrates that the analyst can still determine directionality. Small, satellite spatter and spines are visible in this stain indicating directionality from left to right.

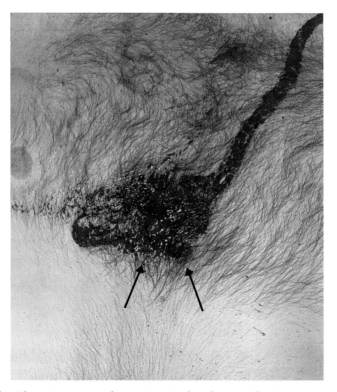

Plate 2 The victim was shot twice in the chest with a 9-mm automatic pistol as he lay on his back in bed. The two wounds to the chest are extremely close together (the arrows point to the wounds). Based on the subject's statement, a minute or less elapsed between the first and second shot.

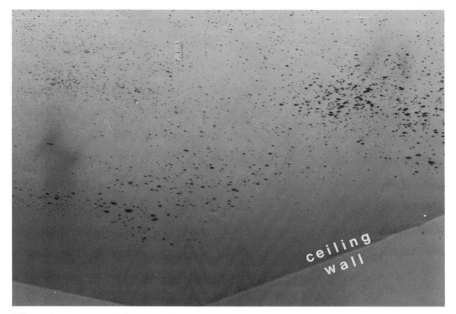

Plate 3   View of the ceiling above the victim shown in Plate 2. The ceiling was 6 feet from the point where the subject lay facing it. This entire pattern is the result of an abnormal backspatter condition. What occurred is a pooling of blood in the first wound track, which was subsequently compressed by the second shot. The compression projected the blood onto the ceiling, causing a pattern well in excess of the volume, size, and distribution expected in backspatter. This type of pattern cannot occur without both the volume of blood present in the wound track and the compression/projection action caused by a second shot.

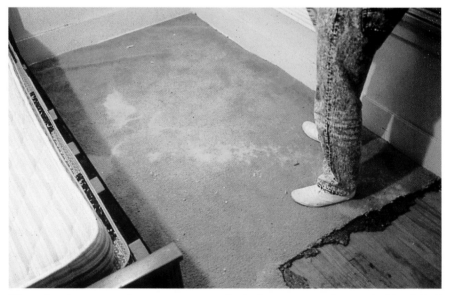

Plate 4   A suspected crime scene in which there was evidence of a bloodshed event, but there were also indications the subject had cleaned the area. The victim, at this point in the investigation, had not been found. This is a standard view of the scene prior to the application of Luminol. (Photo courtesy of Ray Clark, Oklahoma City Police Department.)

Plate 5 The scene in Plate 4 following the application of Luminol. The blue-green luminescence shows various stains including wipes, swipes, smears, a drag mark, blood trails, and spatter. (Photo courtesy of Ray Clark, Oklahoma City Police Department.)

Plate 6 (Left) The back stairs of the same crime scene. This drag mark was not evident in any fashion without the application of Luminol. These photographs were taken in the dark while a flashlight beam was bounced off the surrounding surfaces for several seconds. As a result, the photograph shows both good luminescence and scene detail. (Photo courtesy of Ray Clark, Oklahoma City Police Department.)

Plate 7 (Right) Another shot from inside the scene. Only the large pool of blood was evident without Luminol. Following Luminol application, several additional stains on the carpet and the wipe mark on the wall, which was caused by clean-up efforts of the subject. (Photo courtesy of Ray Clark, Oklahoma City Police Department.)

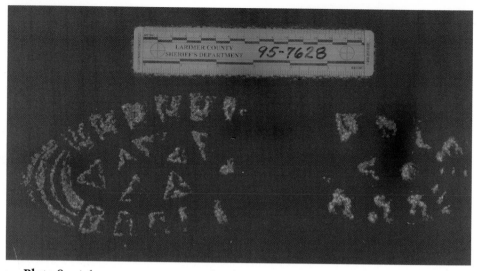

Plate 8 A footwear pattern transfer photographed using another lighting technique and Luminol. In this method, luminescent tape was applied to the back of a clear plastic ruler. Following application of Luminol to the scene, the ruler was inserted giving a visible scale of reference. (Photo courtesy of T. Daniel Gilliam, Larimer County Sheriff's Department.)

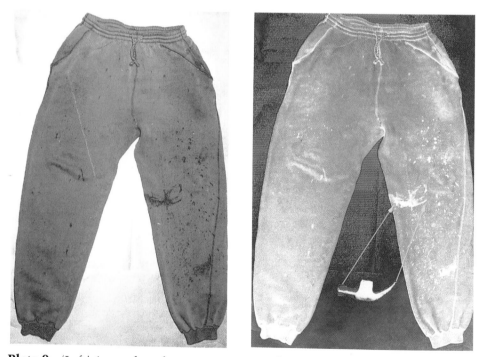

Plate 9 (Left) An unaltered computer-generated image from a photograph of a pair of bloodstained pants. Although the spatter is evident, the dark-colored blood on the blue background makes viewing difficult. (Photo courtesy of Norman Reeves.)

Plate 10 (Right) An enhanced image of the same photograph in which the analyst inverted the colors. The blue background becomes red and the dark bloodstains become white. This increased contrast allows for a more in-depth examination. The analyst further superimposed a weapon into the photograph. This allows viewers to make a general visual comparison between the two.

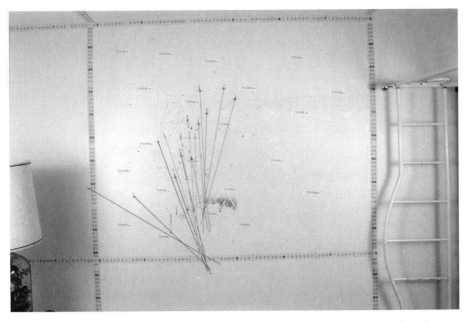

Figure 142   A continuation of the roadmapping method. This time the photographer introduces graphic tape to show a point of convergence for the spatter involved. For clarity, the bed was removed and set aside. (Photograph courtesy of Toby Wolson, M.S., Metro-Dade Police Department, Miami, FL.)

more closely at the evidence.[12] In whatever fashion they are used, the freehand sketches becomes an integral part of the analyst's crime scene notes.

Another method of sketching is the tracing of patterns. The analyst simply tapes tracing paper or an acetate sheet over the stain or pattern in question and traces its characteristics. This allows the analyst a method of creating full-size reproductions, which may be of some use. Unfortunately, depending upon the nature of the pattern, tracings can be very time consuming.

Written Reports

Photographs, sketches, and video tapes certainly enhance our overall understanding of the crime scene, but written reports are the foundation of investigative documentation. For that reason we should not approach the written report in a haphazard manner. The written report is the means by which analysts share much of their knowledge. It should be complete, methodical, and as objective as possible.

The first consideration in the written report should be to describe the information which serves as its basis. The analyst should describe the evidence

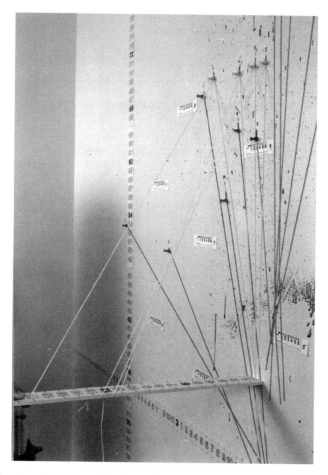

Figure 143 Another example of roadmapping combined with the "stringing" method. This combination allows the viewer to see the likely point of convergence as indicated by the graphic tape, while the stringing indicates the probable point of origin. (Photograph courtesy of Toby Wolson, M.S., Metro-Dade Police Department, Miami, FL.)

that was reviewed and what actions were performed in support of the report. If all observations were made from photographs, the report should state this. If one section of the report is based on photographs and a subsequent section on photographs and on-scene evaluation, the analyst must make this clear. Consider the following example:

> Using photographs provided by S.A. Jones, I conducted an evaluation of bloodstains present at the scene of a rape/attempted homicide. Additionally, a review was made of all crime scene reports and crime scene sketches.

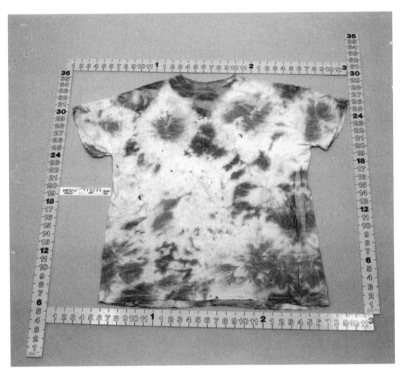

Figure 144 Roadmapping is just as effective for documenting items of evidence after collection. In this instance we have an initial photograph of the overall item, framed by the large scales. (Photograph courtesy of Toby Wolson, M.S., Metro-Dade Police Department. From *J. Forensic Identification*, Vol. 45, No. 4, Aug. 95.)

Each major pattern or stain group is then discussed in the an orderly fashion (e.g., either by numerical order, or perhaps in order of significance). This discussion begins with a complete description, which may or may not include a categorization of the stain in question. For example:

> **Stain Group # 1:** This is a spatter pattern present on the wall adjacent to the headboard.

This categorization is not speculative in any nature. For instance, one would not want to categorize such a pattern as expiratory blood vs. an impact spatter pattern; this is best suited for the conclusion. The pattern should then be described in detail, as in the following:

> The pattern is a spatter pattern, the majority of the stains are circular in nature with very few elliptical droplets. The pattern fits the category of a medium-velocity stain (e.g., spatter stains between 1 to 4 mm in diameter). The majority of spatter present in the pattern are actually under 2 mm in size.

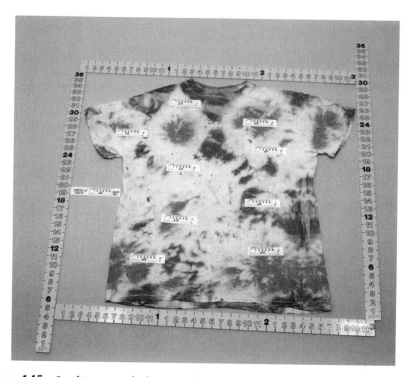

Figure 145 In this second photograph of the shirt, an establishing shot, labels are introduced to identify specific stained areas present on the clothing. (Photograph courtesy of Toby Wolson, M.S., Metro-Dade Police Department. From *J. Forensic Identification*, Vol. 45, No. 4, Aug. 95.)

This pattern is slightly offset on the wall above the single bed and slightly left of a large saturation stain on the bedding. The pattern's overall dimensions are 2 ft by 3 ft. The pattern begins at the level of the mattress and extends up the wall for approximately 2 ft. The pattern extends outward and left along the wall for a distance of 1 ft from the left edge of the headboard. The pattern extends across the wall to the right for another 2 ft.

Based upon documentation provided, no specific point of origin recreations are possible. Nor is any specific radiating effect evident in the photograph.

There are no indications of cast-off patterns associated with the pattern.

There are generally two approaches as to where in the report the analyst should present conclusions. Judy Bunker feels the conclusions should be presented at the end of the report in a conglomerate fashion. Using this method, she saves all major conclusions to the end of the report and does not include them with the description of the stains. The following is an example of a conclusion sheet from Ms. Bunker's advanced course:

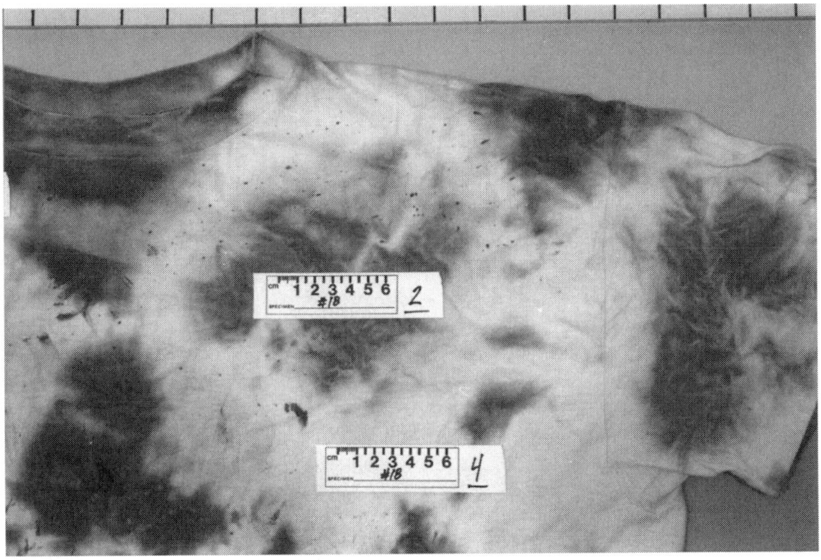

Figure 146 An evidence close-up photograph of Stains 2 and 4 on the shirt. By referring back to Figures 144 and 145 the viewer could easily determine the stain locations even if the shirt collar was not evident in the photo. (Photograph courtesy of Toby Wolson, M.S., Metro Dade Police Department. From *J. Forensic Identification*, Vol. 45, No. 4, Aug. 95.)

Stain #	Conclusion
1	Forceful bloodshed occurred near the east wall of the bedroom and within 26 in. of the floor.
2	Cast-off stain patterns seen on the ceiling describe an object wet with blood being swung in a right overhand fashion. These patterns correspond to the forceful incident described in #1.
3	The subject was upright and in a seated position when blood flowed from her head wounds.
4	The subject was repositioned face down following the infliction of wounds to her head.[13]

Another approach is to simply include a brief conclusion regarding the individual stains after the description. For example, with regard to our Stain Group # 1 such a conclusion might read as:

The spatter pattern on the wall is consistent with an impact which occurred in the vicinity of the bed mattress. The small size of the stains suggest a strong forceful impact. No other correlations are possible at this time.

Obviously, such conclusions should be limited to what that particular stain details for us. Correlation of one stain to another and conclusions drawn

Figure 147   The use of self-adhesive hole reinforcements in a crime scene photograph. The reinforcements highlight the specific locations of very small spatter present on the floor. In instances of small spatter (e.g., gunshot spatter, expiratory blood) the hole reinforcements make it easier to locate the position of the spatter in the photograph.

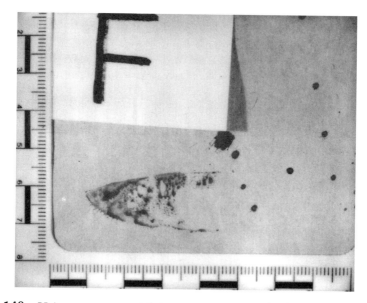

Figure 148   Using a commercial instant camera with the manufacturer's 1:1 copy stand, quality close-up photography is possible. Although these cameras can't replace 35 mm or larger format cameras, they do ensure that the analyst leaves the scene with all critical stains documented in some fashion.

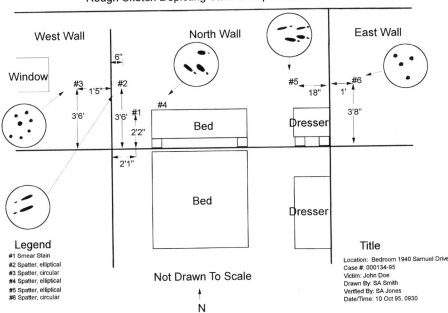

Figure 149 The cross projection sketch. A cross projection sketch allows the viewer to consider evidence present on various surfaces in the scene. For example, Stain Groups 2 and 3 based upon their position indicate a common source as to their origin. This relationship might not be immediately evident to anyone reading the report without the cross projection sketch.

from them should be presented somewhat as Ms. Bunker describes — either as a final concluding statement or in the body of the reconstruction itself.

The written report should give the reader a clear picture of what the analyst observed. Always seek to define specific characteristics that are evident in the stain. Ensure these characteristics are included in the report. The following are more examples of how one might document a stain. We have underlined some of the detail which we feel comprises these specific observable characteristics. Without this type of detail it is difficult for an analyst to support "why" they reach the conclusions they do.

A Spatter Pattern Description/Conclusion

Stain Group 2: This is a spatter pattern present on a nightstand adjacent to the left side of the bed.

The pattern is impact spatter, <u>the largest of which is 5 mm in length.</u> <u>Smaller spatter measure down to the 1.5 to 2 mm</u> range with other smaller spatter present, but too small to measure based on photos alone. Most of the spatter are <u>circular stains on standing articles on the nightstand</u> (e.g., a pitcher, cloth, and bottle). <u>The number of stains is in excess of 100</u>. Those present on the upper surface of the nightstand itself are <u>elliptical and struck the surface at extreme acute angles</u>.

A <u>void/demarcation line is evident</u> in the stain group. This void is evident on a plastic cup behind the pitcher and is also present in the elliptical stains on the upper surface of the nightstand.

Something at the point of the pitcher, either while present on the bed or nightstand, precluded spatter from occurring on the remaining items.

Directionality of the elliptical stains places the origin in the vicinity of the large stained area on the bedding.

Extending the directionality of several of the elliptical stains on the nightstand, a point of convergence in two-dimensional space would be approximately 16 to 18 in. to the right of the bed mattress edge. Once again, this correlates with the observed saturation stain area on the bed mattress.

A Blood Pool Description/Conclusion

Stain Group #3: This is a large liquid pool present on the floor near the entrance of the cubicle in the room.

Although <u>not pure in origin</u> (e.g., not all blood) it represents a flow of some nature. The stain is diluted, but the nature of the dilution is not immediately evident.

<u>Lower sections of the stain show spines</u>, indicating the application of force to the liquid. There is little to indicate the nature of this force itself.

The <u>upper right-hand section suggests linear features which may be more spines</u>. Within the lightest section of the stain (in the central area) is a <u>threefold linear marking</u>.

This stain is not disturbed except for the spines discussed on the edge which faces the bathroom. There are no foot or shoe marks in the stain and the general boundaries are intact.

The blood present within the stain is not the result of drops impacting, either as venous bleeding or spatter. No indication of drips or drip pattern satellites are evident around the stain. The pool received several forceful impacts of some nature, causing the spines. The pool was undisturbed on the side nearest the bathroom, meaning it was deposited then no further action occurred to that side.

A Pattern Transfer Description/Conclusion

Stain Group #7: This group includes numerous pattern transfers on the pillow case. The entire pillow case is saturated with blood, making many patterns marred or blurred to the point that they are of no value.

Within the outer boundary areas of the saturation, however, there are <u>double linear markings</u>. Some of the markings are very short, while others extend for a distance of <u>up to 3 cm</u>.

Three general widths are apparent between these double linear bound-aries: 4.6 mm, 19.7 mm, and 32.5 mm. These measurements were derived from Xerox copies of the stains, in which a 7% enlargement factor was determined and added.

On the pillow case there are one (1) set of lines which closely match the 32.5 width, two (2) sets of lines which match the 19.7 mm width, and five (5) sets of lines which match the 4.6 mm width. These markings suggest a bloody object(s) came in contact with the pillow case. The manner of these sets of stains indicates a random applica-tion of the object(s) to the pillow case. There are many more linear features present on the pillow case, but none provide specific characteristics beyond indicating an object with a bloody edge was in contact with the pillow case.

There was one additional stain of interest, which lacked further iden-tifying characteristics. The stain is a pattern transfer with a curved feature, perhaps a dual boundary. The curve is not typical of any objects evident in the scene (e.g., a bottle) The nature is insufficient for further identification without a specific object to compare it with.

A Mixed Pattern Description/Conclusion

Stain Group #8: This group consists of a saturation stain on the upper sheet of the bedding. It includes pattern transfers evident to the left of the satu-ration stain and spatter evident to the right.

The pattern transfers are linear with dual boundaries indicated, similar to those found on the pillow case. The linear stains range from a few mm in length to 11 cm. The application appears less random than that found on the pillow case, with the majority of the lines angling downward from the saturation stain at about a 30 to 40° angle.

The patterns exhibit the same measurements as those on the pillow case. There are two (2) sets of lines which match with the 4.6 mm width, and one (1) set of lines which match with the 32.5 mm width. Impact spatter is evident throughout this stain, directionality for these limited stains is difficult to determine due to the cotton material.

The spatter evident to the right of the saturation stain is comprised of an area of 8 in. × 3 in. The spatter is much heavier here. The spatter range is 0.2 mm to 2.4 mm. The definition evident in the stain and radiating effect evident in the spatter point to a single action as the source of this stain. The force which created this stain projected the droplets at about a 45° angle down and out from the top edge of the sheet.

The same object which came in contact with the pillow case also came in contact with the sheet. In doing so it was better defined (e.g., length at least 11 cm).

The nature of the conclusions and the level of certainty described in the body of the report are always a major concern. As Ms. Bunker makes the point, "This is a report which will be examined, reexamined, and dissected by others."[14] If you are not confident you can support your findings then do not include them. To support the findings, the analyst must describe every important characteristic evident at the scene.

Summary

Documentation of bloodstains at the scene is truly an important function. Without quality documentation, the analyst may doom any subsequent analysis to failure.

Documentation considerations include the proper collection and preservation of evidence. This demands the analyst understand the needs and desires of the serologist. It also requires an understanding of the chemical detection and enhancement procedures available, to include their limitations.

Graphical documentation in the form of sketches and photographs are equally important. They must clearly show stain detail and define where in the scene the stain was. Without this detail, the analyst is limited in their conclusions. Without knowing where in the scene the stain was, it is difficult at best to make any rational decision about the overall reconstruction. Written documentation is the true backbone of the overall documentation effort. In Chapter 10 we'll provide the analyst with a format for documenting a "reconstruction", but the scene documentation itself must be clear, concise, and detailed. Full descriptions of what the analyst observed are imperative. Each stain should be fully described in a logical order that leads the reader through the scene.

No matter how well intentioned an investigation may be, in the end it will likely be judged on the analyst's documentation. The analyst's efforts at documentation cannot be haphazard.

References

1. Lee, Henry C., et al. The Effect of Presumptive Test, Latent Fingerprint and Other Reagents and Materials on Subsequent Serological Identification, Genetic Marker and DNA Testing in Bloodstains, *J. Forensic Identification*, Vol. 39, No. 6, Nov.-Dec. 1989, pp. 339-358.

2. Svensson, Arne, Wendel, Otto, and Fisher, Barry A.J., *Techniques of Crime Scene Investigation, 3rd ed.*, Elsevier, New York, pg. 173.

3. Sahs, Paul T., DAB: An Advancement in Blood Print Detection, *J. Forensic Identification*, Vol. 42, No. 5, Sept.–Oct. 1992, pg. 412.

4. Anon., *Blood Detection*, document provided by the Rocky Mountain Association of Bloodstain Pattern Analysts, 1988.

5. Gimeno, Fred E. and Rini, Gary A., Fill Flash Photo Luminescence to Photograph Luminol Bloodstain Patterns, *J. Forensic Identification*, Vol. 39, No. 3, 1989, pg. 149.

6. Hetzel, Richard L., Luminol As An Investigative Tool, *The Detective*, Fall, 1990.

7. Ibid.

8. Perkins, Doug, Personal communications, 1995.

9. Gimeno, Fred E. and Rini, Gary A., Fill Flash Photo Luminescence to Photograph Luminol Bloodstain Patterns, *J. Forensic Identification*, Vol. 39, No. 3, 1989.

10. Gimeno, Fred E. and Rini, Gary A., Fill Flash Color Photography to Photograph Luminol Bloodstain Patterns, *J. Forensic Identification*, Vol. 39, No. 5, 1989.

11. Wolson, Toby L., Bloodstain Pattern Documentation Workshop, presentation to the Int. Assoc. Bloodstain Pattern Analysts, Colorado Springs, CO, Sept. 26, 1992.

12. Epstein, Barton P., Examination of Bloody Clothing, presentation to the Int. Assoc. Bloodstain Pattern Analysts, Colorado Springs, CO, Sept. 25, 1992.

13. Bunker, Judy, Documenting and Reconstructing Blood Scenes, Presentation to the Rocky Mountain Association of Bloodstain Pattern Analysts, Advanced Bloodstain Pattern course, Jefferson County, CO, Apr. 22, 1991.

14. Ibid.

Documenting the Reconstruction of a Crime

10

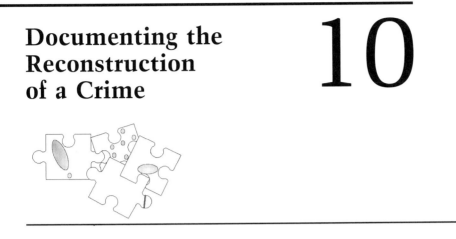

Just as the documentation of bloodstain patterns requires specific effort, a reconstruction report requires a similar level of effort from the analyst. For purposes of the reconstruction report, however, there is a twofold problem. First, the reconstruction is a compilation of information from various sources and reports. It is not based on a single individual's efforts. The analyst must have a thorough understanding of these reports and must interrelate specific facts from all of them in order to reach a reconstruction conclusion. Second, the reconstruction derives its actual form through a reasoning and logic process; a reconstruction is very much a mental product. Unlike physical evidence, it is often far more difficult to point to its subtleties. For this reason it is easy for the analyst to lose focus and often difficult for others to grasp the analyst's underlying decision-making process.

In this chapter we will present several methods for preparing the crime scene reconstruction report and provide guidelines to consider when developing and executing experiments and recreations in support of a reconstruction attempt.

The Reconstruction Report

In effect the reconstruction is a word puzzle derived from the total investigative report. This puzzle is unraveled in the mind of the analyst and then put to paper. For anyone else to believe its final form and conclusion, they must be confident they understand "how" the analyst arrived at the individual reconstruction decisions for the conclusion.

Far too often in investigative reports, this final form is a simple statement such as:

> Smith raped Jones at knife point, resulting in two stab wounds. At the conclusion of the assault Smith then shot Jones while she was lying on the floor.

Although such a concluding statement may well be accurate, it leaves the reader sorting through every document related to the report in order to try and understand "how" the investigator reached that particular conclusion.

Even after reviewing all of the related documents, the "how" is not always evident. Reasoning is an individual mental process. We can never be confident that one reader will see the same significance in each piece of information or put the same bits and pieces together in the same manner. In some fashion the reconstruction report must elaborate on the analyst's reasoning and lead the reader step by step through that process. Only then can the readers of the report properly evaluate the conclusion and determine if they agree or disagree.

Certainly if they disagree with a report of this latter nature, both parties can then point to specific issues and recognize at what point their opinions diverge. What should not occur, although it often does, is an off the cuff dismissal of an opinion regarding some event segment. If two forensic experts are viewing the same evidence, then there is little rationale for completely polarized viewpoints.

The discussions in this chapter are applicable either to bloodstain pattern evaluations or generic reconstruction of crimes. Remember, any bloodstain pattern analysis conclusion is in fact a limited crime scene reconstruction. This is true because the bloodstain pattern analysis conclusion seeks to:

- Define specific actions that caused certain stains.
- Sequence those actions and events.
- Consider whose blood is involved, which will hopefully identify who took the action.

For this reason the analyst should present each bloodstain pattern analysis conclusion in the same format as a crime scene reconstruction report.

Our discussion of Event Analysis in Chapter 2 provides a format for preparing this conclusion. The crime reconstruction report, however, considers more than just the blood evidence in determining these conclusions; it must incorporate all of the forensic information in its findings. It should consider and reference the decisions and reports of other forensic experts (e.g., the pathologist, serologist, and toolmark examiner).

Using Event Analysis as a backdrop, as a minimum the reconstruction report should identify the events and event segments. For each event segment the report should list the critical facts that support that segment. These facts may include physical evidence, testimonial evidence, and other related conclusions. As the conclusions stem from varying sources, the reconstruction report should also include some method of cross reference. This will allow the reader to seek out specific cites within the other documents. A basic format might look something like this:

> EVENT # 1
>   Event Segment # 1A
>   Supporting Evidence   Cross Reference
>   Event Segment # 1B
>   Supporting Evidence   Cross Reference

In this chapter we will discuss three report formats that serve the analyst's needs. All of them use this basic format, but with different levels of detail and in slightly different fashions. These three formats are:

- Event Analysis — outline format
- Statement Comparison to Event Analysis
- Event Analysis — narrative format

Event Analysis in Outline Format

The reconstruction can take the following form, which we refer to as an outline format. Each major event and event segment is described. Specific facts supporting a given event segment are included, along with a cross reference. For purposes of this example the following reports were utilized:

Event analysis
References include:

> CS — Crime scene report
> MR — ER room report
> BP — Bloodstain pattern report
> VS — Victim statement
> SR — Serology report

The reconstruction then would look something like this:

Event, event segments

A: Disturbance occurs within the bathroom. No major bleeding injuries occur here.

1. Beer bottle broken in the tub, probably used as a weapon.
   a. Minor scalp injury consistent with victims claim of head injury. (MR,2)
   b. Broken bottle glass in and around tub (CS,2)
2. No major injuries sustained here.
   a. Complete lack of spatter or blood in this area. (BP,1 CS,2)
3. Victim in the tub/shower at the time of the assault.
   a. Liquid stains present near the entrance to the door. Possible sources are water or alcohol. Officers on scene do not record smelling alcohol, thus water is the most likely source. (CS,3)
   b. Victim claims she was showering and was wet. (VS,1)

Using this portion of the report, the reader understands that Event A was a disturbance in the bathroom. This event included three distinct event segments:

- The event began with the victim in the shower.
- A bottle was broken during the event.
- None of the bleeding injuries occurred here.

To establish the occurrence of this event, the analyst called upon specific information within four other documents. This included Page 2 of the medical report, Page 1 of the bloodstain analyst's report, Pages 2 and 3 of the crime scene report, and Page 1 of the victim's statement.

The cross-reference is particularly important, since it allows the reader to refer back to all of the analyst's supporting facts. Oftentimes small critical pieces of information, which tie together other pieces of information, get lost in the mass of documents collected during the investigation. A single item of this nature, which the analyst is aware of but the reader is not, can make a distinct difference in the conclusions drawn by both.

The following is a continuation of the example report. Note that the capitalized letter represents the event, the number represents the event segments, and the small letters represent the supporting evidence.

Event, event segments (continued).

B: Altercation moves to main room. Bleeding injury sustained, but not a major one.

1. Victim ends up outside bathroom, no indication of standing on her own.
   a. Victim claims being pulled out of the room and falling to the floor. (VS,2)
   b. Large stain on the floor, liquid intermixed with blood. No spatter or droplets present in the pattern. (CS,2 BP,3)
   c. Stain shows no foot marks, other than toe/finger drag marks. (BP,3)
2. Some bleeding occurs.
   a. No spatter or droplets present. Probable source very minor drips or venous flow. (CS,3 BP,3)
   b. Possible source of blood, minor injuries to the feet from glass cuts and/or the minor head injury. If the head, the head was near the ground.
3. Victim pulled from this location by force from the rear.
   a. Edge of the large stain near the bathroom door is undisturbed. (BP,3)
   b. Stain boundary shows evidence of spines, indicating force of some nature was applied to the center. (BP,3)
   c. Drag marks present in stain are consistent with dragging of feet or hands. Marks show motion in the direction of the bed. (BP,3)

C: Primary assault occurs on bed.

1. Victim was on bed with head in the vicinity of the headboard.
   a. Saturation stains in victim's blood type. (SR,2)
   b. All major bleeding injuries on victim's face. (MR,2)
   c. Impact spatter show a point of convergence in this area. (BP,2)
2. Impacts occur here. Minimum of three blows.
   a. Impact spatter on two walls set injuries here. (BP,4)
   b. Spatter establishes a minimum of three blows, but overall distribution is indicative of more. (BP,4)
   c. Wounds on victims face indicate at least three blows. (MR,2)
3. Probable weapon is either the leg support or center supports of broken chair.
   a. Three sets of pattern transfers show characteristic measurements which are consistent with the leg support. (BP,5)
   b. These stains indicate such an object was bloodied, rebloodied, and each time placed in contact with the bedding, near the victim's head. (BP,5)
   c. Wounds present on the victim's face indicate a weapon with a linear edge, consistent with the support. (MR,3)
   d. Size of impact spatter indicates a clear application of force. This spatter is inconsistent with mere hand strikes. (BP,5)

D: Subject departs via window.

1. Window open with items on the ledge disturbed here. (CS,6)
2. Pattern transfer present on outer window ledge in blood.
   a. Pattern has dual linear boundaries which are consistent with one measurement of the cross and leg supports. (BP,5)
   b. Pattern transfers indicate the object which made them came in contact twice at this location. (BP,5)

Using the five source reports, the analyst defines to some degree four specific events and their supporting event segments and sequence. In this instance, the victim, brutally attacked and nearly killed, is unable to provide much detail regarding the actual assault. The reconstruction "fills in" sections where the victim's memory lapses and corroborates the remainder of her story.

Statement Comparison to Event Analysis

A second approach in crime scene reconstruction is to consider a subject or victim's statement as the reconstruction. In this method we take a statement presented as the "facts" surrounding some circumstance and apply event analysis to them. We then attempt to determine if the described events are supportable and whether they match the given sequence.

Accepting a subject's statement as the "reconstruction" is not that wild a thought. Those experienced at interrogation know that suspects don't always weave intricate and completely concocted statements when asked for information. As Avinoam Sapir reminds us, even when trying to hide the truth suspects will often provide very specific and factual information.[1] In terms of event analysis, when they talk to us they simply interject or leave out events and event segments or change the overall event segment sequence. Thus it is not the entire content of what they tell us that concerns us most, rather it is the disjointed segments within the story we wish to identify.

Viewing the statement as a whole, these disjointed segments may not be evident. When viewing the statement against the context of event analysis, however, it becomes easier to determine if the statement is possible given the evidence available. The first step is for the analyst to create a complete picture of how the witness claims the event transpired. Often this is difficult as the witness may have given several statements which must be combined to form the "reconstruction". Once this first step is complete the analyst, using event analysis, takes the evidence and applies it to each event and event segment. Contradictory events and disjointed segments will normally become self evident in this process. If discrepancies exist between the analysis and statement this will provide the interrogator areas to concentrate subsequent questioning on.

The only difference between this method and simply comparing a reconstruction against a statement is that in this method we accept the statement as the reconstruction. We don't develop the reconstruction independently.

Event Analysis in Narrative Format

Both of the methods discussed are quite functional as a format for the reconstruction report, but neither conclusively leads the reader through the entire logic process. Some of the analyst's decisions may or may not be self evident in these formats. The following is an example of the third approach, the narrative event analysis. It provides a clearer indication as to the specific reasoning used by the analyst. The narrative example that follows is just a small part of the total reconstruction report concerning a double murder: For this reconstruction the reference key is as follows:

BA — Bloodstain Pattern Analysis Report
CS — Crime Scene Report
FE — Firearms Examiner's Report
ME — Medical Examiner's Report
FM — Family Members
RA — Reconstruction Analyst's Report
SR — Serology Report
PR — Police Arrest Report

Event Segment Issues

Event Segment # 1 — How did the subject gain entry to the residence?
There are four possible options.

A. Entry with a key.
B. The door was left unlocked.
C. One of the victims let the subject in.
D. The subject forced entry.

Related information

A key to the lock was found in the suspect's vehicle.	PR
The victim was terrified of the subject.	FM
The victim was known to always keep the doors locked.	FM

The child victim was too young to open the door.	ME
The attack started at the bathroom.	CS, RA
No evidence exists of a forced entry anywhere in the home.	CS

Evidence/information relationships: The attack suggests surprise as the victim was preparing for the day. There are no defensive wounds and no evidence of struggle. If entry were forced, some evidence of that process would likely exist. The child victim was too young to reach or work the door lock and knob. The victim reported she was terrified of the suspect and, although not impossible, it is unlikely she would knowingly open the door and allow him in. A key was found in the suspect's vehicle.

Most probable occurrence: The lack of forced entry, the victim's prior behavior, and her known level of concern with regard to the subject make it unlikely events B, C, and D occurred. The presence of the key on the suspect and his knowledge of the residence layout make it likely he entered unnoticed using the key, catching the victim off guard as she was preparing for the day.

Event Segment # 2 — Initial contact: were the victims awake or sleeping at the time of the attack?

Two options exist in this instance. The victims were either awake or asleep.

Related information

The bed appeared slept in and was unmade.	CS
The normal schedule for sleep had passed.	FM
The curling iron was plugged in and hot.	CS
The victim was on her period and a fresh unstained panty shield was in her underwear.	CS,ME
There is specific evidence that both victims were present in the hallway at the beginning of the attack.	CS
Victim 1 had fresh makeup on her face.	

Evidence/information relationships: There is little to suggest that the victims were sleeping at the time of the attack. The condition of both the victims and the home make it almost a foregone conclusion that they were awake at the time the attack began.

Most probable occurrence: The victims were awake when the attack began.

Event Segment # 3 — Mode of attack: in what order were the three modes of attack used on Victim 1?

There are three methods of wounding evident:

A. Gunshot
B. Knife wounds.
C. Blunt trauma to the face.

As we have three events with some sequence, there are several possibilities for that sequence. Using standard probability equations, these three options present six different possible orders, as evident in the following matrix:

Order #	1	2	3	4	5	6
	A	A	B	B	C	C
	B	C	A	C	B	A
	C	B	C	A	A	B

Related information
Relating to A:

There is evidence of one gunshot to Victim # 1 after she was dragged to the bedroom.	BP, SR
There is no visible blood trail in the hallway leading there.	BP, CS
If shot, there is no need to strike the victim.	RA

Relating to B:

There is evidence of cuts to Victim # 1 in the bedroom.	BP, SR
The stabs and cut are peri-mortem.	ME

Relating to C:

The blunt trauma was the least damaging injury, causing a minor lip bruise.	ME
This blow would not render the victim unconscious.	ME
The victim's glasses were on the floor in the hallway.	CS

Evidence/information relationships: The least injurious blows are usually the first struck in the altercation. There is no indication of Victim # 1's blood in the hallway outside the bathroom, but there is evidence of her blood from both cutting and gunshot events in the bedroom. As all knife wounds are peri-mortem they most likely occur last. Based on information evident in Event Segment # 4, it is likely that Victim # 1 was unconscious when moved to the bedroom, thus there would be no resistance.

Most probable occurrence: The most likely order for this sequence of event segments is No. 6, with a strike to the face coming first, followed by at least one gunshot, followed last by the knife wounds.

Event Segment # 4 — Mode of death: what is the order of the fatal wounds to Victim # 1?
There are three different fatal wounds:

A. Gunshot to the left ear.
B. Stab to the heart.
C. Gunshot to C-2.

Once again, three possible events produce six different possible orders as indicated by the following matrix:

Order #	1	2	3	4	5	6
	A	A	B	B	C	C
	B	C	A	C	B	A
	C	B	C	A	A	B

Related Information:
Relating to A:

The shot to the left ear would have lowered the victim's blood pressure.	ME
Such a wound would not cause paralysis.	ME
There is the time to use a pillow to muffle the noise for this gunshot.	RA
If first, the blood flow on the face should be different than as found.	BP
This is a distant shot, left to right.	ME

Relating to B:

There are no arterial spurts present.	BP
This is a peri-mortem wound.	ME

Relating to C:

This wound would lower the victim's blood pressure.	ME
This wound would cause paralysis.	ME
There is time to use the pillow to make this shot.	RA
This wound would cause little external bleeding.	ME
The wound is soft contact, left to right and back to front.	ME

Evidence/information relationships: B, as the only peri-mortem wound, must occur last. This limits the orders to two (i.e., # 2 and # 6). Evidence indicates the victim was dragged by the left wrist and forearm without indication of resistance. There are bruises present to support this. These bruises could form after paralysis, but would not occur after a drop in blood pressure. The blood flow supports A having occurred after the drag from the hallway. Thus C must occur before A.

Most probable occurrence: Sequence # 6 is the most probable: gunshot C followed by gunshot A, followed by the stab to the heart.

Using the narrative style report, note that for each segment the analyst defines the evidence considered, how that evidence relates to other evidence and information, and provides at least a glimpse into the reasoning process used to derive the conclusion.

The narrative report, although more difficult to prepare than the previous formats, doesn't require further action on the part of the analyst. All of the efforts detailed in the report are an integral part of basic event analysis. Whether using an outline or narrative format the analyst must still accomplish each step. When using the narrative format, the analyst simply describes everything in a little more detail. For each event segment in the narrative report, the analyst:

- Establishes the issue or question being considered.
- Establishes the various possibilities.
- Considers sequence as necessary.
- Describes the information relevant to each possibility.
- Describes pertinent relationships evident which impact on the conclusion.
- Describes the most probable occurrence.

In considering these issues, the analyst may wish to use a Segment Analysis Worksheet similar to Figure 150. This document helps keep each issue in question in focus.

Whatever method the analysts use to detail a reconstruction, it must allow them to follow their own logic and decision process. All of the relevant information which supports the decision should be evident and the report should have a clear cross reference which allows any reader to refer back to specific investigative documents supporting a given decision.

Remember, the reconstruction product or conclusion is not infallible. What the reconstruction report offers the analyst is a greater level of self scrutiny. Links between evidence become clearer and analysts can often discover weaknesses in their own decision making. In particular, the analyst is

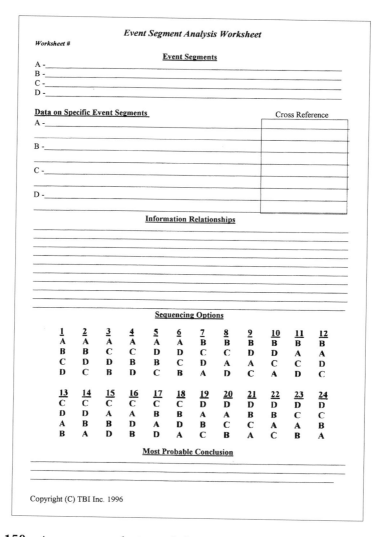

Figure 150 A segment analysis worksheet. It is helpful if the analyst creates a worksheet of this nature for each investigative issue in question. The document keeps all pertinent data in focus while working up an investigative conclusion for that particular issue.

far more likely to recognize situations in which they use contradictory arguments. Such a product also makes it easier for analysts to revisit their reasoning processes in preparation for court. No small detail of the original analysis is forgotten, nothing is left out. The reconstruction report also provides a format for trial, presenting the investigative conclusion in a logical and structured form which is easily followed and understood by the jury.

Guidelines for Maintaining Objectivity During Case-Specific Experiments

In unraveling the investigative puzzle, the analyst must oftentimes conduct some manner of experimentation in order to clarify a given event or event segment. This is particularly true for the bloodstain pattern analyst, who must often decide if a particular event can create a given stain.

The goal of any such experiment, whether developed for bloodstain pattern analysis or crime scene reconstruction, is to simply include or exclude some event or set of events as a source of the questioned pattern or result. With this in mind, lets consider some guidelines and pitfalls that affect the reconstruction. The following factors and guidelines will assist the analyst in maintaining investigative focus. These guidelines may also prevent the reconstruction from becoming too subjective.

Define what is at issue. What exactly are you trying to establish or learn. Be clear from the start and maintain your focus throughout the effort.

Consider all possible explanations for the result or pattern. The analyst can't go looking for "their" answer. As such it's best that the analyst at least consider all possibilities, even if they appear improbable.

Eliminate the ridiculous. Particularly when considering bloodstains, given a little time and a little ingenuity the analyst can reproduce a particular pattern in any number of ways. For instance, a misting stain is easily created using a spray bottle, but was a blood-filled spray bottle found in the scene? Certainly consider all possibilities, but don't waste investigative resources and time on flights of fancy.

Brainstorm with others. Don't rely on yourself to maintain objectivity. Ask investigators, analysts, attorneys, or individuals not directly involved for input.

Concentrate on "elimination". Concentrate your efforts on eliminating from your possible list those things which are "not consistent". Don't put too much emphasis on "identifying" an event. It is not always the case that the analyst can associate a set of circumstances to a specific event and absolutely exclude all other possibilities. Simply by eliminating impossible circumstances, however, a level of clarity is brought to the situation.

Using these guidelines, analysts are unlikely to find themselves lost in the maze of possible event sequences without a specific investigative focus. Just the same, they are also more likely to maintain their overall objectivity and not follow a singular investigative theory. No matter how experienced the investigator may be, this is a delicate balance to maintain.

Recreating Human Anatomy

In many instances of bloodstain pattern analysis, the need arises to recreate an event that was directed at a specific part of the anatomy. In considering attempts to recreate the structure of human anatomy for such evaluations, the first question of concern is: Is it necessary? To the analyst trying to recreate some specific event, this is certainly a critical question. The question, however, assumes that human anatomical structures **can** be recreated. We doubt this is really possible nor do we think it is necessary.

Even if analysts could replicate anatomical structures (e.g., general bone and tissue structure), what they cannot replicate is the dynamics of the underlying circulatory system. In most instances this is the most relevant issue, since analysts are concerned with the dynamics of the force and its effect on the blood (e.g., can a given force produce a specific size of spatter). They are less concerned with the force's effect on the anatomical structure (e.g., can the force cause the same damage to the bones and skin). The true volume of blood present due to the injury and the pressure behind the flow of that blood are all factors which no one can reproduce, yet these factors obviously affect the ultimate pattern observed by the analyst.

Given the discipline's combined knowledge from live subject experiments, cases where the manner of wounding was known, and the experiences of "wounding" sponges, we have found that bloodstain patterns are reproducible. Thus, analogies from bloodstain pattern experiments seem to be more than adequate, making the accurate replication of human anatomy unnecessary.

Recreating Event Particulars

Just because we don't think it necessary to recreate human anatomical structures doesn't mean the analyst should ignore other particulars of the event.

First, we need to return to our consideration of what is at issue. Wherever the analyst has an investigative question, it must be considered with an appropriate focus. For instance, a pattern transfer recreation is usually concerned with the manner of application of the object, while a spatter recreation is more likely to consider the nature of the force. In order to maintain the focus, the analyst must recreate the event particulars to the best of their ability.

Wherever possible match the particulars of the event to the recreation. If the recreation involves blows, the analyst must consider the range of force. If a pattern transfer is in question, the analyst must either use the instrument in question or find one which matches it closely (e.g., same model or construction).

Certainly surface characteristics need to be matched; for example, matching a particular tile, fabric, or material on which a pattern is found. Orientation may also be of significance, so don't assume the way you use the object or bring two items together is the only way to do it.

Pitfalls to Recreation/Reconstruction Attempts

There are many pitfalls in a recreation or reconstruction attempt. The following are some of the more common to consider.

Group think. The group involved may form a type of tunnel vision and collectively eliminate concerns that individual members clearly recognize as important. In recreations we often employ a group effort and "group think" concerns are common. Any concerns or criticism by team members of the methods employed should be objectively considered.

Designing an experiment to prove your result. Since analysts control the variables its entirely possible that they may either consciously or subconsciously create a circumstance that defines exactly what they want. For instance, if trying to disprove that a beating caused a stain, the analyst could fail to use enough blood to create spatter. Thus the weapon involved obviously will not cause spatter.

Failing to take a holistic viewpoint. Tunnel vision in the individual or the group can eliminate objectivity and doom recreations to failure. Design the experiment around the case facts. Consider the results with those same facts in mind. If analysts know they're dealing with a contact wound, then recreating a noncontact wound fails to consider the case facts. The analyst must consider all known facts and information, then ensure the experimentation accounts for and includes that knowledge.

Finally, be cautious in the exclusion of events. If you choose to exclude some event or segment as being possible, then know exactly why you feel the exclusion is warranted. "Gut feelings" and "Because I think so" are not adequate reasons for absolute exclusion in a reconstruction.

Case Examples

The following are two case examples which may allow the reader to gain a greater appreciation of how to apply these guidelines and exclude the pitfalls.

Case Experimentation Example # 1

Facts of the case. A female was found in bed on her back. A .38 revolver was on the bed beside her. There was a hard contact entry wound to the right temple, with a right to left and down to up trajectory. There was no apparent exit wound. (See Figure 151.)

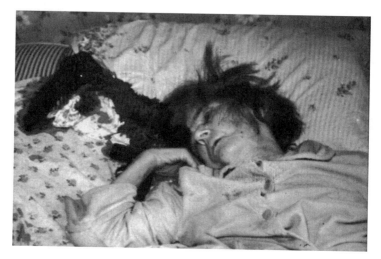

Figure 151 The victim of this incident died as a result of s single gunshot wound to the right temple. There was no apparent exit wound found at autopsy.

Issue in question. The primary question in this case is how the bloodstains on the wall (see Figures 152 and 153) could have been created from this shooting occurrence. The stains were approximately 6 ft away from the victim's head as she lay in her final position on the bed. The stain indicated a distinct volume of blood was involved, with directionality evident upward and slightly to the left. There was a large number of micromillimeter stains surrounding the main area of bloodstains. There was also a bullet ricochet to the right edge of the main area of bloodstains. The blood was tested and found to be consistent with the victim.

Brainstorming by peer input. Photos, a scene diagram, and a synopsis of the facts were sent to two peers. Two different opinions were returned for consideration. One felt that an exit wound was missed at autopsy. To check this possibility the Medical Examiner's office was asked to check the X-rays for any overlooked wounds. None were found. The second peer felt that the victim was standing up in bed and the bullet fragmented upon striking the skull. To check this, the bullet extracted at autopsy was weighed and compared to the weight of a whole .38 round. This information excluded this possibility.

Brainstorming by the investigative group. A round-table discussion was held between the firearms examiner, bloodstain analyst, serologist, detective, and crime scene technicians to consider possible occurrences. One thought offered was that the weapon, while resting on the bed, received a volume of blood down the barrel. The gun was then held up toward the wall and fired a second time by another party.

Initial test design. This possibility was tested using the same weapon and ammunition. About half an eyedropper of blood was placed into the barrel

Figure 152   Present on a nearby wall, but over 6 ft away from the victim, was this pattern. The blood present in the stain was determined to be consistent with the victim. Given the victim's final position, the lack of an exit wound, and the atomized nature of the stains in the pattern, it obviously could not be reconciled with the known facts.

and it was fired at a white cardboard target. The weapon was held approximately 18 in. away and at a 45° angle. The blood did not produce a similar pattern. In fact, very few bloodstains resulted.

Second brainstorming. At a subsequent discussion, one of the members mentioned that all of the variables had not been considered. They offered that any passage of time would congeal and thicken the blood in the barrel of the weapon. It was felt that congealing might affect the resulting stain pattern.

Redesign of the test. A similar test was conducted — this time allowing the blood to set in the barrel for successive intervals of 30 min. After a cumulative period of 3.5 h the questioned stained pattern was replicated, complete with a bullet hole, to the edge of the main pattern area. (See Figure 154.)

Conclusions. It was later determined that the husband assisted his wife in her suicide. When placed on the bed after the suicide shot, the barrel filled with blood. This blood then congealed. The gun was left on the bed for 3.5 h, after which the husband reentered the scene and fired the gun into the wall. The combination of time, congealing, and the second shot were all factors in the ultimate pattern observed.

Figure 153 A close-up photograph of the stain in question. The stain reflects distinct features typical in high-velocity impact spatter, but it also indicates that some volume of blood was involved. Adding to the analyst's concern is the presence of a bullet ricochet in the pattern. The reader may note in Figure 152 a distinct ricochet pattern present on the ceiling above this pattern. This also indicates the level of volume involved in the creation of the pattern.

Case Experimentation Example # 2

Circumstances. A passenger in a fleeing vehicle shot a .30-.30 rifle at the pursuing police officer, striking his vehicle three times. At the end of the chase both vehicles collided and came to rest 33 ft apart on opposite sides of a roadway. The officer, unable to free himself from the seat belt, observed the driver of the vehicle standing in front of the open driver's door. The suspect was attempting to recover a rifle from the driver's side floor area. While seated, the officer drew his service weapon firing five shots out the window. The suspect was hit twice in the upper and mid back.

Issue in question. The defendant's family filed suit against the officer and his agency for wrongful death. The suit alleged that if the suspect had been located as claimed by the officer, the two bullets exiting him would strike the vehicle. No such strikes were evident, nor were the bullets found.

Peer input. An investigative team reviewed the photographs, a scene diagram, autopsy report, accident investigation, and a synopsis of the facts. One consideration was that the bullets, on exiting, might have gone through the open window of the driver's door. A second issue for consideration was the actual condition of the area between the front edge of the driver's door

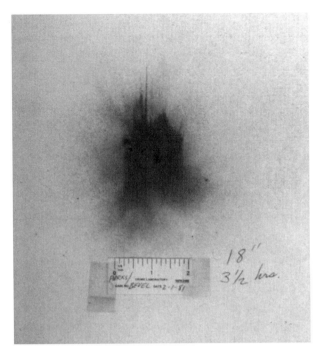

Figure 154   A photograph of the stain created during the recreation. By allowing the blood to sit and congeal in the revolver for a period of 3.5 h, the subsequent pattern produced was quite consistent with the pattern found in the scene (Figure 153).

and the vehicle. To understand the relationships, the investigative group decided to try a reenactment in order to help come to a proper conclusion.

Test design. Using an individual similar to the subject and similar vehicles, the autos were returned to their positions at the time of the shooting. A laser sight was chosen to recreate the "weapon". Bright colored patches were placed on the simulated suspect at the point of entry of both wounds. This allowed the investigative team to see and document the laser. All parties were then placed in the scene as they were alleged to have been.

Reenactment. Using all information available, the vehicles were placed in the same positions as on the night of the shooting incident. The officer was positioned in the driver's seat of the police vehicle. He drew his weapon with the laser sight and aligned it with the patches on the simulated suspect.

Conclusions. In considering the officer's position and possible positions for the subject, it was evident that:

- If the suspect was away from the vehicle during the shooting (forward of the position claimed) it was unlikely the exit bullets would hit anything.

- If the suspect was in front of the open driver's door as claimed, it was still possible for bullets exiting his person to miss the vehicle. This was due to the angle and difference in elevation of the vehicles combined with the height of the suspect. The bullets exiting would actually travel above the top edge of the driver's door.

The idea that the bullets would take this latter path was not considered in the original group discussions. As is often the case only through a reenactment did the total dynamics of the situation and scene become apparent.

Summary

Ultimately the final form of any investigation is a reconstruction of some nature. To be useful to the court, the reconstruction must be clear, concise, and to the point. The reconstruction report is a written account of the logic process the analyst utilized to reach the conclusions and should lead the reader through each point of the analysis.

Incorporating our concept of Event Analysis from Chapter 2, the reconstruction should include each supportable event and event segment. The analyst should include details regarding specific items of evidence which support these event segments, then briefly explain their interrelationships.

As the reconstruction report is a compilation of many different sources of information, the analyst should also cross reference this information. The cross reference serves an important function in keeping sight of all supporting evidence. It is often small, minute details scattered throughout the investigative report that allow some specific conclusion to be reached. Without a cross reference, these small details are often lost or forgotten in the total package.

In seeking a conclusion, the analysts will often have to recreate events or conduct some form of experimentation. In these instances, the analysts must know what they are trying to establish. Pragmatic objectivity is the key to success. Don't arbitrarily rule out any possibility, but then again don't try to prove the foolish. When designing experiments and recreation attempts keep the focus clear, seek the advise of others, and maintain an open mind.

By following the guidelines and format explained in this chapter, the analyst's reconstruction report will ultimately serve any fact-finder in determining the most probable sequence of events for a given incident.

References

1. Sapir, Avinoam, *Scientific Interrogation Course Manual*, LSI Inc., Phoenix, AZ, pg. 31.

Automation Applications in Bloodstain Pattern Analysis and Crime Scene Reconstruction

11

Computers abound in our society and as we become more cognizant of their capabilities we seek to automate more and more processes. This is certainly true in forensics. The reader may recall the discussion in Chapter 6 of programs that allow us to define the point of origin for a given set of bloodstains. This type of software is just one example of how automation resources are making the analyst better able to conduct analysis. In this chapter we'll consider some of the ways in which automation supports crime scene analysis, bloodstain pattern analysis, and overall crime scene reconstruction.

Automation Usage Considerations

Although some may see the application of computer resources in analysis as inappropriate or unnecessary, that is a far too limited viewpoint.[1] In fact, computer analysis is really nothing new to the reconstruction business. Using high-end graphics packages, engineers have conducted accident reconstruction for a number of years. The typical limitation for such usage was simply access to a "mini" or "mainframe" computer and of course the money to fund the expertise for such an endeavor. Access is no longer at issue, nor for that matter is expertise. The average desktop computer can now run similar if not the same software packages and, given time, nearly anyone can learn to use many of these programs.

However, those who voice concerns about automation advances are not completely wrong. Certainly there must be acceptable uses and even limitations in their application. Unfortunately, little effort has been put forth to

251

explore and thus define the computer's future in the field of reconstruction. Although we recognize that automation serves a very functional purpose in reconstruction, there are still many issues that need resolution. Are all 3-D presentations scientifically valid? Are they too prejudicial? Will a jury, in "seeing" rather than "hearing" an expert's opinion place more credibility in it than it deserves?

We don't claim to have answers to these questions, but just as we see the potential of using automation in reconstruction, we also recognize a need to consider the downside of its use. To some, the answer has been "let the court decide". If forced to, the court will certainly set limits for the analyst, but forcing the court to act is probably not the discipline's best response. That attitude removes the responsibility of the discipline's experts to consider and set appropriate standards. We have no doubt this issue will receive a distinct amount of attention over the next few years, if not by the discipline itself, then certainly by lawyers.

Types of Applications

From author to author, the breakout for generic groupings of software applications is different. Reese saw animation applications as one of simulation, tutorial function, and illustration.[2] Alexander saw four groupings for applications: Category 1 — basic mathematical solutions which are tedious (e.g., velocity determinations) but easily verified by human examination; Category 2 — graphics for illustration of opinion; Category 3 — simulations based on standard equations; and Category 4 — experimental simulations not easily verified by human examination.[3] Gardner saw the grouping in a similar fashion as Reese, making three distinctions in software: teaching tools, computer-aided analysis, and illustrative tools.[4]

For purposes of discussion here, we'll use three groupings: tutorial, simulation and computer-aided analysis, and illustration.

Tutorial Applications

Tutorial applications allow the analyst to instruct someone on a given concept or theory relevant to the discipline. Although Reese saw this solely in the setting of the court, tutorial software is also available to assist those learning about bloodstain pattern analysis.

TRACKS® is one such program. Designed by Dr. Alfred Carter of Forensic Computing of Ottawa, *TRACKS®* allows the user to adjust variables regarding blood droplets (i.e., speed, angle, size) and discover what these changes do to the droplet's flight path. The reader may recall seeing several figures produced from *TRACKS®* models in Chapters 4 and 7. Although primarily intended for students, *TRACKS*® may eventually find its way into the court-room to clarify teaching points to the jury.

Currently there are few other true "tutorial" applications available in the field of bloodstain pattern analysis. The creation of an Expert System offers one possible area for development. The Expert System is an early form of artificial intelligence (AI) programming techniques. It consists of a database of knowledge held by a given expert or group of experts. This database is combined with a rule base, which is the logic process the "expert" applies to solve issues or questions. Together the information and methodology walk the student through a given problem, typically by the system asking specific questions and the student giving answers.

Simulation and Computer-Aided Analysis Applications

Simulation or computer-aided analysis is an up and coming function of automation. Simulation applications allow the analyst to take basic data from an event and then using known equations create a simulation of what the event may have looked like. Computer-aided analysis takes data from the scene and allows them to be viewed in a different manner. Both methods let the analyst test their beliefs regarding an event, determine if the data available match the circumstances, and all in all allow for a more in-depth analysis.

As discussed in Chapter 6, both *BACKTRACK*® and *No More Strings*® are simulation software packages which allow the user to evaluate spatter patterns. The software, using standard equations, does the tedious math necessary to define the point of origin. The software then presents the data in both text and graphics. Each uses standard equations and physical laws to determine where a droplet may have originated. Although not absolutely accurate, the programs provide a fairly accurate estimate or representation of the spatter event.

A developing area in computer-aided analysis is the use of imaging software. Too often analysts are presented with poor quality photographs of evidence, stain patterns, and the like. Imaging software allows the analyst to clean up these photographs and view them in a more functional fashion.

Image processing software, although relatively new to bloodstain pattern analysis, is not new to forensics. Document examiners and other forensic scientists have used these software systems for some time.[5] Some of the image manipulation and enhancement routines available to the analyst in off-the-shelf software packages include pattern elimination, color modification, edge determination, and adjustments to contrast, brightness, or intensity.

In pattern elimination the analyst identifies a color belonging to some unwanted pattern and then removes it. As a result, unwanted patterns are diminished in the image. This allows the analyst to better view adjacent patterns or see the pattern as a whole.

Color modification and manipulation are very similar and well suited to bloodstain pattern analysis. In this instance, a particular color in the image is chosen and modified so it stands out more clearly. Color manipulation works well because the computer distinguishes between colors or shades of colors better than the human eye. The analyst simply points to the area in question and the computer modifies the given pixel color at that location to whatever color the analyst desires. This kind of modification allows better human discrimination by increasing the contrast or color shade of all similar pixel colors in the picture. Of particular note, this method often enhances transfer patterns, allowing far better visualization.

A simple form of this process is color reversal. Consider Color Plates 9 and 10,* which demonstrate this technique in enhancing a spatter and transfer pattern. In the original photograph (Plate 9) the dried bloodstains appear dark and do not stand out well against the blue color of the pants. Reversed (Plate 10), the pants become red while the patterns become white, making their form and boundaries much more evident.

Edge determination is a method in which the computer analyzes the image looking for specific edges in the patterns. Once again, the identified edges are enhanced, allowing better visualization. Since the system identifies these edges mathematically, it may locate patterns not immediately evident to the human eye.

A major concern in image enhancement and manipulation is the difference between alteration and enhancement. Reeves, in a presentation to the IABPA, made the point that enhancement increases the value, while alteration implies a change to the original image. The difference between the two is not that great.[6] As such, the analyst walks a very fine line in the business of image enhancement — one where the court may or may not approve of the methods. To counter these concerns, the analyst should document each manipulation routine employed, its overall effect, and wherever possible create an exhibit reflecting each stage of the enhancement.

Another area new to scene reconstruction combines both image enhancement with a process that might best be called a simulation. At a joint training meeting of the IABPA and ASCR in Oklahoma City, E-Systems of Dallas presented an image enhancement process clearly suited to both bloodstain pattern analysis and crime scene reconstruction. The method employs techniques and algorithms originally developed for space reconnaissance imaging. E-Systems refers to this process as perspective transformation.

In a case involving one of the authors (Bevel), E-Systems enhanced a photograph of a tile floor with a large bloodstained area. (See Figure 155.) Within the bloodstain is a voided section of specific interest since it shows

---

* Color Plates 9 and 10 follow page 216.

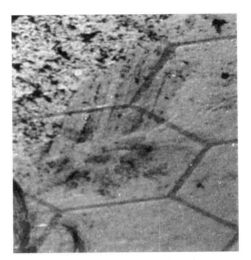

Figure 155   In this crime scene photograph, there is evidence of a footwear impression in the stained area. Unfortunately, the oblique angle at which the photograph was taken causes major perspective distortion, making the photograph of no use to the analyst. Note also the lack of a scale of reference. (Photograph courtesy of Henry Muse, E-Systems, Dallas, TX.)

indications of the presence of a footwear pattern. The problem associated with the photograph is the oblique angle at which it was taken. This angle introduces obvious distortion to the voided section and presents the viewer with a glancing view. Unfortunately, this was the only photograph available of this critical evidence.

Henry Muse and Nancy Jackson of E-Systems, using advanced photogrammetric techniques, were able to correct the view to the point that one could actually look down onto the floor.[7] Although no scale of reference was included in the original photograph, the computer model used the dimensions evident in the tiles of the floor to build a control grid. (See Figure 156.) This allowed a projection of the original oblique perspective to the vertical perspective. The pattern transfer itself was then enhanced in the image, using a mathematical model that corrected imprint detail missing from the original image. Figure 157 is the enhanced version of the photograph.

These methods go far beyond the simple image enhancements available using off-the-shelf computer software programs. To some extent, E-Systems' methods actually allow the analyst to correct photographic mistakes made during the initial scene processing.

Illustration Applications

This area of automation use is a bit more open. Illustrations range from simple graphics to detailed animations. Their function is always the same:

Figure 156 Using the tiles as a scale of reference, the computer program was able to create a control grid, which allowed the transfer of the perspective from the original photograph to the vertical perspective.

such methods help illustrate the expert's opinion to the court. For that reason they are generally held to be demonstrative evidence, which is important for reasons we'll discuss later.

From the graphics perspective, analysts have used illustrations to show wound characteristics, bloodstain pattern characteristics, crime scene layouts, and other similar information. The most typical approach is to digitize a photograph, which the analyst then enhances by adding "highlights, labels, croppings, overlays, or scaled comparisons."[8] A specific benefit of graphics is to show a wound characteristic without the accompanying gore, which the court often finds prejudicial. Graphics allow for both the isolation and demonstration of a specific characteristic and the elimination of the offending images.

Another illustration application is the three-dimensional sketch program, which is gaining popularity over traditional crime scene sketching methods. Several years ago, such programs were generally run on computer-aided

Figure 157   E-Systems of Dallas, Texas was able to enhance the original photograph (Figure 156) to this end product. Using a mathematical model, they filled in detail missing from the pattern transfer and highlighted the entire enhanced pattern in white. Although certainly an "alteration" of the original image, this is an example of a substantive type programming technique that may well serve analysis and reconstruction in the future. (Photograph courtesy of Henry Muse, E-Systems, Dallas, TX.)

design and drafting (CADD) software, with high-end memory and processor requirements. Since 1989 criminalists have seen the creation of numerous crime scene sketching applications running on the PC and MAC platforms. These applications allow the analyst to recreate the scene in two-dimensional and three-dimensional perspectives. Many also incorporate a low end virtual reality or animation approach. After creating the scene the analyst can choose a position from which to view the scene or combine a series of views. In this fashion the analyst or jury can make a virtual "walk through" of the scene.

Most of these crime scene programs allow the analyst to create two views: either a line drawing rendition or fill-in drawing. The first is typical of the graphics seen in a standard CADD view, where transparent objects are like those found in Figure 158. The fill-in view presents the scene and information in a more realistic perspective, such as that found in Figure 159.

More complex animation and design programs allow the introduction of people into the scene. Not only can the analysts recreate the scene, but they can introduce scaled victims and subjects, placing them in any position desired. Analysts often use these applications to illustrate the relationship of the individual at the moment of wounding. This is particularly effective for demonstrating an expert's opinion on possible and impossible positions.[9,10]

Animation, although clearly linked to our discussion of three-dimensional scene viewing, is an application in and of itself. Forensic animation developed

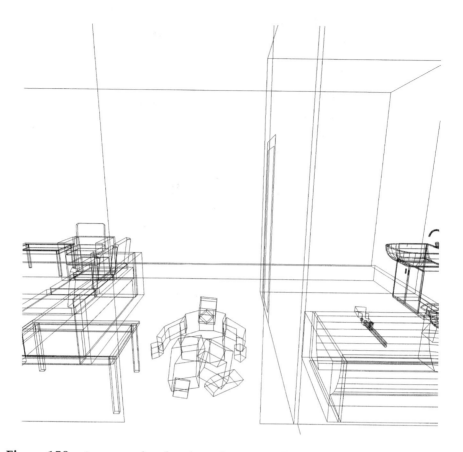

Figure 158 An example of a three-dimensional view of a crime scene. This example is a line drawing rendition, in which all objects are transparent. Various courts have shown a preference to this view as compared to a more realistic view like that in Figure 159.

out of the efforts of accident reconstruction, particularly in the area of vehicular collisions.[11]

In animation not only are the scene and players recreated, but the players (e.g., victim and subject) are repetitively positioned within the scene. Different views are created, showing event segments, then the entire series is shown in sequence. Its important to recognize that this process is distinctly different from showing people or objects in static positions within the scene.

The intent of forensic animation is to show the reconstructionist's view of how the events proceeded. Once again, used in this fashion the animation is demonstrative only. As Reese points out "[the animation] does not determine 'what happened'. The accuracy and credibility of a forensic animation is a product of the skill of the animator... and the accuracy of the expert or

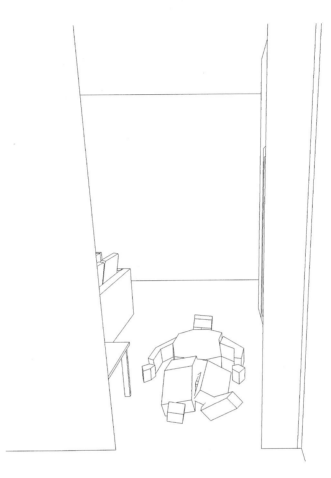

Figure 159   A "painted" view of the same area. In this example, the computer hides all lines which would not be evident to the viewer if standing in that position, providing the viewer with a more realistic view of the scene. Many crime scene sketching programs allow the analyst to create a number of such views and then show them in sequence. In effect, this method allows the jury or other parties to "walk through" the crime scene.

lay witness who will authenticate the animation."[12] If the basis of the crime scene analysis and reconstruction are tainted, then the animation serves little purpose.

Views regarding the use of forensic animation in the criminal justice system vary. We personally feel full-fledged animation is too subjective. If you recall our discussions of event analysis, the analyst is probably lucky if a majority of the specific events which make up a given incident can be defined. Obviously, full animation requires the analyst to fill in the unknown event segments and it often assumes that no other actions occurred. Unfortunately, the analyst has no real assurance that this is true. It may simply be

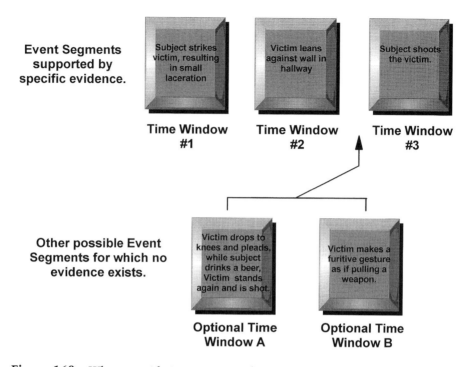

Figure 160 When considering Event Analysis and animation, the analyst must be cognizant of the limitations in using animation. We rarely ever know enough to claim that we can recreate the entire incident. For instance, the evidence may establish clearly that Time Windows 1 through 3 occurred. We may also be confident of their overall sequence, but we can never be absolutely sure that other actions did not occur. Between the moment the victim leans against the wall and the point when the subject shoots, either of the optional time window actions may have occurred. Full animation often demands that we make an assumption that nothing else occurred in the course of the event.

a situation where evidence indicating the occurrence of the other actions is obscured.

In considering this concern, look at Figure 160. Imagine a situation where we have three distinct time windows, all based on specific physical evidence at the scene. All of these established event segments occur in a small area within a hallway and appear to be sequential. With no other evidence to suggest any other action on the part of participants, the animator would likely sequence them one after the other with little or no time in-between. Unfortunately, there is nothing which precludes optional windows A or B, or both, from having occurred between time windows 2 and 3, nor is it likely the analyst would ever find evidence to support these actions. Either action, however, could drastically alter the jury's or court's beliefs with regard to the entire incident.

Animation often demands major assumptions and these assumptions impose a level of subjectivity into the reconstruction. Granted, it can be argued that even if we present the reconstruction in the storyboard method (one graphic for each event segment, shown sequentially, but not animated), we still would not be aware of these other actions. Whether we would or could discover their occurrence is not the point. The presentation of the reconstruction, however, is. In the animation method the analyst is forced to introduce obvious subjectivity concerns, while in the story-board method the reconstruction remains accurate to what the evidence actually establishes.

In some instances, full-fledged animation is both possible and perhaps viable in presenting event reconstruction. For instance in a case in San Francisco, Alex Jason combined the timing of a series of shots recorded in a 911 call along with physical evidence from the scene. Taken as a whole, this allowed a somewhat solid basis on which to present an animation of the actions of the victim during his murder.[13] In this particular instance the establishment of a very clear time line, with little intervening time between each shot, allowed this. Nevertheless, the analyst can never be sure whether some other action was taken in-between these established events. This concern will remain the most aggressive argument against full-fledged animation in forensic reconstruction.

As indicated, an alternative to full-fledged animation is in demonstrating event analysis with animation software. Established event segments are created and shown in a series, which become true "snapshots" of the crime. Figures 161 through 164, created by Ken McCracken of Video Solutions in Norman, Oklahoma demonstrate this process.[14] Each snapshot is then presented, one at a time, as the reconstructionists explains their theory. These images are shown in the appropriate sequence, either using a still video mode or by using hard copy. In a way, we are physically creating Rynearson and Chisum's concept of a "story board".[15] This approach to animation usage is perhaps best, as it eliminates subjective fill-in by the analyst. It also precludes many of the arguments against animation, while still allowing the court to "see" the reconstruction.

Another benefit of this technique is adjusting to successful objections by opposing counsel. If the judge rules that a specific image or event segment is inappropriate, the analyst need only remove that particular image from the overall reconstruction. With animated reconstructions, this is much more difficult. A full-fledged animation can rarely be edited in a timely manner and certainly not on site.

Court Acceptance

A critical concern in using automation is the fashion in which it is presented. If demonstrative, that is, the evidence is used to illustrate and demonstrate

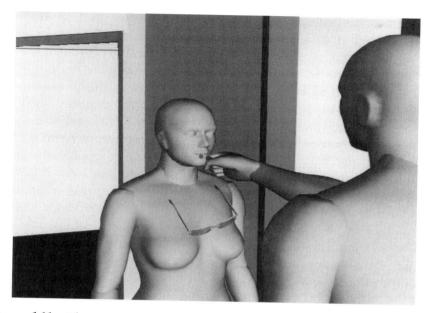

Figure 161 This computer-generated snapshot depicts a single-event segment relating to a multiple murder. This particular segment depicts a blow to the face. This is Event Segment # 3 from the case example provided in Chapter 10.

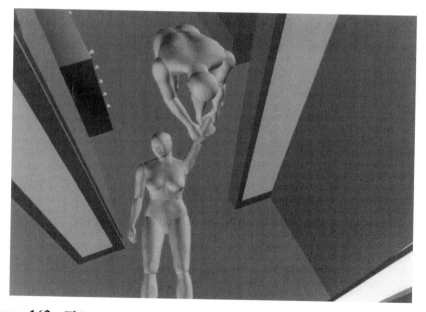

Figure 162 This segment depicts the subject dragging the victim to another room. Once again, it is a specific snapshot of the crime established by specific facts and knowledge. This segment relates to Event # 4 from the example in Chapter 10.

Figure 163 This segment depicts the sexual mutilation of the victim, following several other fatal wounds. Although certainly graphic, the computer-generated image is often more easily accepted. In fact, three jurors from the subsequent trial commented that they were better able to listen to the testimony when viewing these images. They found it difficult to follow verbal testimony when viewing the actual photographs, as they were very graphic and disconcerting.

a given expert's opinion, the evidence will face fewer challenges in the courtroom. On the other hand, if the evidence is substantive it is likely to be judged in a more critical light.

There are few true substantive applications available at the moment. Alexander's description of Category 3 and Category 4 modeling applications are perhaps the best explanation for a true substantive program. He described such applications as situations where: "Known variables are given to the computer, and from these variables, a computer is able to construct an illustration based upon standard equations programmed into the computer."[16]

The concept of a substantive application is distinct from the demonstrative application. For instance, where *BACKTRACK®* might assist the analyst in defining the probable point of origin for a spatter-producing event, the analyst could then demonstrate this knowledge using a three-dimensional crime scene. *BACKTRACK®* helps the analyst establish the point of origin — it gives the analysis something new; therefore it might be considered substantive. On the other hand, the crime scene sketch application doesn't "tell" the analyst anything with regard to the analysis, it merely helps to show his or her opinion based on the information derived from the substantive application.

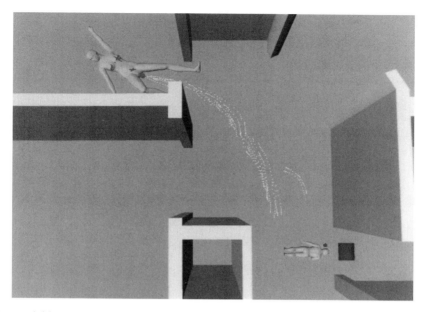

Figure 164 Computer imaging with virtual reality software allows the analyst to create a view of the scene from any position. In this image the viewer is provided with a "birds eye" view of several rooms within the scene. This allows them to orient the position of the two victims and a blood trail discovered using Luminol.

Nonetheless, just because a demonstrative program is not held to the same rigorous test for admissibility as the substantive one doesn't mean that anything goes in the courtroom. The court has put clear limits on the use of this technology. Any application or evidence presented must be relevant to the inquiry and be reliable. Two areas in which the court has taken specific issue with such evidence are the passage of time, and the validity of the actions demonstrated.

Although a "walk through" of the three-dimensional crime scene is generally accepted, the introduction of movement by parties in the scene is viewed more negatively. The experiences of Dr. Daniel Davis, a medical examiner in Minneapolis, demonstrate that the court can be picky in this regard, and rightfully so. In one instance when he used diagrammatic footprints in a scene to show the most likely path an assailant took, the court argued that Dr. Davis didn't really know how many steps the assailant took in moving along this path nor that the assailant took the most direct route. Aside from this concern, the judge found the remaining demonstration acceptable and, after removal of the offending footprints, allowed its use.[17]

In another instance, Peter Barnett encountered a judge's objection while trying to use animated figures to demonstrate the position several shots were fired from. The objection was based on the issue of time. The judge had no concern with the positioning demonstration, but argued there was no evidence to support the time depicted by the animation. In the end the animation was allowed, but only after the jury was clearly advised of the judge's concern.[18]

Summary

It should be evident to our discipline that there is a growing body of decisions which reflect the court's desires and limitations. Whether judged by a Frye or Daubert test, the court will apply some level of scrutiny to the use of automation. The best guidance for the moment is to apply automation objectively and cautiously to any analysis. Steer clear of subjective considerations and present only those facts which are easily supported. As Dr. Davis comments on this issue, "just because its possible to [demonstrate something] on a computer doesn't mean that its realistic to push it on the court. It may be 'cool' but it may also be imprudent."[19]

Analysts are just beginning to recognize the full benefit of automation applications to analysis. The concern for the future should be in defining acceptable methods of application. If the discipline fails as a group to take a lead in this process, then we can be certain the court will impose limitations of its own without the benefit of the discipline's insight.

Whatever the outcome of this concern, the analyst should recognize that automation brings distinct benefit to the reconstruction effort as it allows the analyst to look at and present information in a completely different light. To that end, the keyboard and screen may well be one of the most valuable tools available to the analyst in the future.

References

1. MacDonell, Herbert L., *Bloodstain Patterns*, Laboratory of Forensic Science, Corning, NY, 1993, pg. 42.

2. Reese, Andrew, The Trial Lawyer's Guide to Forensic Animation, Autodesk Inc., 1992, pg. 17.

3. Alexander, Richard, Computer Simulation and Animation in the Courtroom, available at the Alexander Law Firm Homepage, WWW.

4. Gardner, Ross M., Computer Aided Analysis Limitations and Capabilities, *International Association of Bloodstain Pattern Analysts News*, Vol. 11, # 3, Sept. 95, pg. 16.

5. Hicks, Frank, Computer Imaging for Questioned Document Examiners. I. The Benefits, *J. Forensic Sciences*, Vol. 40, Number 6, Nov. 1995, pp. 1045-1051.

6. Reeves, Norman H., Computer Digitizing and Ehancements of Photographs, Presentation to a joint training conference of the Int. Assoc. Bloodstain Pattern Analysts, and Assoc. Crime Scene Reconstruction, October 6, 1995, Oklahoma City, OK.

7. Muse, Henry and Bowden, Ron, E-Systems Forensic Image Processing: A Case Specific Example of Softcopy Exploitation, Presentation to the joint training conference of the Int. Assoc. Bloodstain Patterns Analysts, and Assooc. Crime Scene Reconstruction, October 7, 1995, Oklahoma City, OK.

8. Davis, Daniel W., M.D., Personal communications, 14 Dec. 1995.

9. Barnett, Peter D., Personal communications, 28 November, 1995.

10. Davis, Daniel W., M.D., Personal communications, 14 Dec. 1995.

11. Reese, Andrew, The Trial Lawyer's Guide to Forensic Animation, Autodesk Inc., 1992, pg. 11.

12. Ibid., pp. 11-12.

13. Jason, Alex, Forensic Animation, Presentation to the Assoc. Crime Scene Reconstruction, Oklahoma City, OK, October 1, 1994.

14. Video Solutions, Norman, Oklahoma, (405) 321-4500.

15. Rynearson, Joseph M and Chisum, William J., *Evidence and Crime Scene Reconstruction*, J.M. Rynearson, Shingleton, CA, 1983, pg. 105.

16. Alexander, Richard, Computer Simulation and Animation in the Courtroom, available at the Alexander Law Firm Homepage, WWW.

17. Davis, Daniel W. MD, Personal communications, 14 Dec. 95.

18. Barnett, Peter D., Personal communications, 28 November, 1995.

19. Davis, Daniel W., Personal communications, 14 Dec. 95.

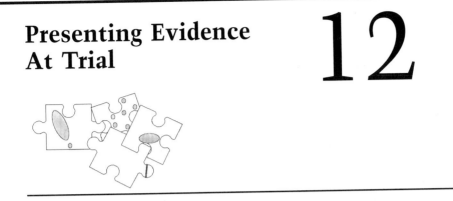

Presenting Evidence At Trial

12

Preparation for court begins long before any actual court date. Having failed to prepare properly, analysts should not be surprised when a skillful attorney cuts them to shreds on the witness stand. After such a mauling, and usually while nursing a bruised ego, the analyst is likely to blame the situation on "that unmerciful attorney". However, if we step into the witness chair unprepared or oblivious to the nature and expectations of the court, then perhaps we deserve such treatment. The culmination of any analysis is to demonstrate in court the conclusion drawn from the analysis. In meeting that end the analyst can never take preparation for trial lightly.

General Concerns

Analysts should investigate and prepare reports in every case with an eye on the witness stand. Their own report can often come back to haunt them; so it must not contain inaccuracies, discrepancies, exaggerations, and unsupported theories. When writing the report the analyst must keep the question in mind: How can I substantiate this in court?

When presenting an opinion to the court be prepared to use demonstrative evidence, such as large photographs or charts, as a method of educating the jury. It is not uncommon nor inappropriate for an analyst to use stage blood or other inert substances to demonstrate bloodstain dynamics. This may include dripping blood onto angled targets or creating spatter. As discussed previously, computer resources are also helpful in this regard. They can effectively illustrate specific events and points related to the analyst's testimony.

The ability of the analyst as an instructor is a concern that can't be overemphasized. An expert opinion that the jury fails to understand is a worthless opinion. Conversely, if a conclusion is clear, logical, concise, and understood, the jury is likely to find such testimony extremely valuable. Therefore, analysts should use all appropriate illustrations to let the jury "see" and not simply hear their testimony.

Maintaining Objectivity

It's important to maintain objectivity throughout the trial. Remember, the analyst's role is that of a witness, not an advocate. It is not their job to help an attorney win the case and such an attitude often leads analysts to include unsubstantiated details in their conclusions. The jury will view this behavior as a bias or prejudice, and rightfully so. In the end it can destroy the analyst's overall credibility.

Nevertheless, pressures to be "one of the team" will be present. Police organizations employ many bloodstain analysts directly within the structure of the agency. As such, it is easy to identify singularly with the goals of the investigation. Additionally, the analyst may team up with the prosecutor, building the particular case against the defendant. In the process, the analyst is subjected to the "Us and Them" attitude found in the adversarial court system.

It takes a conscious effort by the analyst to remain impartial, but reconstruction and analysis demand this impartiality. This might seem at odds with our purpose, as certainly the analyst will eventually conclude that something happened and that someone was involved. Being adamant in the conclusion isn't a bad thing, but the analyst becomes adamant only by evaluating all evidence and considering all possibilities. Their ultimate conclusion objectively recognizes inherent strengths and weaknesses. This kind of impartiality is a far cry from pursuing only that evidence which supports a specific theory. Impartiality demands we recognize the difference between the two and pursue the holistic approach.

Analysts often find the legal system intimidating since it has its own unique purpose and values, and even its own logic.[1] The search for truth in the context of the law is simply part of the process by which the goal, "justice", is sought. On the other hand, in analysis, truth is the goal. All the analyst is concerned with is being confident that they have the most probable sequence of events established based upon all evidence available. Of course, the court works in a slightly different fashion. As Peterson explained: "The principle objectives of the litigants is to win the case, often at the expense of truth ... counsel tries to extract a slanted picture from the witness, and, on cross examination, opposing counsel seeks to slant the picture the other way."[2]

As Alan Dershowitz, one of O.J. Simpson's defense attorneys, commented, "A criminal trial is anything but a pure search for truth. When defense attorneys represent guilty clients ... their responsibility is to try by all legal and ethical means, to prevent the truth about their client's guilt from emerging."[3] Truth then, is very often the unfortunate victim of this wrangling, but analysts can ill afford to play this game. They must present their knowledge factually and objectively, no matter how it may be used. If by answering a counselor's question they harm their own position or conclusion, then so be it. Truth is truth, the jury or judge are the ones who must decide if they believe a conclusion. The analyst simply gives them knowledge on which to base that decision.

Analysts can never allow themselves to forfeit their own or their department's integrity. No matter how perturbing the judicial system may be, no matter how adamant their belief in the guilt of some particular subject, they can only report what they know. In the recent past there have been unfortunate cases in which forensic experts, to support a particular position, modified or manufactured "evidence". There is absolutely no room in forensics for this type of activity. The analyst owns their integrity, no one can take it from them. To lose it, you have to make a conscious decision to give it away. Guard your integrity carefully, for every time you take the witness stand both the court and society are relying on it.

Settling In and Establishing a First Impression

Often, it is the first few moments in the witness stand that are the most disconcerting. Unfortunately, these are the same moments when the jury is defining their first impression of the analyst. The following actions may assist the analyst in establishing a more positive image.

In preparation for voir dire and subsequent testimony, the analyst may wish to assist counsel in preparing qualifying questions. Since analysts know their own qualifications better than anyone else, they can create questions that place them in a positive light. Of course it is imperative that the analyst not embellish their credentials in any fashion. Areas to be covered by these questions include:

- Training and years in the discipline
- Position in and years with a given agency.
- Articles published or studies conducted.
- Schools taught on the subject.
- The number of times previously qualified as an expert witness.
- Membership in professional organizations related to the field.

Preparing these questions in advance and providing them to the appropriate attorney ensures two things: (1) the analyst knows what the questions are and knows how best to answer them, and (2) by knowing the nature of the initial questions, the analyst can relax somewhat and will become more comfortable on the stand.

A relaxed attitude is critical since both the analyst's appearance and demeanor are being evaluated by the jury. The court's first impression of the analyst may set the tone for acceptance of the entire testimony. To address this issue the analyst should always dress conservatively, preferably in a business suit. Don't wear items such as sunglasses, or anything that might be considered flashy. This has a way of stealing the jury's attention from testimony. If at all possible do not testify in a police uniform, as the jury may perceive this as demonstrating partiality to the prosecution.

Demeanor is difficult to maintain and the analyst constantly walks the "demeanor tightrope". One cannot be "cocky", but just the same one shouldn't be viewed as "timid". Analysts must appear confident in their knowledge, experience, and conclusions. By acting like professionals on the stand, the jury will hopefully perceive them as professionals.

To present this professional appearance, analysts must use every action in the courtroom to their advantage. As they walk into the courtroom, all eyes are on them. The analyst should walk in with their heads up and shoulders back. When taking the oath the analyst should stand at a position of attention. Their affirmation should be in a voice that is confident and loud enough that a jury can hear them. The actions and manner of the analyst must say, "I am here to be honest and to tell the truth." If done well, the jury's initial impression of the analyst is that of a serious professional.

Attacks on analysts come in a variety of ways, but quite often counselors simply set the stage and allow analysts to impeach themselves. Trained to bring out any attitude of animosity or bias, the opposing attorneys will seek to do so during cross examination. If this can be accomplished, the attorneys can feel more confident in their own argument knowing that the jury's opinion of the analyst is diminished. If the analyst refuses to be drawn into such encounters and remains objective and calm, then the jury is unlikely to view the analyst in a derogatory manner.

Remember, objectivity and impartiality are critical. If questioned about a weakness in the case, admit it. It's not the analyst's job to convict, but rather to give whatever testimony that can honestly be given and nothing more. The analyst's credibility will suffer if there is any attempt to hide a weakness or subjectively dismiss it.

When responding to questions that are short, such as "yes" and "no", look at the attorney asking the questions. Don't look back and forth from the attorney to the jury during a series of such questions. The jury may find the motion of the analyst disconcerting. On longer answers, the analyst should look to the jurors. In doing so, the analyst builds rapport and further establish an image of credibility. The analyst should not forget to look back at the attorney, particularly when listening to the questions being asked.

One often observes that even the most experienced witnesses will eagerly answer the questions of their own attorney, then become immediately defensive or hostile when the opposing attorney asks questions. No matter how aggressive an attorney becomes, the analyst should never get mad nor display hostility. If the analyst simply ignores this aggressiveness and continues to answer with confidence, the jury will tend to view the analyst in a more credible light.

Understanding Cross Examination

For those unfamiliar with court, it is often difficult to understand that a trial has little if any relationship to the investigative process. Truth has only a limited place in court. What does count is the manner in which each opposing counsel is able to turn the facts to support their own position. For that reason, the analyst must understand and be prepared for the rigors of cross examination. Counselors use cross examination to meet any number of objectives, which include:

- Discrediting the witness.
- Discrediting the discipline or methods used.
- Discrediting the ultimate conclusions or opinion given by the expert.

Direct questioning in the initial stages of a trial is like a walk in the park when compared with the antagonistic manner evident in cross examination. In preparation for this ordeal, the analyst must read and know their own report. They should review all related reports and any articles or books which have a bearing on the conclusions drawn. Additionally, analysts should know or be cognizant of concepts or theories of other authors that might be counter to their own. Finally, analysts must be able to verbalize under adverse conditions "why" they reached the conclusion they did.

Event analysis is the best method we know of for assisting the analyst in accomplishing this end. By referring to the event analysis reconstruction report, the details and specifics remain evident to the analyst. No matter how flustered or hurried the attorney makes them, the supporting information is always at the analyst's fingertips.

During cross examination expect the opposing attorney to dwell on those areas for which the analyst is not qualified. An example may be the attorney who asks if the analyst has a degree in physics, math, or biology. Often, the attorney will attempt to make the analyst answer simple questions, those which the analyst may know the answer to. Using these answers the attorney will then try to further the impression that the analyst is claiming to be an expert in that area. During cross examination these easy "little" questions have an ugly habit of turning into big complex questions, that ultimately leave the analyst embarassed. For example, in bloodstain pattern analysis, even though the analyst is not a serologist a serology question will likely be asked. The analyst's best response is to state a lack of qualification in the area and request the attorney ask the question of someone who is qualified. If others should answer the question, then let them!

The analyst should never consent to conducting examinations of "new evidence" on the witness stand. It should be evident to the reader by now that analysis demands proper examination in an appropriate setting, with sufficient work space, lighting, magnification, equipment, and time. Off the cuff examinations are exactly that ... off the cuff. They have no place in the ultimate analysis, and they certainly don't belong in court.

An associated ploy is to hand the analyst a reproduction from some book, lab manual, or bloodstain experiment, and then ask if the analyst can determine from the item what produced the stain. Once again, the analyst should explain that this cannot be done out of context. Obviously more information is necessary such as: what was the original surface; was it vertical or horizontal; what were the associated stains surrounding those presented; what injuries caused the bleeding; and what other physical evidence was present which might support or refute any opinions made. An analyst doesn't make opinions based on tunnel vision, but rather by utilizing a holistic approach. Hopefully, the judge will preclude an attorney from conducting such "expert testing" procedures. They serve little if any function. In the same way, if the analyst is forced to answer a question about a specific book or article, he should always demand to see the cite before answering.

An attorney won't often use leading questions during direct examination. Conversely, on cross examination the attorney wants to control the witness and is likely to use leading questions. There are generally three types of leading questions; mildly leading, fairly leading, and brutally leading. Mildly leading questions often begin with words such as "is", "are", "was", "were", "do", and "did", while fairly leading questions start with words such as "aren't", "weren't", "don't", and "didn't". Brutally leading questions either begin or end with phrases such as " Isn't it true...?", "Isn't it a fact ...?", "Won't you admit ...?" or "Won't you concede ...?"[4]

When these words come out of the attorney's mouth, listen to the questions carefully. If the analyst is unclear what was asked, he should not answer.

The analyst should state clearly that he did not understand the question and ask that it be repeated. If the question is a compound question, take each part separately; answering the first, then the next. If this is not possible, then try asking the attorney which question he would prefer to have answered first. The analyst must recognize the attack for what it is and respond. The attorney doesn't want answers, he is trying to confuse the witness. A good counter to this technique is to simply pause after every question. Since the analyst is charged with answering the attorney's questions, they also have some control over the pace. Should the attorney interrupt the analyst while he is talking, the analyst can simply stop and wait. Once the attorney stops talking, the analyst can then ask the court to allow him to complete the answer if needed. Slow the pace down and don't become flustered by the attorney's actions.

In answering any question be cautious of offering "yes" or "no" responses, as the attorney will often go to great lengths to keep the analyst from answering with anything more. Never start an answer with "Yes ... but," or "No ... but.". By doing so the analyst has already answered; the only chance to provide the full details considered necessary is to explain the answer first.

Summary

If the reader remembers nothing else from this chapter, remember always that the analyst is a fish out of water in the courtroom. The rules, in effect, have little to do with the analyst's own. It is easy to be drawn in by a skillful attorney who will turn a simple slip of the tongue or minor mistake into a major production. In doing so, they know the evidence will lose center stage as the jury becomes enraptured by the melodrama.

By remaining within comfortable limits in the conclusion itself, by preparing properly, and by applying careful attention to the manner in which they testify, analysts can preclude many opportunities to be party to such courtroom theatrics. Once the evidence is heard, so long as the analyst remains an unbiased and objective expert the court or jury who must ultimately decide the issue will likely accept the testimony.

References

1. Jones, H. W., *Law and the Social Role of Science*, Rockefeller University Press, New York, 1966, pg. 124.
2. Peterson, J. L., Ethical Issues in the Collection, Examination and Use of Physical Evidence, *Forensic Science*, 2nd ed., American Chemical Society, Washington, D.C., 1986, pp. 35-48.

3. Dershowitz, Alan, As quoted by William F. Buckley, Jr., in Simpson Lawyer Ambiguous on Verdict, United Press Syndicate, June 9, 1996.

4. Arizona Prosecuting Attorneys' Advisory Council and Arizona Law Enforcement Officers' Advisory Council, *Courtroom Demeanor,* Phoenix, AZ, 1982, pp 21.01-21.15.

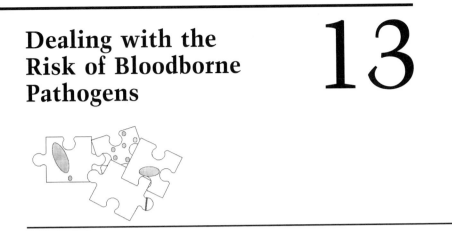

Dealing with the Risk of Bloodborne Pathogens

13

It is imperative that analysts recognize the risk involved in processing blood-stained scenes. The very nature of the medium in which the bloodstain pattern analyst works represents a specific health hazard. Unfortunately, police organizations have been slow to develop programs to deal with this particular issue, and slower still to establish comprehensive training programs to teach effective risk controls to their employees. In an informal survey in 1993, Stewart found 43 out of the 70 departments he queried without any comprehensive policy in place. Over 50 were unaware of Occupational Safety and Health Administration (OSHA) regulations governing employer responsibilities with regard to at-risk employees.[1]

In this chapter we'll discuss the basic issues and provide some limited guidelines that may assist the individual analyst or department in establishing methods for operating and managing bloodstained crime scenes.

Bloodborne Diseases

There are two specific diseases which pose an immediate hazard to the analyst. These are HIV and hepatitis B.

The human immunodeficiency virus or HIV is the most talked-about threat to law enforcement officials who work in bloody scenes. For those exposed to the virus, it very often results in Acquired Immunodeficiency Syndrome or AIDS. The virus destroys the host's ability to fight off other microorganisms, which allows the development of other diseases in the host.[2]

Current research indicates that HIV is transmitted only by exposure to blood, semen, vaginal secretions, or breast milk. In terms of accidental exposure (other than through consumption of breast milk or sexual contact) the nature of the exposure required is not great. A simple needle stick injury is sufficient contact to cause infection. In fact, Stewart goes so far as to caution against contact with chapped skin or mucous membrane areas as these may also represent infection avenues.[3]

Of specific concern to the analyst is the virus' ability to survive. The HIV virus can survive outside the human body for up to 15 days in a liquid state. Dried, the virus survives for periods of 3 to 13 days, with more conservative estimates at about 3 to 5 days.[4] Temperature has a direct effect on survivability: refrigeration delays the degradation of the virus while heat speeds up its demise.[5]

The second threat, hepatitis B, is a virus which causes mild to severe liver damage in the infected host. It results in jaundice, cirrhosis, and in some cases, cancer of the liver.[6] In the more severe instances it can result in death. The virus is transmitted in the same fashion as HIV, through contact with blood, semen, vaginal secretions, and additionally saliva.

Crime Scene Considerations

As indicated, the survival of these pathogens at the scene is not an uncommon event. Therefore, those working within the scene must consider possible exposure risks and take effective measures to reduce them.

A major concern for the police or lab supervisor is who to allow in the scene. Scene integrity considerations require that we limit the number of people who enter and move about the crime scene. The health risks imposed by these pathogens is an additional consideration which demands that we exclude all unnecessary personnel. With regard to exclusion, the supervisor must consider not only an individual's function at the scene, but also the time necessary for them to accomplish it. This concern is particularly important during the collection of dried blood evidence, when the likelihood of airborne particles in the scene is temporarily high. By removing unnecessary personnel, even for a short period while the collection takes place, the supervisor effectively reduces the overall risk.

Additionally, supervisors and analysts must consider personal injuries or wounds, as both represent a source of exposure to the virus. Cuts, abrasions, or sores offer potential access routes for infection. If an individual has such injuries they should approach the scene with extreme caution and, if practical, they should avoid the scene completely. Certainly as a minimum protective measure the individual should be using double-layer protective clothing for the area concerned.

The individual analyst should show a distinct concern for preventing exposures that result from accidents. Crime scene processing and searches are filled with possible sources of injury and exposure. The analyst should move cautiously to avoid accidental needle stick injuries, cuts, or punctures from weapons, sharp-edged articles, and the like. Any accident or lapse in concentration can open the analyst to an immediate exposure risk.

As protection against these types of accidents, protective clothing for the analyst is an absolute must. Clothing concerns and solutions include double-layer techniques whenever possible. The purpose for the clothing is actually twofold: protection from accidental exposure at the scene and from subsequent incidental contact with blood products tracked out of the scene. Disposable booties, outer garments, and gloves are the minimum requirements. Additionally eye goggles and face masks should be used to reduce possible contact from splashes or airborne particles, particularly during operations in which this risk increases (e.g., during the collection of stains).

Unfortunately, methodologies clash in this regard. The most appropriate methods of collecting dried bloodstains for DNA analysis is by scraping and collecting the entire stain. This scraping also increases the overall risk of the collector, as small particles will flake off and often become airborne. Such particles can be ingested, breathed in, or make contact with the eyes. Until procedures change, the analyst should remain cognizant of the increased risk and take some action to protect themselves.

We should also consider the personal actions of officers and analysts at the scene. Eating, drinking, smoking, and the application of cosmetics while in the crime scene are all considered risky behavior and should be prohibited.[7]

To reduce the risk from subsequent incidental contact with contaminated items outside of the crime scene, the analyst must control the collection of contaminated articles and protective clothing used at the scene. A single, controlled collection point prevents these articles from contaminating other areas and equipment. At the collection point, articles are discarded into biohazard bags and destroyed in an appropriate fashion. Generally, a local hospital can deal with the small amount of biohazard materials resulting from the crime scene processing, but we suggest coordinating such support before the need arises.

After use in the scene, any nondisposable clothing or equipment should be thoroughly cleaned. Although common, use of items such as favorite pens and notebooks increase the risk to the analyst. If accidentally contaminated, these items are not discarded and remain in close contact with the individual over extended periods. To preclude this concern consider using only disposable items inside the scene.

For those items of equipment and clothing which require cleaning or laundering, bleach is the most effective disinfectant method. Bigbee reported that the HIV virus is very susceptible to common forms of disinfectants and suggested cleaning solutions of household bleach and water mixed in a 1:9 or 1:10 dilution.[8] He adds the caution that either bleach or alcohol solutions may be used, but never together.

Dealing with Accidental Exposures

No one can guarantee a method of dealing with accidental exposure which will effectively eliminate the risks involved. We offer the following guidelines, however, as a basic response to accidental exposure. First of all, remember that all exposure situations should be promptly reported to both medical personnel and employers.

As far as vaccination prevention goes, some level of prevention is possible in terms of the hepatitis B virus. Currently a three-shot vaccination is available. This vaccination is highly recommended for anyone who works in bloody scenes. *OSHA Regulation 1910.1030 — Bloodborne Pathogens,* requires some public safety employers to provide this vaccination free of charge to at-risk employees who request it. Unfortunately, no such vaccination exists for HIV at this time.

In situations of on-scene injuries where accidental exposure to blood or body fluids occurs, the analyst should allow the wound to bleed freely for a few moments. Afterwards (or in cases of simple contact) wash the affected area immediately with a antimicrobial detergent or a solution of 50 to 70% isopropyl or ethyl alcohol. Obviously, this action is dependent upon the area injured or affected. Allow the solution to remain in place for a minimum of one minute. Finally, wash and rinse the wound or affected area with liquid soap and water, then promptly seek medical attention.

Packaging Biohazard Evidence

As discussed in Chapter 9, proper packaging of serology evidence ensures that no loss of evidence occurs. Proper packaging also effectively eliminates subsequent contamination risks to those who must handle the evidence.

Once again, methodologies for packaging present a contrast. Clothing and other bloodstained items are generally packaged in paper products to ensure the samples do not degrade. In these instances the blood can seep through the paper prior to drying. Even if completely sealed, such seepage may represent a possible avenue of exposure.

As a result of concerns over exposure to biohazard materials, authors such as Bigbee suggest returning to plastic packaging. However, plastic means the increased possibility of degraded samples, which is also unacceptable. In the end the analyst or police department must consider both the evidential considerations and exposure risks, then develop a packaging policy that best fits their organizational needs.

Whatever methods are used for packaging, ensure that containers allow some level of assurance to those opening them at the crime lab that the exposure risk is minimal. Double packaging of inner containers and the proper labeling of outer containers prevent surprises to those who may need to handle the evidence at a later date.

Exposure Risks in Training and Experimentation

Exposure risks are not limited to crime scenes. Those involved in training, those attending training classes, and those conducting experimentation should avoid unnecessary exposure. Although most blood used for this purpose comes from blood banks, the analyst should apply universal precautions and consider all products contaminated.

A recent development in training is the use of animal blood as a substitute for human blood during training courses. Daniel Christman presented an interesting study to the International Association of Bloodstain Pattern Analysts in which he compared different types of animal blood. Neither the HIV nor Hepatitis B virus are transmitted through animals such as horses, cows, and sheep. Although such animals may harbor other pathogens (e.g., brucellosis), these pathogens do not represent the level of risk associated with human blood. For this reason, Christman feels these sources may be very appropriate for use in training police and others in the discipline of bloodstain pattern analysis.[9]

Other Sources of Information on Managing Bloodborne Pathogen Risks

The discussion of the problem and issues related to bloodborne pathogens in this chapter has been a general one. In seeking to establish a comprehensive risk management policy, there are several documents that provide a more in-depth discussion of the subject. We suggest seeking out all of them for further guidance. One of the best documents available for the individual analyst, is David Bigbee's manual entitled *The Law Enforcement Officer and AIDS*, which is available through the U.S. Government Printing Office. Other documents which may be of assistance in establishing a pathogen risk management policy, include:

- A Curriculum Guide for Public Safety and Emergency Response Workers — a Centers For Disease Control publication.
- AIDS and the Law Enforcement Officer: Concerns and Policy Responses — a National Institute of Justice publication.
- OSHA Regulation 1910.1030 — Bloodborne Pathogens.[10]

Summary

The danger that law enforcement personnel and analysts face from blood-stained scenes is not likely to be eliminated in the near future. Processing a scene demands that someone make contact with the evidence, and contact means exposure risk. It is imperative, then, that both analysts and supervisors recognize this danger and introduce steps to reduce the risk. The only rational means of dealing with this problem is to take proactive measures as part of a comprehensive risk management policy; business as usual in the crime scene is no longer a viable option.

Research on the treatment of individuals exposed to the various blood-borne pathogens is ongoing. As a result of this effort, methods and guidelines are likely to change. The best advice we can provide the analyst or supervisor is to remain vigilant to reducing accidental exposure risks. A few simple steps, a little education, and the purchase of basic protective gear will effectively eliminate the majority of accidental exposures. The **prevention** of exposure is always preferred over treatment of individuals for exposure — not only in terms of the well-being of employees, but also from a financial standpoint. When and if prevention fails, simply pattern any treatment plan on the advice of health care professionals.

References

1. Stewart, Jerry D., Bloodborne Diseases: Developing a Training Curriculum, Compuserve Law Enforcement Forum, May 1993.
2. Bigbee, David, The Law Enforcement Officer and AIDS, 2nd ed., U.S. Government Printing Office, Washington, D.C., Nov. 1988, pg. 2.
3. Stewart, Jerry D., Bloodborne Diseases: Developing a Training Curriculum, Compuserve Law Enforcement Forum, May 1993.
4. Bigbee, David, The Law Enforcement Officer and AIDS, 2nd. ed., U.S. Government Printing Office, Washington, D.C., Nov. 1988, pg. 10.
5. Op. cit.
6. Bigbee, David, Collecting and Handling Evidence Infected with Human Disease-Causing Organisms, FBI Law Enforcement Bulletin, July 1987, pg. 1.
7. Drayton, Larry, Guidelines for Personnel Handling Potentially Contaminated Evidence, HQS USACIDC Policy Message 015-87, Jun. 1987.
8. Bigbee, David, The Law Enforcement Officer and AIDS, 2nd ed., U.S. Government Printing Office, Washington, D.C., Nov. 1988, pg. 11.
9. Christman, Daniel, A Study To Compare and Contrast Animal and Human Blood Products, Int. Assoc. Bloodstain Pattern Analysts and Assoc. Crime Scene Reconstruction Joint Training Conf., Oklahoma City, OK, 5 Oct. 95.
10. Stewart, Jerry D., Bloodborne Diseases: Developing a Training Curriculum, Compuserve Law Enforcement Forum, May 1993.

APPENDIX A

Weight/Measure Conversion Table

To Convert	Multiply By	To Get	Symbol
Linear Measure			
Inches	25.4	Millimeters	mm
Inches	2.54	Centimeters	cm
Feet	30	Centimeters	cm
Yards	0.9	Meters	m
Millimeters	0.04	Inches	in
Centimeters	0.4	Inches	in
Meters	3.3	Feet	ft
Meters	1.1	Yards	yd
Liquid Measure			
Fluid Ounces	30	Milliliters	ml
Quarts	0.95	Liters	l
Gallons	3.8	Liters	l
Microliters	0.001	Milliliters	ml
Milliliters	1,000	Microliters	µl
Milliliters	0.03	Fluid Ounces	fl. oz.
Liters	1.06	Quarts	qt
Liters	0.26	Gallons	gal
Weight			
Ounces	28	Grams	g
Pounds	0.45	Kilograms	kg
Grams	0.035	Ounces	oz
Kilograms	2.2	Pounds	lb

Trigonometric Functions and Their Application in Bloodstain Pattern Analysis

Mathematics by definition is the systematic treatment of magnitude, relationships between figures and forms, and relationships between quantities expressed symbolically.[1] Mathematics allows us to recognize relationships in real objects in order that we may better understand them.

Bloodstain pattern analysis draws on mathematics in several areas which were outlined in Chapter 6. In particular, the analyst uses the trigonometric functions. These functions define the relationships between the internal angles that comprise a triangle and the length of its sides. Although the analyst may not fully appreciate these relationships, their specific application to our discipline is relatively easy to understand.

We'll only consider the trigonometric functions related to the right triangle and not those which define the plain triangle. The latter may be of some interest to the analyst, as other authors have described methods by which the analyst can determine a convergence point using these relationships.[2] These methods are generally used in the algorithms of software designed to determine point of convergence.

To properly consider the trigonometric functions, the analyst must first understand four terms and accept two basic facts true to all triangles. The terms of importance are

- **Right Triangle:** a triangle in which one of the three angles measures 90°. (Refer to Figure B-1.) In the figure the angle at A is a 90° angle, making the triangle a right triangle.
- **Hypotenuse:** this term designates the side of the triangle opposite the 90° angle. Thus in the figure the side labeled a is the hypotenuse.
- **Side Opposite:** this term designates the side of a triangle opposite a given angle. The side labeled c is the side opposite angle C.
- **Side Adjacent:** this term designates the side of the triangle adjacent to a given angle, but not the hypotenuse. The side labeled b is the side adjacent for the angle C.

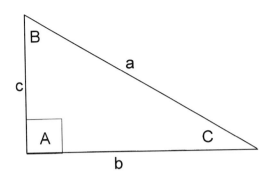

Figure B-1   A right triangle is any triangle in which one angle measures 90°. In this figure, the angle "A" is 90°.

Two basic facts which assist us in understanding the application of the trigonometric functions are

- For any triangle, the sum of the three internal angles is always 180°.
- For every combination possible for these three angles, there is a distinct ratio between the angles and the lengths of the triangle's sides.

The relationships of concern to the analyst are known as the sine and tangent. Based on these two functions, we know that for any value of the angle C in Figure B-1, the following is true:

$$\text{Sine of C} = \frac{\text{opposite}}{\text{hypotenuse}} \quad \text{or} \quad \frac{c}{a} \qquad \text{(B.1)}$$

$$\text{Tangent of C} = \frac{\text{opposite}}{\text{adjacent}} \quad \text{or} \quad \frac{c}{b} \qquad \text{(B.2)}$$

These ratios are displayed in a trigonometric function table. Generally, such a table shows the ratios for every angle between 0 and 90°, in increments of at least 1°. If you recall the discussion on determining the impact angle, that level of detail is unnecessary. The impact angle determination is generally accurate only to about 5° to 7°. Table B-1 is an abbreviated Trigonometric Function Table, in increments of 5°.

Lets begin with the sine function, which helps establish the angle of impact for a given droplet. In Figure B-2, note that the orientation of the right triangle is rotated. The right angle is now at the top of the triangle.

Given our discussions in Chapter 4 and considering Figure B-2, we should feel confident that:

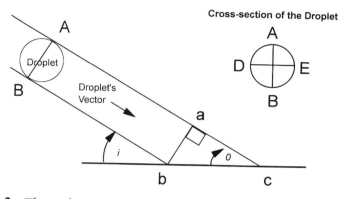

Figure B-2   The path at which a droplet strikes a target in combination with the target defines the right triangle abc. Using this triangle, we can draw an analogy between the dimensions of the resulting stain and the triangle, which allows the analyst to define the impact angle.

- The droplet in flight is generally spheroid in shape.
- Therefore any measurement of the diameter dimension of the droplet will be equal. Thus in the figure AB = DE.

In Figure B-2, the triangle we'll use to solve the problem is formed by the vertical dimension of our droplet (line ab), the path of the droplet (line ac), and the area on the target surface between the point where the droplet first touches and the termination of the path (line bc). Also note that when viewing Figure B-2, the angle *i* is the same as angle *0*. The angle *i* defines the impact angle and is what we seek to determine.

In Figure B-3, we transpose the triangle and now compare it to the resulting stain. We can draw an analogy between the length of the hypotenuse (bc) and the length of our stain (JK), and the width element of the stain (LM) to the side adjacent (ab). Using the measurements of JK and LM in the stain we can define the angle at *0*, where:

$$\text{Sine of } 0 = \frac{\text{opposite}}{\text{hypotenuse}} \quad \text{or} \quad \frac{\text{ab}}{\text{bc}} \quad \text{or} \quad \frac{\text{LM}}{\text{JK}} \qquad (B.3)$$

The result of this division is a ratio. The analyst then finds this ratio on the trigonometric function table and identifies the closest corresponding angle. If the analyst has a scientific calculator the inverse sine of *0* or arc sine function (ASN), which converts this ratio to the angle, can also be used.

One important note: in viewing the diagrams it may appear that a 1:1 relationship exists between Line LM and Line ab or between Line JK and Line bc. This isn't true. As the droplet impacts, the liquid laterally displaces

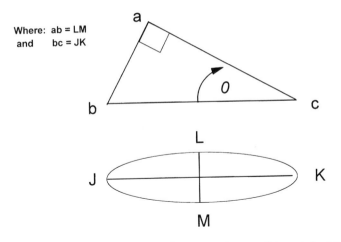

Where: ab = LM
and   bc = JK

Figure B-3 The relationship we draw between the resulting stain and the right triangle. The side opposite (Line ab) is analogous to the width of the stain (Line LM). The hypotenuse (Line bc) is analogous to the length (Line JK).

outward. So the droplet's diameter in flight is much smaller than the resulting stain width; however, since this displacement occurs in both the length and width axes of the resulting stain it has no effect on the application of the trigonometric functions.

Our application of the tangent function is a little more direct. (See Figure B-4.) Given several droplets which impact a surface as a result of a single event, we may want to define the point of their origin (B). To do this we need to determine the length of the side opposite the two angles c and d, which is the line AB. In the figure, the line AC is the side adjacent the angle c while the line AD is the side adjacent the angle d. Since AB is simply a straight line projected from the unknown point of origin back onto the target surface, the angle at A for both triangles is a right angle.

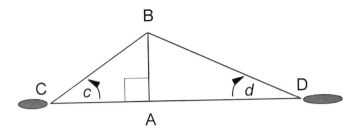

Figure B-4 The relationships of our scene to another right triangle when using the tangent formula. The probable point above the target where the stain originated is defined by the Line AB. The Line AC is equal to the distance from the base of Stain C to the point of convergence (A). The angle c is the impact angle for Stain C.

If we wish to solve for the angle c in Figure B-4, the tangent function tells us that for every right triangle:

$$\text{Tangent of } c = \frac{\text{opposite}}{\text{adjacent}} \text{ or } \frac{AB}{AC} \qquad (B.4)$$

We can easily determine the two impact angles (c or d) using the sine function. By measuring from the base of each stain to the point where their paths intersect, we can also determine the length of the side adjacent of each triangle. Using these two known values we solve for the unknown length of the side opposite (Line AB) by balancing the original equation.

For the triangle ABC and the angle c that means:

$$\text{Side Opposite} = \text{Tan } c * \text{Side Adjacent}$$

$$\text{or} \qquad (B.5)$$

$$AB = \text{Tan } c * AC$$

By considering the triangle created by each droplet's impact we can establish a general distance above the target surface for point B. If all of the droplets are from the same origin and event, then this distance should be the same. To understand the limitations of the tangent relationship in defining the point of origin, please review the discussion in Chapter 6.

Table B.1 Trigonometric Function Table

Angle	sin	tan	sec	csc	ctn	cos	
0 degrees	0.000	1.000				1.000	90 degrees
5 degrees	0.087	0.087	1.004	11.474	11.430	0.996	85 degrees
10 degrees	0.174	0.176	1.015	5.759	5.671	0.985	80 degrees
15 degrees	0.259	0.268	1.035	3.864	3.732	0.966	75 degrees
20 degrees	0.342	0.364	1.064	2.924	2.747	0.940	70 degrees
25 degrees	0.423	0.466	1.103	2.366	2.145	0.906	65 degrees
30 degrees	0.500	0.577	1.155	2.000	1.732	0.866	60 degrees
35 degrees	0.574	0.700	1.221	1.743	1.428	0.819	55 degrees
40 degrees	0.643	0.839	1.305	1.556	1.192	0.766	50 degrees
45 degrees	0.707	1.000	1.414	1.414	1.000	0.707	45 degrees
	cos	ctn	csc	sec	tan	sin	Angle

Accuracy, Precision, and Significant Digits

No matter what we choose to measure: bloodstains, football fields, or our own height, there is always a level of uncertainty in any measurement process. The nature of the uncertainty is affected by two concepts: accuracy and precision. Accuracy in a measurement is a statement as to the level of certainty the measurer has for the final measurement. The greater the level of uncertainty in the measurement, the lower the accuracy. Precision on the other hand describes the ability of the analyst to repeat the measurement. The more likely the measurement can be repeated, achieving the same result, the higher the level of precision. Accuracy is affected most by the nature of the thing being measured, while precision is affected most by the method of measurement employed.

In considering the determination of droplet impact angles using the formulas discussed, accuracy and precision both effect the level of trust the analyst has for the resulting impact angle. In terms of accuracy, it should be self evident that because we apply straight line geometry to define an angle that is created by a parabola, the level of accuracy is not great. It is not so much the precision of the measurements used by the analyst, but rather the manner of measurement and the nature of the thing (the impact angle) being measured. The authors generally accept that impact angles are accurate to ±7 degrees. Not everyone will agree with that limit of uncertainty, but ranges of uncertainty for the accuracy of impact angle determinations are usually given between 5–7 degrees.

Precision in measuring the bloodstain is also a factor. Remember, precision speaks to the ability to repeat the measurement and achieve the same result (the same measurement). The manner of measuring the stain is critical in defining precision. For instance, if the analyst uses a ruler scaled to 1 mm to measure small bloodstains, then precision will likely suffer. In viewing such a scale in relation to the stain, the analyst is estimating the final digit of the measurement down to the nearest .5 mm. On the other hand, should the analyst use a micrometer, scaled to the nearest .1 mm, precision of the measurement increases. Now, the analyst is estimating the final digit for the measurement down to the .05 mm level. Just as important to the precision of the measurement is the knowledge of skill of the measurer. As discussed in Chapter 6, if the analyst inappropriately includes portions of the tail or scallops in the measurement, precision of the measurement will suffer.

The result of any impact angle or point of origin determination will ultimately be given as a measurement; either as an angle of impact (e.g., 65°) or a distance from a target (e.g., 2.5 ft). In accepting this measurement, the analyst must recognize the significant digits in the result. This significant digit is always the estimated digit. For instance, given an impact angle determination of 64.5°, the analyst cannot assume the significant digit is 5. The uncertainty present in the accuracy component (±7 degrees) tells us the answer is estimated to the second digit (e.g., 4). Due to the level of uncertainty in the accuracy some might even argue that the significant digit is the 6. Recognition of the significant digit in an equation's answer is a recognition of the overall uncertainty of the answer itself. To be objective, the analyst must keep in mind the effects of accuracy and precision on the measurements, and then represent their investigative findings appropriately. This means keeping an eye on the significant digit, and not alluding to a level of certainty that does not exist.

References

1. Stein, Jess, *The Random House Dictionary of the English Language,* Random House, New York, 1980, pg. 825.
2. Carter, A. L. and Podworny, E. J., Bloodstain Pattern Analysis With a Scientific Calculator, *J. Can. Soc. Forensic Sci.*, March, 1980.

Stop-Motion Photography Techniques

In order to study droplets and impacts in depth, it becomes imperative to photograph them. Unfortunately, that is not easily accomplished under ordinary circumstances. The action is far too fast. Bevel and Leonard Conn, formerly with the University of Oklahoma Police Department, perfected a trigger mechanism which allows the researcher to use bulb settings on a camera with a strobe flash to capture these impacts.[1]

The process is relatively simple. Working in near-darkroom conditions, a light beam is set up to illuminate a small phototransistor. The beam is placed in such a way as to cross an area where the initiating action will occur. For example, it might be placed so that a blood droplet crosses the light beam, or in such a manner that the closing of a mousetrap device crosses the beam. The method of initiation is limited only by the desires of the researchers and the nature of the event they wish to photograph (e.g., low-velocity droplets or impact spatters).

As long as the beam illuminates the transistor, the circuit to the flash unit remains open. Once the beam of light is interrupted, this closes the circuit causing the flash to fire.

Two potentiometers allow the researcher to adjust the time to the flash. The two potentiometers used are a 500K ohm which allows for coarse adjustments, and a 50K ohm which allows for fine adjustments. Using these controls, the researcher can adjust the time between the beam interrupt and the flash in increments of between 10 to 560 ms.

To expose photographs, the researcher places the camera on the bulb setting and locks the shutter open. The droplet or mouse trap is then released, which interrupts the beam, initiating the flash. Once the photograph is exposed, the researcher closes the shutter. The trigger mechanism provides for approximately a 0.5 s delay before the flash can fire again. This gives the analyst sufficient time to close the shutter without risking a double exposure.

Synchronization of the flash to the action one wishes to capture is the most difficult part of the process. Before wasting film, the researcher should practice and ensure the image captured is the one intended.

This "practice" technique is relatively simple to master. The researcher simply focuses his eyes on the area in which the action will occur. The droplet is released and the flash goes off. After a few attempts, the individual observing this is able to see well enough to get a good indication of the image they'll end up with.

Parts required for this device include:

3 in. × 2 in. × 1.5 in. plastic housing box
3 in. × 2 in. perforated board
Q1 — Phototransistor RS-276-145
IC1 — 4093BCN or RCA SK4093B
SCR1 — C106D2 SCR or RCA SK 3598
R1 — 1K ohm resistor
R2 — 3.3K ohm resistor
R3 — 10K ohm resistor
R4 — 330K ohm resistor
R5 — 680K ohm resistor
R6 — 500K ohm potentiometer
R7 — 50K ohm potentiometer
C1, C2 1 mfd/35 volt capacitors
Male PC sync cord

At the time of writing, costs were under $30. The parts are arranged as indicated in Figure C-1.

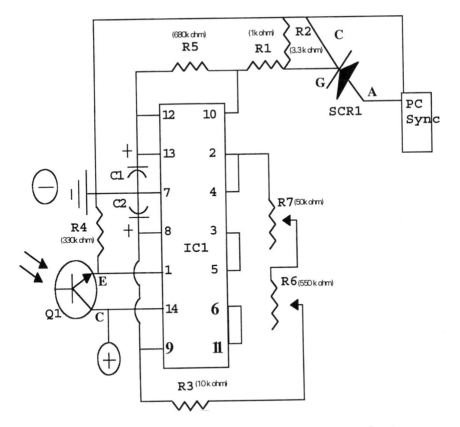

Figure C-1 The wiring diagram for a flash trigger mechanism.

References

1. Bevel, Tom and Conn, Leonard, Stop Motion Photography of Bloodstains, *International Association of Bloodstain Pattern Analysts News*, July 1987.

Index